WOMEN
WITHOUT
CHILDREN

THE REASONS
THE REWARDS
THE REGRETS

SUSAN S. LANG

ADAMS MEDIA CORPORATION
Holbrook, Massachusetts

For Bea Lang

*who devoted her life to being a mother
and continues to excel in that role,
and for that I will always be
deeply grateful.*

Published by Adams Media Corporation
260 Center Street, Holbrook, MA 02343
Originally published in 1991 by Pharos Books.

ISBN: 1-55850-597-0

Printed in the United States of America

J   I   H   G   F   E   D   C   B   A

Library of Congress Cataloging-in-Publication Data
Lang, Susan S.
Women without children : the reasons, the rewards, the regrets /
Susan S. Lang.
p.   cm.
Originally published: New York : Pharos Books, 1991.
Includes bibliographical references and index.
ISBN 1-55850-597-0 (pb)
1. Single women—United States. 2. Childlessness—United States.
3. Childlessness—United States—Psychological aspects. I. Title.
HQ800.2.L36   1996
306.87—dc20   96-6395
                                              CIP

Grateful acknowledgment is made for permission to include excerpts from previously published material:
Douglas, Marjory Stoneman, *Voice of the River*. Copyright ©1987. Permission granted by Pineapple Press, Inc.
Klepfisz, Irena, *Dreams of an Insomniac: Feminist Essays, Speeches, and Diatribes.* Copyright ©1990. Published by Eighth Mountain Press. Permission granted by author.
Landers, Ann, Oct. 29, 1989 column. Copyright ©1989. Permission granted by Ann Landers, *Chicago Tribune*.

Interior design by Janet Tingey

*This book is available at quantity discounts for bulk purchases.
For information, call 1-800-872-5627 (in Massachusetts 617-767-8100).*

Visit our home page at http://www.adamsmedia.com

CONTENTS

ACKNOWLEDGMENTS

With all my heart and soul, I first want to thank my husband and my best friend, Tom Schneider. I am ever so grateful for his unwavering love and support throughout this project and for his keen insights as a compassionate and perceptive psychotherapist.

Special thanks also go to Ellen Friedman for her role in inspiring this project and to my agent Bob Silverstein for making it happen.

Many people went out of their way to help me find women to interview, and I thank them again for their time and effort. These include Millie Rosoff, Fran Epstein, Bryna Fireside, Maida Gierasch, Fefi Barno-Ross, Lauren Goldman, Margo Hittleman, Leslie Cohen, Andrea Brown, Hope and Hazel Mandeville, Jane Powers Levine, Meg Ambry, Susan Neiberg Terkel, Jamie Catlin, Joan Slatoff, Rebecca Pirto, Carol Skawinski, Renee Heider, Margie and Mitch Bloomberg, Paul Lang, Bea Lang, Donna Dempster-McClain, Laurie and Bob Thomas, Nancy Treadmill, Rick and Jackie Zelman, Jessica Fitzpatrick, Rick Lamport, Anna Primavera, Gail Jaspen, and Judy Long.

To all the women whose names do not appear but whose voices ring out in this book, my special thanks for their generosity in sharing their lives, thoughts and feelings.

SUSAN SCHNEIDER LANG
Ithaca, NY
April 1991

PROLOGUE

Just after my fortieth birthday, I had lunch with an old acquaintance who had a long history of infertility. Seven years earlier, after endless medical procedures, she had been told she couldn't have children. After some soul-searching, Terri and her husband chose not to adopt a child. She worked hard to change her priorities and carve out a child-free* lifestyle. Even though several newborn babies were later offered to her through doctors in her family, Terri was already entrenched in her child-free life and couldn't see turning it around at that point.

As we were reflecting on how our generation was about to start leaving its childbearing years behind, Terri told me she was enjoying her child-free life and was confident she had made the right decision. But she felt bitter that she had had to go through the decision-making process alone. The transition from assuming she would one day be a mother to coming to terms with the

---

* I don't like using the term "childlessness" because it infers a lack, that you're "less" if you don't have a child. Words like "nonmother" and "unchilded" are awkward and also connote a state of missing something. "Child free," on the other hand, is usually used to convey an active choice to not have children. For lack of a better term for a woman who defines herself as simply without children, I have used "childless" more often than I would have liked.

fact that she was not going to be one had been fraught with emotional isolation and upsetting upheavals. Men react to these issues so differently from women. Her husband did the best he could, but Terri still felt she had made her transition basically alone. She was angry that there had been so little information available about other women before her who never had children.

In making her decisions regarding children, Terri had wanted to know how older women without children felt about it when they reached their fifties or eighties. What is life without children like after the childbearing years? She couldn't find much written on the subject. Granted, these women are what one researcher calls an "invisible minority," but she knew there were millions of women who didn't have children. And she knew there were many more younger women who wanted the answers to the questions that she had asked, such as: How did not having children affect their lives? Were other women without children well adjusted and living satisfying lives, or were they haunted by lingering doubts? Were they fulfilled, lonely, or somewhere in between? Did they have regrets? Did the rewards remain liberating or had they become limiting? What about their old age? Were they loved, connected, and cared for, or, as younger women fear, were they feeling lonely, deserted, and uncared for?

This book was written for those who want to know what it is like for women to not have children. It explores this issue with sixty-three women, ages thirty-six to one hundred. I interviewed women in each decade of life beginning with the late thirties, when the childbearing decision crystallizes and begins to finalize. Within each decade, I looked for women who didn't have children for different reasons, including single women, late brides, infertile women, wives of husbands who didn't want children, the divorced, the widowed, and lesbians, as well as women who had consciously chosen their child-free state.

Although my sampling is not as racially diverse as I would have liked, my primary focus was on finding representation among different ages and different reasons for not having children. The women do, however, come from diverse socioeconomic backgrounds, all within the broad range of the middle class.

I found the women through my network of personal acquaintances—a friend's mother's former workmate, my lawyer's client's daughter, my neighbor's great-aunt, my brother's ex-roommate's friend from college, my husband's friend's mother's friend, an acquaintance of someone I interviewed. I also put a query in a women's writers' newsletter and a wonderful group of thoughtful and articulate women mailed me their thoughts in response to my questionnaire. As I met people over the course of writing this book and mentioned my topic, many volunteered a name, and many of those casual referrals became my future interviews. Although I originally planned to interview several celebrities, I later decided that the lives of "ordinary" women were far more relevant.

◆ ◆ ◆

Never before have women been able to control so effectively when and whether to have a baby. Many women spend their twenties exploring their talents, seeing how far their hard work can take them, traveling, and trying out different lifestyles. Many put off thinking about whether or when to have children, for they believe there's still plenty of time.

The biological clock ticks urgently in a woman's thirties. During that decade, women begin to realize that their time to have a child is quickly slipping away. They may be gripped by the fear that the open window of opportunity to have a child may soon slam shut forever.

Women today have options that no previous generation has ever had. Never before have so many women pursued fulfilling, demanding careers that can require lifelong commitments and yield rich and rewarding lifestyles. Never before have birth control and abortion given women so much control over reproduction. Never before has child-free living been such a real option. Yet given such a menu of choices, women have never before been so tormented by the decision over whether or not to raise children.

The decision to have children is probably one of the few irrevocable choices a woman can make. You can't take it back. There are ex-husbands and ex-jobs, but there aren't ex-children. Having a child is a permanent commitment, yet the decision to do so is often a blind one, and the outcome is unpredictable. To have a child requires a giant leap of faith. There is no way of knowing whether a child will be a source of love, comfort, and inexpressible joy, or a source of worry, pain, and torment.

Whichever it is, and it's usually a blend of them all, a child becomes a part of a woman's life forever. To be a mother is a lifelong role. Thinking about the decision to become a mother can be complicated and confusing, confounding and contradictory. In many ways, to have or not have a child will be the deciding factor in hundreds, perhaps thousands, of other little decisions down the road—what job you'll take, what house you'll buy, what neighborhood you'll live in, how you'll spend your days, your money, your weekends, holidays, vacations; where and when you'll travel, who your friends are, who's in your kinship network, and so on.

Although most women think they have an idea of what motherhood is like (although we'll see just how wrong they were), few know many women who did not have children. There are dozens of books about having kids, yet there are few that present the stories of women over forty who have not had children, either by choice or by circumstance. I hope the stories of the women in this book, told through their thoughts and feelings, will be of value to other women grappling with this emotional life issue.

In writing this book, I feared separating women into two camps: those who have mothered and those who have done other things. I did not mean to create a polarity or schism between the two. But as a journalist, I strove to sort out how the lives of women who do not parent differ from the lives of women who do. Women who are not mothers have room for other choices to enter their lives. I wanted to know what some of these choices were, how women satisfied certain needs, whether there were regrets, and if younger women could benefit from their lives. I sought to not only integrate much of the research about women without children, including issues such as marital satisfaction, health, wealth, how time is spent, and the implications of not having children in later life, but to give the data human faces and voices of women at different times in their life cycle.

This book does not try to convince the reader to have or not have children. That decision is highly complicated, personal, and very much a function of each individual woman's circumstances. My purpose, instead, was to find out about women without children and how and whether they differ emotionally, biologically, or financially from women with children. How, for example, do their marriages, health, happiness, lifestyles, and social supports differ from those of mothers? Is their time spent differently? What are the costs and benefits of not having children in middle and old age?

But even more importantly, I wanted to know how women— single, married, divorced, widowed, straight, and lesbian—*feel* about not having children. Did their decisions come about purposely or circumstantially? How did their feelings, whether of loss, relief, or the fear of growing old, change as they aged? What issues have become important to them because they didn't have children? What have been the rewards of being child-free? What are the regrets? What have the outside pressures on them been like? If they had to do it over again, what would they do?

◆ ◆ ◆

Since this book came out in hardcover five years ago, the first wave of baby boomers, who were then pushing forty-five (the age that typically marks the end of childbearing years) are turning fifty. Murphy Brown might have had a baby in TV-land but in the real world, more than 16 percent of the oldest baby boomers do not and will not have children.[1] That's more than one out of every six women. This is the highest rate of foregoing children since the women who came of age before and during the Great Depression; some 22 percent of these women did not have children.[2]

The next wave of baby-boom women, those between thirty-four and forty-three years in 1996, are expected to have a comparable, perhaps even higher rate of foregoing children. About 5

---

[1] Bureau of the Census, *Fertility of American Women: June 1992.* Current Population Reports, Population Characteristics, Series P-20, No. 454. Written by Amara Bachu, pp. xi-xxi.

[2] Ibid., pp. 22–32.

percent more of these women did not have children in 1992, compared with their older counterparts at the same age in 1982 (19 vs. 14 percent). Although many will still have children, demographers predict that 15 to 20 percent of these women will leave their childbearing years with no children. And as is consistent with previous reports on women without children, these women will tend to have finished college and married later, and to have jobs.[3]

All told, baby boomers are twice as likely as their parents to never have children. It's too early to predict the trends among younger women, except that even more of them are putting children off than their counterparts in 1976. (Forty-one percent of women between ages fifteen and forty-four didn't have children in 1992, compared with thirty-five percent in 1976, suggesting that they may continue these trends.

On a larger scale, there are more households without children living in them than there have been in decades (including couples with children who have left home). In fact, couples without children are one of the fastest growing segments of household populations "and their lead is widening," according to *American Demographics.*[4] By the year 2,000, 60 percent of married couples will have no children under age eighteen living with them; only 40 percent of married couples will be raising children.

Although many of these households without children are "empty nests" and single parents without children living with them, this trend means that households without children are becoming increasingly common and soon will be the norm. No longer will women without children in their twenties, thirties, and forties feel isolated and surrounded by households with children. Women sixty-five and older without children will also feel less isolated. Today, some 20 percent of women in this age group have no living children.[5] Chances are that number will grow, since women these days have much smaller families than did today's older women.

[3] Bureau of the Census, *Fertility of American Women: June 1992.* Current Population Reports, Population Characteristics, Series P-20, No. 454. Written by Amara Bachu, pp. xi-xxi.

[4] "The Future of Households," *American Demographics,* December 1993, p. 35.

[5] Baine Alexander, Robert Rubinstein, Marcene Goodman, and Mark Luborsky. "A Path Not Taken: A Cultural Analysis of Regrets and Childlessness in the Lives of Older Women," *The Gerontologist,* Vol. 32, No. 5, pp. 618-626, 1992.

As the segment of the population without children continues to grow, women without children are feeling less isolated. More and more magazines and book publishers periodically offer articles and books on life without children. *Glamour, Redbook, Newsweek, New York,* and *Health* have all had articles about not having children in the past few years. Several thoughtful books have been published since mine, including *Unwomanly Conduct: The Challenges of Intentional Childlessness* by Carolyn Morell, a book about middle-aged married women who decided not to have children[6] and Linda Hunt Anton's *Never To Be A Mother,* a ten-step self-help program for women who view not having children as a loss and want to learn how to cope better with that loss.[7]

Two national support networks have also sprung up. Childless by Choice provides support, humor, and social commentary for and about people who have chosen not to raise children (PO Box 695, Leavenworth, WA 98826, 509-763-2112). The ChildFree Network in Roseville, CA (916-773-7178) is a relatively young support network and is intended for women, men, and couples who do not have children for whatever reason.

In the past few years, a new issue for women without children has emerged—a sense of feeling discriminated against in the workplace. Some women without children report that as parenting co-workers take time off from work because of their children, they're left "holding the bag" and expected to take up the slack, simply because they don't have children. Yet they receive no recognition or payoff for the extra work. Leslie Lafayette talks about members of her ChildFree Network who feel compromised by the sense of entitlement parents receive in the workplace. Some airlines, she says, grant free airfare to children of employees but no comparable freebies for employees without children. In other companies, workers without children are sometimes assigned the unwanted business trip because others use their families as reasons why they can't go.

Lafayette also points out that while people without children generally don't complain about having to pay property taxes to

---

6 Carolyn Morell, *Unwomanly Conduct: The Challenges of Intentional Childlessness,* New York and London: Routledge, 1994.

7 Linda Hunt Anton, *Never To Be A Mother,* Harper: San Francisco, 1992.

support public schools or helping to subsidize the tax deductions parents get for their dependent children, they find it unfair when their companies subsidize day care in the workplace without providing comparable benefits for the child-free. She calls for companies to offer a "menu" of benefits, so that workers who do not need benefits such as day care or health insurance for five can choose other benefits instead, such as extra time off to take classes or extra days of vacation. Lafayette says: "Colleagues without children are not here to ease parents' ways. We gladly contribute equally in taxes toward schools and social programs that benefit children, even though we may never have any. It's offensive to assume that our time is less valuable than that of parents, or that we are making less of a contribution to society."[8]

Today, we still live in a very pro-motherhood (pronatalistic) society, but with a growing band of women taking a very different path. They are trying to make their way in a society that still largely views the biology of women as their proper destiny and makes prejudicial assumptions about women who don't have children—a society where many women embrace choice and reproductive freedom but forget to accept as readily the choice not to reproduce. In this society, child abuse and neglect is rampant among all the socioeconomic classes, yet women who are not driven to motherhood are given little respect for resisting the pressure to procreate. And other women who have missed their chance to become parents—either through unresolved infertility, early divorce, late marriage or no marriage at all—have a hard time finding support for their child-free lifestyle.

The book is not only intended for women who do not have children, but also for friends and relatives of of these women. I have received several letters from mothers, for example, whose daughters or daughter-in-laws had chosen not to have children. Although initially hurt and angry that their daughters had rejected motherhood and deprived them of grandchildren, they said they now better understood this difficult decision.

[8] Leslie Lafayette, "What Childless Women Put Up With at Work," *Glamour,* December 1993. p. 158.

The book is also meant for younger women who are ambivalent about motherhood. They see mothers all around them, but few have any insight into the hearts and minds of older women who did not have children. To make the best possible personal choice, a woman needs good information. I hope this book fills the gap for these women as well.

◆ ◆ ◆

I launched this project with a combined sense of humility and fear. Humility, because I was prying into the private recesses of women's hearts and minds. I was also fearful that my probing might open emotional wounds that had been laid to rest years or decades before. I was gratified that the overwhelming majority of women were enthusiastic that a book of this nature was to be written and were therefore frank about their personal histories. For many women, the topic of not having children was easy to discuss and they were not particularly heavy-hearted about it. For a few, the interview brought tears when buried sorrows rose to the surface. I thank them for their willingness to share their lives with others, and I deeply regret if the experience caused them any pain. I want to thank all the women who let me into their hearts and minds.

Hopefully, this book will help provide a variety of voices that many women without children can't find in their personal networks. I hope that the women's thoughts and feelings in these pages will be of value to others and will help provide the validation that for so long has been unavailable to women—the chorus of other women who, like them, are pursuing the less-trodden path of a life without children.

Susan S. Lang
Ithaca, N.Y.

CHAPTER ONE

Three Women Without Children

Thirty-Six and Engaged, Loves Kids But Won't Have Any

Andrea Brown is one of the youngest women I interviewed. At thirty-six, she's a successful literary agent for children's books with her own business based in Manhattan and San Francisco. Engaged to be married for the first time, Andrea knows she'll never have children though she's young enough. As with most of the women interviewed for this book, Andrea's reasons form a web of contrasting threads that depict her life's story.

One of those threads was sewn even before Andrea was born. Her mother took DES (diethylstilbestrol) while pregnant to avoid a fifth miscarriage after fifteen years of trying desperately to have a baby. With the birth of Andrea, her mother finally had the baby for which she yearned. Without DES, could this dreamchild ever have come to be? There's no way to know.

What is strikingly clear, though, is that the drug warped Andrea's ability to have a baby. Doctors give her only a fifty-fifty chance of being able to carry a baby to term. (So far, she's been compensated a mere $2,500 in a DES lawsuit for her injuries. As part of the "guinea pig" generation, Andrea also has reason to fear that she might develop cervical cancer.)

But Andrea will never even try to get pregnant to find out. Dave, her fiancé, has never wanted children. When Andrea met him five years ago, he was just getting over the bitter ending of a fourteen-year marriage. He and his ex-wife had agreed before their wedding that there would be no children. But when his wife hit her mid-thirties and all her friends began having babies, she was smitten, too, and wanted a baby. They found out that Dave's sperm had a motility problem, so she pressured him to have surgery, but it didn't help. Dave knows he probably can't father a child, and it turned out that his ex-wife couldn't have them either. But by the time she found out, the marriage was falling apart. To top it off, Dave has diabetes and a fifty-fifty chance of passing the disease on to a child. Said Andrea:

> He was very clear at the beginning: "I definitely don't want kids." After we were in the relationship a few months, he said it again: "If you think you want kids, we should break this off now."
>
> Well, I figured I couldn't have them so that was okay, but then a few years passed and all my friends and cousins started to have kids. They were happy, good kids, and I got along with them great. Here I was in my mid-thirties. If I was going to do something about having children, it had to be now.

Ironically, Andrea remembers never wanting kids when she was a child. "I used to babysit and all that, but I didn't really like it," she recalled. "I never really took to babies much or thought they were cute. I never saw it for me."

And even though Andrea was the answer to her parents' dreams for a baby, she had always had a turbulent relationship with her mother, especially when she hit her teens:

> I remember in the middle of these fights—and we fought constantly, night and day—my mom would say, "I can't wait until you have your own kids and you see what it's like."
>
> "Ha, ha," I'd say. "I'm not going to have any, I'm not going to go through this. Who needs it?" My mother adored us; we were her whole life. She waited so long for us, but she tried too hard. She was so overprotective. I knew I didn't want to be that kind of mother but probably would be.

When Andrea was eighteen, her mother died, and Andrea became the "little mother," doing the shopping, cooking, and housekeeping for her father and little brother. Like many women who later don't have children, Andrea got an early preview of "motherwife" life and it didn't particularly enthrall her.

In college, Andrea laughed at her friends who were desperate to find a husband:

> At that point, I didn't even think I'd get married. I couldn't imagine being with just one man. I was rather promiscuous and never monogamous until I was in my late twenties. It never occurred to me that I'd really find a guy that I'd want to stay with, every day, all the time. And since I didn't really want kids, it didn't matter to me if I got married, or so I thought in my early twenties.

After three long-term, far from perfect relationships, Dave came into her life. His insistence on never having children didn't bother Andrea until she hit that critical mid-thirties crunch. The idea of the window of opportunity for having children slamming shut forever made her very nervous. She had to think twice, thrice, and many more times before she softly closed the window herself.

> After Dave and I had been serious a few years, I went through the baby crisis. I went to Florida for a few weeks to visit my father and stepmother and to get away from Dave and really think about it. For a few weeks there, I thought about breaking up with him and finding a guy so we could adopt, or someone who had a child.

Andrea asked a dozen or so older women in Florida if they thought she'd regret not having children when she was sixty. The mothers and grandmothers told her that they loved their children and most said they were glad they'd had them. But they warned Andrea that her spouse must come first. Kids grow up and leave home. All that's left is your husband, and women who had put their kids first find themselves emotionally stranded later on.

> In looking back, they said their lives had been most enriched by their marriages, not so much by their kids even though they loved them a lot. I asked them would I be missing out on something that

I'd regret? I remember one said, "Andrea, you can't miss something you never had."

That made a lot of sense to me. Do I want kids so badly that I'd be willing to leave a great relationship? What will be more important to me when I'm older and I look back?

Quite a few, including my stepmother, told me that they wouldn't have kids if they had to do it all over again and lived in these times with all the choices women have now. That hit home too.

Andrea realized that her relationship with Dave was far more important than her ambivalent feelings about wanting babies. "I thought I wanted a baby because I didn't want to miss that life experience," she said. "But that wasn't a good enough reason to have a baby."

Andrea's very comfortable launching her marriage without the motherhood part of it. Trying to fit kids into their lifestyle now, anyway, would turn the hectic into the insane.

With the way my life's turning out, it's craziness. We just moved to San Francisco because Dave's career is up and down, I have my own business, and I'm setting up and running a household. Children really wouldn't fit in.

I'm doing something good through children's books—each book I sell is a baby. You see it grow and enjoy how it continues to grow with paperback or film rights. I'm doing something very satisfying and I love it. I'm pretty much at peace that this is a good decision.

Andrea's life beats in rhythm to the tempo of her times. She is young enough to have benefited from the mind-boggling new choices that have opened up as a result of the women's movement, and she will always cherish her pre-AIDS swing in the singles fast lane through her twenties and her career as a children's book editor and literary agent in New York City.

But there's also an alphabet soup of by-products from growing up in Andrea's times: DES, IUDs, STDs, PID (pelvic inflammatory disease). They have created an entire sub-generation of women who can't have babies simply by going to bed with their mates. In Andrea's case, her mate didn't want one.

I'm sure in the future, I'll look back at times and think, too bad I didn't have kids. But it wasn't ever a good time or the right guy. I made a lot of choices when I was young and I'm glad for them.

Whatever point I'm at in the future, I'm only there because of all the decisions and choices I made in my twenties and thirties that were only possible because I didn't have a child. You can't really miss what you never had. I did all those other things—living an exciting singles life in Manhattan, partying, taking advantage of the theater and concerts, staying out all night.

I'll never be sorry I did all that rather than marrying and having children. I'm one of those people who believes you can't do it all.

Fifty, Widowed, With No Children: Mild But Haunting Regrets

Dusk's fading sunlight cast Randy's charming brick home in an eerie glow when I interviewed her. She bought the house more than a decade ago with her second husband. Two years later, he was fatally shot during a robbery. Randy was shot too but survived. As she told me her story, I was taken by how much her life, too, was a reflection of her times. Randy came of age during the nascent stage of the women's movement.

I was born in 1939, just before the start of World War II. My mom was 34 and my dad was 32. They'd been married eight years. They always said they waited because it was the Great Depression and my father didn't have a good, full-time job, but I think they were reluctant to have children. My mother was a reformer, a working woman, which was very unusual at that time. She was working as an academic librarian full time when I was born, and I was put into child care almost immediately.

Just as the war started, Randy's sister was born—Randy still teases her that she was born only to hold off the draft a bit longer. But their dad went to war anyway. It was 1944 and Randy was four. While her mother worked full time, Randy and her little sister spent the days at grandma's. Randy's grandmother died in 1946, the same year Randy's father came back from the war. Her mother quit her job.

I think there was a fair amount of social pressure for my mother not to be working anymore. She says it was a child-care problem, but I think it was social pressure.

Around that time, I went from a semiprivate school into public school and was put ahead two years. I think that was a giant factor in my not having children later because I was precocious intellectually. I ended up in therapy when I was twelve. Everyone else was fourteen and talking about boys, but I just wanted to play soft ball. I felt very left out, very alone at that time.

Randy remembers one night when her parents' closest friends were over. The women were working in the kitchen while the husbands smoked in the living room. Randy felt indignant that after working all day, just as hard as their husbands, these women had to come home and keep working while the men put their feet up:

These women were getting screwed at the workplace and they were getting screwed at home, and I saw having kids as something extra. I remember later on saying I was never going to have kids, and they'd all say, "Oh, it will be different when you're on your own, you'll see."

In a sense, you could say I was living an ordinary American, midwestern little kid life, with a mom and dad who had two kids, a garage, house, and all those things on the surface that say middle America. But what was different was that my mother had been a career woman, had worked, and missed it when she had to go home. She finally went back when I was fifteen but then retired early because my dad made her.

Randy went on to college and then straight through to graduate school for a masters in economics. In 1961, she headed for Washington, D.C. Because she was an unmarried woman, her prospective employers knew she wasn't about to have babies, and she easily landed a good job. She remembers how she felt:

I said to myself then, okay, I've gone as far as I can go in terms of being different. I was the youngest of my classmates—all my sorority sisters were married. I was determined to work first in the big world, but once I got out there I just thought, I can't push this any further, I don't want to be some weird old lady, so I got married.

He was eight years older than Randy, drove a sports car, and Randy tried hard to feel how everyone said she should feel. He wanted children, and she agreed . . . but not yet. She wasn't ready, and she recognized they had different values and feared they'd butt heads over issues regarding children. Then they went to Europe on vacation, and Randy fell in love with France and its language and culture. She threw herself into French lessons.

So here I was, married to this good-looking man with a wonderful job who treated me like a princess. I had more than I ever thought I could ever have. But I was hyperventilating. Something was wrong. It was fall, 1967. By this time, all my sorority sisters were in their own houses with babies. I quit my job and told my husband I had to go back to Europe and get something out of my system. .

On her own for the first time, Randy jubilantly explored Paris. She met several American women in their forties whose last kids had just left for college. They had been finally able to leave the "bums," as they called their husbands, to go to Paris. "I guess I said to myself, I'm not going to wait to live my life until it's too late," Randy said. "I was young; I could have romance, and I did." First, there was a love affair with a Parisian cellist, and then with a psychology student.

I was twenty-eight and living in Paris during the Vietnam demonstrations. I was in a sort of hyperintellectual world, and it was all very exciting. Here I was supposed to be getting it all out of my system and going back to the grand middle-class, nonintellectual life. Well, my husband came over to talk but it just didn't work out.

They divorced during that supposedly high-risk seventh year of marriage. Randy went back to graduate school, where she spent the next seven years earning her Ph.D. in French literature and working part-time as a business writer to support herself. It was the late sixties and early seventies, and Randy spent most of that time living with a musician, going to rock concerts, smoking pot, and having fun.

But by the time Randy was thirty-five, she was ready to settle down. She'd gotten her wanderlust out of her system and had completed her education. But her musician boyfriend wasn't the right man, so they broke up. "Suddenly, I was living by myself, and I hated it," she said. Within a year, however, Randy met the love of her life. When they married, she was thirty-seven and he was thirty. She got pregnant almost immediately.

> But my instant feeling was, get this out. I just didn't want it at all. My instant feeling was that I'd like to have kids, but it'd have to be an egalitarian thing. He was just getting started in his career, and he said he felt he hardly had enough time to give to me. So I had an abortion.

But a few years later, a baby seemed more timely. Randy's husband was always careful about contraception, but one night, Randy made love to him while he was sleeping—a "half-hearted try to get pregnant, maybe," she said. Randy thought she was pregnant again, and she was delighted that the timing might be perfect now. She could freelance from home, and by the time the child was ready for school, she'd be ready to go back to work full time. But her husband, an assistant professor, was feeling overwhelmed by his job. His career meant a lot to him, and he just wasn't interested in having a child yet. They debated the issue, but then Randy discovered that she wasn't pregnant after all. The following year she had to have a hysterectomy, and the year after that, her husband was shot.

> And that was it. My feeling is, *now* I regret that abortion, but if he had lived, I don't think I would have regretted not having a child. We had a very, very tight relationship, and I don't think I would have wanted to share him. I think he would have wanted a child later on, but I would have been too old by then and I don't know what would have happened.
>
> Looking back now, I think having a child is the most responsible and one of the most important things you can do. I think I had so much respect for it that I didn't do it, and it may have been the only mistake I made. But I made my decision in good faith and did the best I could with the information I had at the time. Now I think society allows you to have a child and do other things, too. It doesn't close doors to you the way it would have for me earlier.

Today, Randy lives alone with a cat she adores, who "brings me a mouse on Mother's Day," and is a top editor at a national news magazine.

Unlike other people I knew growing up, I'd say that I have done everything I've ever wanted. I have lived abroad, traveled, been married, worked, had lovers, and am now full blast in my career and very successful. I go around the country to give talks, am picked up in limousines, interviewed almost every day by reporters, and quoted all over the country. My life is fully used. Except for my husband's death, I've had an extremely good life.

Even though I say now that I regret not having children—I'm very aware that this is a dead end—I regret I wasn't mature enough to make that choice at a time I could have had them. If I had had them when I wasn't mature, though, I would have made a terrible mother; I wouldn't have enjoyed motherhood. In fact, I still don't feel all that comfortable with kids, and I was never one of those people who'd be devastated if she found out she couldn't have children. So my regret is that I wasn't mature enough. But I've really enjoyed my life.

In a sense you could say I'm now paying dues, but being a mother was never my most important goal. I'm actually very happy. The regret is maybe five percent in a 100-percent scale. I've had, and continue to have, a great life.

Randy is an interesting case because although she's not a baby boomer, she saw early that she had choices, probably because her mother had a career and provided Randy with a different kind of role model. But she also shows how not having children can be the unforeseen consequence of a series of unrelated decisions and circumstances. Randy's reasons for not having children run the full spectrum: she's voluntarily childless because she postponed children; she has no children because her second husband didn't want them, at least not while she could have them; and she's a victim of infertility and widowhood.

Randy's life shows how, for many women, the issue of children doesn't fall into a neatly defined package of simply wanting or not wanting children, of having or not having regrets. Shades of grey speckled with ambivalence have colored her life and her choices, and continue to affect her feelings about her chances, choices, and circumstances.

One Hundred Years of Near Solitude and no Regrets

Marjory Stoneman Douglas was one hundred years old when I saw her, the oldest woman I interviewed. Although she was almost totally blind and wore thick glasses for farsightedness, Mrs. Douglas lived alone in a dark, cool, Hansel-and-Gretel-type cottage in Coconut Grove, Florida. Off the road down a grassy path and tucked back into a grove of southern Florida pines, the cottage was barely noticeable among its neighbors of opulent Spanish-style mansions.

I arrived on time and banged the enormous knocker on the heavy, carved wooden door, but she didn't answer. Her secretary had warned me that she dozed off often and might not hear me. So I knocked again and again, calling her name loudly.

After twenty minutes of knocking and waiting, I started peeking into her windows, calling her name to try to rouse her. Although her secretary had confirmed my appointment with her just two hours earlier, Mrs. Douglas was definitely not there to meet me. I sat on the stoop and waited for half an hour.

She was forty minutes late for our appointment, but not because she had forgotten. She had been treated to lunch by two admiring acquaintances. They had had several Manhattans and just couldn't rush back for our interview. They pulled up and apologized for their tardiness. I was so grateful that my trip wasn't wasted, I assured them it was okay.

I had never even seen anyone one hundred years old before, much less interviewed a centenarian. But on that 90°, humid June day in southern Florida, Douglas was a sight to admire. She moved slowly from the car to the cool comfort of her spacious living room in a hot pink, long-sleeved polyester dress. Her living room was overpowered by her desk, and cassette tapes were strewn everywhere. Antique furniture adorned the spacious, cool room.

I noticed a tiny bedroom with a single, unmade bed off a simple, green kitchen that was small and messy. The kitchen sported just a simple two-burner camping-style stove. Two cats slinked around in the summer heat.

I expected either a gentle, grandmotherly type or a cranky, cantankerous old woman. I was glad I had prepared myself; on the subject of children, she was cranky and impatient with me.

> I never wanted children. Why should I bother? I could never see why everyone wanted children. Why should everyone have them? That would be terrible. Stop asking me about children. I don't want children, I never wanted children, and I don't want children now. And it's none of anybody's business.

I asked her what the rewards have been for never having children. What curves had her life taken because she had never had them?

> I think that's the silliest question I ever heard of. I've been busy all my life doing things that have nothing to do with children or grandchildren and yet you ask me that. That's silly. You know what I've been doing all my life and it's had nothing to do with children.

Yes, I had read her autobiography, *Voice of the River*. I knew that she had spent her twenties as a reporter for the earliest editions of the *Miami Herald*, and her thirties and forties as a freelance magazine writer. In her fifties, she authored her first book which helped save the Everglades from development doom. She became a local and national spokeswoman for the Everglades' miles of swamps, a precious refuge for nature.

As an author and avowed environmentalist, Douglas spent her seventies, eighties, and nineties giving speeches to inspire Floridians to respect and preserve the Everglades. She had been named a Woman of the Year by *Ms.* magazine in 1986 and had been featured in *National Geographic*.

But why the lack of interest in children? I had assumed that most of my older interviewees would have been raised to want children and to assume they would have children. What were the threads of her life that had woven a different pattern?

Marjory Stoneman was an only child born in 1890 in Minneapolis. When she was five, her mother left her father after financial problems set them back. Marjory's mother sought refuge with her parents and unmarried sister in Massachusetts. She suffered a nervous breakdown and proceeded to take a passive mothering role. Marjory's maiden aunt took over the care of her child. Marjory talks about it in her autobiography:

> My Aunt Fanny was in many ways my caretaker, and the caretaker of the entire family. In those days in New England, the youngest daughter was almost always sacrificed in this way. She didn't marry and stayed at home to help the parents in their later years. Up and down our street were at least thirteen old maids, sometimes two to a family. So many men had been killed in the Civil War and so many others had gone West, there were 60,000 unmarried women in New England alone. This made it a very female society. I was brought up in that. The only men I really knew until I got to high school were my grandfather and my Uncle Charlie.[1]

Aunt Fanny, Marjory recalls, was very pretty and attracted men in flocks, but Aunt Fanny would have nothing to do with them. She just wasn't interested. She cared for her parents and did the bookkeeping for her father's brass foundry. Her passions were the "young ladies" bicycle club and astronomy. As Marjory's mother became more and more withdrawn, Aunt Fanny became increasingly important to Marjory. Marjory writes that "she did everything in the world for me. It was my aunt who saw that I got up in the morning and had a good breakfast, who, along with my grandmother, sewed my clothes, and who tried and failed to teach me arithmetic."[2]

But her mother's problems cast a pallor of gloom over the little girl. She became a shy teenager with a rich inner life, based on reading and daydreaming. Reared in a feminine society and on a street full of unmarried, childless women, Marjory described herself as plump and unattractive. But she was smart, and Aunt Fanny's secret stash of cash allowed her to go to Wellesley College in 1908.

> . . . [A] woman's college was the answer. It freed me of the pressure of the boys' presence, which made me very self-conscious. Since I was still unattractive to them, at least at Wellesley they weren't around to remind me of it. I could forget all that. I could be myself as an individual, as opposed to a young girl. There were no men to

take over. And men do take over, bless their hearts, they've always had to take over, they're out there in front, in the cold as it were, sticking their necks out. When men are in an institution, they tend to dominate it. It's their nature. I don't object to it, it's just that they can't help it. . . .

Men remained an elusive part of Marjory's life for several more years.

I don't think anybody can imagine how ignorant, how innocent girls of my kind were in those days, in the winters of 1913 and 1914. We were an ignorant and an innocent generation. The word sex was not spoken in respectable families. I knew nothing whatsoever about reproduction. In junior and senior year, we had lectures behind locked doors. It was supposed to be sex hygiene but it wasn't about sex at all, it was about pregnancy. Nothing was said whatsoever about how you got pregnant, except that it was a secret process.

I'm sure that other young women in my class knew as little about sex as I did. One girl fainted when the lecturer showed a picture of a pregnant woman. Nobody explained, even in whispers. . . . outside of the general idea that something had to happen between the male and female, we were completely vague. I had some dim idea it had something to do with the navel.[3]

All through college, Marjory never had a date. Not only was she seemingly unattractive to men and somewhat overweight, she also had a nervous giggle which she's sure put the young men off, too. She writes that "secretly, of course, I was immensely attracted to them, and suffered a great deal."[4]

After college, Marjory went to work as the educational director of a giant department store in New Jersey. One day, when she was twenty-three, she casually met a man thirty years older. A friend of hers was walking down the street "obviously impressed with herself" for being accompanied by this six-foot-tall, attractive, and well-mannered man who was an editor at the local newspaper. When Marjory ran into him at the library some time later, they exchanged pleasantries. Marjory was dumbstruck by what happened next:

. . . [A]s I started to walk away he spoke to me again. No man had ever spoken to me again. I turned and looked at him, and realized he was staring at me with intense personal interest. It was

startling, something I'd never experienced. After that he began calling me up, coming to the store, asking me to lunch. This was un-
heard of, bizarre, completely unlikely, and also spectacular. In
about three months we were married. . . .

On my part it wasn't love exactly. It was sheer delight. I didn't
know Mr. Douglas well enough to have loved him. In fact, I couldn't
have told you anything about him at all. It was all so overwhelming . . .

I discovered sex. I came to the experience not so much with love
or even passion, but with a wild, eager curiosity. There must have
been a good deal of latent passion in me. At last, I'd found out about
men.

I thought sex was a little crazy, really. It almost made me laugh.
My husband had excellent manners always. . . . He was kind and
instructive and the whole thing was very successful.[5]

But her marriage was not. After a year or so, her husband was
carted off to jail for six months for something to do with bad
checks. When released, the couple went to New York City, where
Marjory read a lot and didn't do much else.

In my marriage I was completely dominated. Since then I've
never wanted to give myself over to the control or even the slightest
possible domination of anybody, particularly a man. I know I'm one
of those women who's susceptible to giving up. It's antithetical: I'm
so independent a person basically, but I drifted through this queer
limbo of life in Kenneth's tow.[6]

An uncle visited one day and informed Marjory that her husband had been forging her long-lost father's bank drafts. He con-
vinced her to walk out on him and to go see her father in Florida.
Marjory hadn't heard a word from him since she was five. He had
started a newspaper in a distant, isolated town of fewer than 5,000
residents called Miami. It was 1915; Marjory was twenty-five years
old, and the thunder of World War I was starting to roll across
Europe.

Marjory met Andy and they became engaged. But war was taking over everyone's lives. Andy went overseas, and Marjory en-
listed, too, becoming the first woman in Florida ever to enlist in
the armed forces. After a year of impatience with Navy clerical

work, she was honorably discharged and joined the American Red Cross in France. She became engaged to another man while there, but things didn't work out. She was delighted to return to Florida, not far from where Andy was. But then she was working at a job at her father's newspaper that was far superior to the dead end jobs he could find. When he was offered a job in the north, he took it and never called for her to join him.

Marjory writes in her autobiography:

> In time, I heard Andy was married and had children and a happy life. It was inevitable. I was beginning to realize that I was not the marrying kind. In my secret heart, I didn't want to get married again. I never wanted children. I wanted books. I couldn't see why every woman had to have children. It wasn't necessary. I didn't want a normal family life, I wanted my own life in my own way. I was too interested in writing editorials and in writing my column.[7]

Marjory worked her way up in the newspaper business, had her cottage built in 1926, wrote stories for the *Saturday Evening Post*, and then quit the paper to write a novel. At 51, she wrote her now famous book, *River of Grass*, about the Everglades. She has never stopped writing since.

I asked her how old age was without children and grandchildren to look after her. Unlike most of the older women I interviewed, Ms. Douglas was an only child, so she had no brothers or sisters. She also had no nieces or nephews. In fact, she had no living relatives she could think of. But family didn't seem very important to her; and she makes that clear in her autobiography:

> We make such a fetish of the family. I think we've created a tremendous mythology about it. We believe the family must be maintained, it's the basis of society, etc. Yet for a great many of us, the family has been difficult. Many of the troubles of mankind are family troubles, more devastating and more lasting than other kinds of troubles. Almost any well-run orphanage would be better than some families I've known. There are countless unjust and narrow-minded families, and parents who bring up children in hatred for reasons that are invalid.
>
> Just being a family is not enough.[8]

And what about children?

> You don't have to have children. I've got lots of friends. If you're lonely in your old age, it's because you've failed to make friends. I don't need a family. I have friends. And if you think you can always count on children, you are much mistaken. Because I know a lot of families who can't count on their children at all. It's too bad if you didn't make arrangements for your old age—you planned your life very badly if that is the case.

During our half-hour conversation, Ms. Douglas's phone kept ringing. I could see that she had a network to call upon. I knew her philosophy and strategy from her autobiography:

> When you do things for yourself, you'll have more people to come see you because you'll have something to talk about. And you won't be complaining, which is a bad habit to acquire. Complaining about being old, nobody loves you, nobody comes to see you is a big mistake. Maybe people don't come to see you because you bore them to death. Reading books and having something to talk about will save you and your friends some trouble.[9]

I also knew from her autobiography that Ms. Douglas had inherited the cottage next door. She had rented it out and, while in her eighties, had rented it to a younger man who became her friend. As her health failed and her needs grew, he looked after her. They had an arrangement, she wrote, in which he was to be an heir. The bulk of her estate is willed to the Friends of the Everglades.

For Marjory Stoneman Douglas, the fact that she was single most of her life partly accounts for her never having children. But two other factors also played an important role: she was an only child with an unhappy childhood. Both factors predominate in the life histories of women who don't have children.[10] Men were minor characters in Ms. Douglas's female-dominated society, and she grew up with female role models galore. She wrote that many of her teachers in high school and at Wellesley had a powerful influence on her, and that most were single and childless.

Furthermore, Ms. Douglas was living an adult-centered lifestyle with strong supports for not having children. With so many role models around her, her way of life was easily accepted. She moved in adult-centered circles, writing for the newspaper, being active in her community. Her career was important, and she never got close to marrying again.

She clearly had no regrets and would not speculate about what she would have done had she married the war-torn veteran, or another man she loved. Looking back like that, she said, "was stupid."

CHAPTER TWO

Tracking the Trends
Before the Baby Boomers

Give me children or else I die.
—RACHEL
in Genesis

"Be fruitful and multiply," God commands in Genesis. Sex is forbidden if it's not for reproductive purposes, the Roman Catholic church preaches. "He who has no children is as if he were dead," the Jewish Talmud condemns.

Yet, there have always been some women who have defied the norm of getting married and having children. Although the reasons for each woman may be complex and highly individual, a woman's circumstances are largely molded by her times.

Reproduction, of course, is vital for the survival of the species. In years past, large families were not only unavoidable but actually made life easier. More children meant more laborers and more people to form a family version of social security. Families took care of each other, or so the idea went. And since so many infants and children used to die young, the more babies the better. Birth control was primitive and children were useful and necessary, so many a married woman had babies continuously until she or her husband died at a relatively young age, usually before all the children were grown. Even in the early 1900s, when fifty was the average life span, married couples could expect less than a year with an "empty nest" before one of them died.[1]

To raise a brood, mothers labored from dawn to dusk. Unmarried or childless female relatives were expected to help out. As many hands as possible were needed, after all, to carry on the perpetual cycle of tending to the needs of the young. Aunts without children often became "surrogate" mothers for nieces and nephews whose parents were overburdened with making a living and caring for so many children. And when aging parents grew feeble and ill, it was usually the daughter without children, if there was one, who nursed them.

Working-class women without children (and even many with children) typically worked in middle-class homes as nannies, housekeepers, or maids. Middle-class women without children tended to devote their lives to low-paying, but nurturant and rewarding jobs as teachers, nurses, social workers, and missionaries. Rural women went on to do both kinds of jobs. In either case, these women were expected to provide care both for their families and in their professions. These patterns defined the lives of women who are today in their eighties and never had children.

Carol, for example, born in 1898, was the eldest of eight children. She remembers when she was as young as fourteen thinking she would never have children. She lived on the family farm until she was fifteen, when she left to go to high school. She never really went home again. Right after school, she moved in with a family to take care of their five small children; she stayed with them for twenty-two years until she was forty and met her husband. He was a boarder in the home of one of her married sisters.

By that time, she was weary of taking care of children, having also helped to raise her seven siblings throughout her childhood as well as five children for twenty-two years. The country was already in debt and she worried that it would only get worse, and it did. When she was thirty-seven, she remembers her biological clock alarming her briefly that she might not have children, but the feeling of alarm passed. When Carol and her husband got married, they knew they didn't want children.

> We had practically no money, and children cost a lot. We were older by then, but just in case, I was sterilized. It never bothered

me that we were different. Sometimes, I think it'd be nice to have children, but then again, children can be awful bossy when you're old and take over your life. I've seen it happen again and again.

Carol's husband died of lung cancer four years after they married, and Carol bought herself a gas station where she also opened a small store. "Dear, if I'd had young children then, it would have been so very hard for me," she told me, adding, "No, I didn't feel more alone, I felt less burdened."

Her brother and his family and her parents lived close by. When World War II broke out, Carol wrote to her customers in the service, trying to send them some good cheer from home. Only one ever answered. She married him within months, while he was still in the service. She was forty-five years old. They sold the gas station, bought a farm, and Carol worked in a florist shop until she retired.

Today, Carol is ninety-two and still lives with that husband in a small apartment in a senior citizens housing project. She's in excellent health and still uses the stationary bike next to her bed. Abundant plants crowd her small apartment. Passionate hunters, Carol and her husband, eighty-eight, spent fifty years enjoying the freedom to go on extended hunting and camping trips. They've been hunting in every state in this country, every province in Canada, and Australia. Carol often traveled with her brothers and was always the only woman on the trip since all her sisters-in-law had to stay home to care for the children. This summer, her husband is taking her on a "mystery trip"; Carol has no idea what he's cooking up, but she is eager to take off as they've done every summer for more than half a century.

Carol never feels deprived about not having children, and besides, she's still very close to the five children she helped raise:

They are my family, I'm very much in contact with them, especially one girl—seventy and widowed now—who's very close and dear to me. They took the place of my children. I think I've gotten all the benefits of having children through them. I still worry over them. The widowed one expected us to move in with her when we moved a few years ago, but we'd already made up our minds to move here.

Since Carol lives within ten miles of where she has resided for the past seventy years, she knows many people in the area. Several of her sisters and brothers or their widowers/widows live nearby, as do several of the "youngsters" (all retired now) she helped raise. Carol feels no lack of people looking in on her.

> I suppose if I'd married at thirty I would have had children, because that would have been normal. But I haven't missed them, really. And it doesn't bother me now either. For me, not having children has meant I could travel a lot and be a lot better off financially. I can't think of any drawbacks for me in not having them; I never felt a lack. I've had a good life and I have no regrets.

Carol says she seldom thought about the fact that she didn't have children. In fact, one of her sisters who married never had children, and Carol and she never even discussed it. To this day, Carol has no idea why her sister never had children. The topic was too taboo to talk about. People never asked about it; it was assumed that you were "barren," which was too painful or too embarrassing to discuss.

Clara, born on a farm about eight years later than Carol, never talked about it much, and she says she didn't think about it that much either. She was the youngest of six born to her forty-four-year-old mother. She left home to go to high school, and started teaching at eighteen. She married at twenty-five, never got pregnant, and never knew why. She was too busy to dwell on it much, though, she says. Her four brothers and sisters lived close by and had large families themselves. They eagerly welcomed Clara's help whenever it was offered. She spent her middle age helping to take care of more than two-dozen nieces and nephews *and* assuming full care for her aging parents.

"I remember I used to go around from house to house taking care of them. They all lived nearby," Clara recalled. It was the depression and her husband didn't have a job, so they had to move in with her parents in their ten-room house. Her teaching salary kept them going. Shortly after Clara married, her mother became ill, and Clara and her husband nursed her until she died several years later in 1938. Her father's health and sight started failing immediately; within several years, he got worse. Although all her brothers and sisters live nearby, his care fell to Clara, the only one without children. She quit teaching to take care of him full time until he died. Clara was forty-three; her husband was fifty. Clara figured it was too late to adopt a child:

> I expected we'd have children, but I guess God didn't see fit to send me any. We had thought seriously about adopting, but my father lived to be 87, and he was blind the last eleven years and needed so much help. We didn't think it was fair, living in the same house and all, to bring a baby in in his condition. Even feeding him was a problem.
>
> I guess God just left it to me to take care of a lot of other kids.

All told, Clara spent twenty years teaching all eight grades in a one-room schoolhouse, twenty-three more years teaching the fourth grade, and fifty years teaching Sunday school. She's been a widow now for fifteen years but still lives in the same rural Pennsylvania town she's lived in for sixty-four years. All her brothers and sisters have died, yet she lives within a few miles of at least fifteen to twenty families of relatives—her nieces and nephews who are now retired themselves. "I speak to or see relatives every day, and I see my former children (students) everywhere I go," Clara told me. "Just last week, one of my students from California was visiting the east coast and he rented a car to come visit me. I had him from first through eighth grade." Today, he's a seventy-year-old retired Baptist minister.

Most of Carol and Clara's peers married and had children. Only about ten percent remained childless. But then the disaster of the Great Depression struck this country and shattered the lives of millions. An entire generation of young women came of age during that dark hour in American history. For many, it was too bleak for children.

The Depression's Dip in Fertility

The early 1930s were among the gloomiest years Americans have ever known. No matter how hard people worked or tried to find work, the economic forces of the times were overpowering, and most Americans became dragged down in the undertow.

Men would wait outside employment offices all night to be the first in line in the morning. Families could be seen rummaging through garbage heaps, gnawing on discarded bones and sucking on dirty watermelon rinds. Social historian William Manchester describes these consequences of destitution in his tome *The Glory and the Dream*. Bands of men prowled the back alleys of restaurants, scrounging for scraps, hunting for anything remotely edible to fill the empty hole gnawing in their guts.

Manchester tells of one child too drowsy from hunger to pay attention in school one day. She couldn't go home and eat, she explained to her teacher, for it was her sister's turn to eat that day. Parents would tremble from self-starvation, Manchester writes, so that their children would not go hungry. It was a bitter father who said, "A worker's got no right to have kids any more."[2]

Edith was a pretty young woman of twenty-two when the Great Depression clenched its iron grip on America. Edith's life would be forever affected by those bleak years. She was of marrying age but dreamed of studying medicine. Her mother burst her fantasies, harshly telling her such ideas were absurd. Children listened to their parents then, Manchester reports. Youngsters were loyal to their families and did what they were told. There was no teen culture to pull them away from family influence. The only media was radio, and the only news was dreary and depressing.

So Edith, a good Jewish girl from Brooklyn, did what her mother thought she should and went to secretarial school right after high school instead of thinking about attending medical school. After three months, she'd had enough and quit, then lied her way into her first job. She was lucky, for in those days even elevator operators were required to have bachelor degrees. But she was a legal secretary and didn't lose her job during even the worst of times. At her mother's insistence, she showed attention to a young man whose mother had just died. When he asked her to marry him, she accepted.

There was no money. It was so rough, you can't imagine how bad it was. It was a very dire time.

Edith became pregnant in 1932, what Manchester calls "the cruelest year":

It would have been a terrible time to have baby. My older brother had a friend who was studying medicine—I don't know if he was a doctor or not—I was so young and so frightened.

Anyway, I had an abortion. I never regretted it. My husband didn't give a darn. I didn't want much sex after that. I was scared to death of having children then. Things were so bad we had to move in with my family; they were trying to keep their house. That was the beginning of the end. My two brothers lived at home, and the oldest was always arguing with my husband. It got very, very bad.

We finally got another apartment, my husband and I, but neither one of us could talk much. We'd just sit there morose, not saying much. I realized this wasn't going to be successful.

Edith, now eighty-two, divorced her husband seven years after her wedding vows. She never remarried or had any children. Like thousands of other women her age, having children would have made hard times even tougher.

Despite the fact that most businesses were collapsing during the depression, a few boomed. One was the contraceptive business, which had sprung up in 1916, when Margaret Sanger opened the first birth-control clinic. Although Sanger was jailed nine times for distributing her "obscene" materials, women were finally able to take some control over their reproductive lives.

Edith and her peers set the record for the highest rate of childlessness ever recorded in this country. As lives fell apart in the wake of the 1929 stock market crash, record numbers of women put off marriage and children as part of their strategy to survive. Almost one-quarter, twenty-two percent, of the women of childbearing age at that time—about sixteen percent of married women—never had children.[3] Married black women experienced a record-breaking twenty-eight percent childlessness rate.[4] Some sociologists have noted that although postponing children is an understandable way to survive dire times, it's a mystery why these women didn't have babies later. Of course, some never married or later divorced, but at least one Census Bureau demographer has speculated that many of these women perhaps ended up valuing their freedom from children and didn't want to disrupt an already contented condition.[5]

In Edith's case, after her divorce, she went into the family business in New York's garment district. As the outside seller, working with fashionable designers, she did very well. "After my divorce, I had a good time," she said. "I didn't stop to think that children should be part of my life. That never changed."

Edith worked in the business until she retired. She has traveled to Europe, South America, the Orient, Scandanavia, Switzerland, and even through the Soviet Union. Although she knew very few other women in her circumstances—unmarried, well-off, and childless—it never bothered her. She said, "I never felt a stigma although I didn't know anyone else really who didn't marry or have children. In fact, I think a lot of my friends were very jealous of me."

Edith moved to Florida to retire and worked as a hospital volunteer for seventeen years, consoling families with loved ones in surgery. She remained close with her brothers and especially intimate with a cousin and her children. Today, that beloved cousin is dead, but Edith's friendship with her cousin's children is special to her. "They call me, I visit them," she said. "I get three- and four-page letters from them. They are very dear to me. I tell you, I have never regretted the fact that I don't have any children; that's the truth."

Lillian also married at the beginning of the depression. She waited until she had finished college and had worked several years before marrying her high-school sweetheart in 1930. Although they'd been engaged for ten years and times were getting harder, they didn't think they should put the wedding off much longer. He was a medical student, and Lillian could work to support him through school. Lillian assumed that once he finished, she'd never work again or be anything but a loyal, devoted doctor's wife and mother to his children.

It was just assumed that I'd have children. We'd sometimes talk about it after we got married. At one point I thought I couldn't wait to have a family, but he was so busy, and there was no money to have a child. The depression was peaking and it just wouldn't be the right time until we knew he'd be firmly established.

But the pressure of medical school coupled with the effects of the depression became too much for him. He started drinking, and Lillian couldn't take it anymore; she left him in 1932, that blighted year in American history. She was twenty-nine years old and had no means to support herself.

An old friend from Buffalo had just lost her job, so the two women pooled their resources to try to make it through those harrowing years.

I don't think I ever thought much about having children after that. Getting through the depression was really difficult. All you thought about at that time was where your next meal was coming from.

First, Lillian and her friend sold Compton's Pictured Encyclopedias in a college town where faculty salaries had just been cut. Things were "touch and go" for three years; Lillian worked wherever she could, washing dishes, collecting bills, selling salted peanuts by the bag, and then landing a job with the Work Projects Administration writing a bibliography of game birds and animals. In 1935, she opened a tearoom and a year later began a decade-long job working for the new Old Age Assistance Program; later she became a probation officer, a reporter for a local newspaper, and a public relations officer for a college. She's proud of being a founding member of a host of community organizations, including a state crafts guild, local writers' group, and a local spiritual group that now serves as her extended family.

Her friendship with her friend flourished, and the two lived together in what has been called over the years, a "Boston marriage," (two unmarried women living together) until 1975, when her friend died of cancer. Today, Lillian is eighty-seven years old and lives alone in a retirement home. Her room is cluttered with wall-to-wall bookshelves and stacks of magazines and books. Until last year, she wrote for a local newspaper. This year, an earlier book of hers was republished.

On the topic of children, she said:

> Not having children has never been a factor in my life. It isn't that I don't like children. I love kids, but I never had a maternal drive or anything. In my era, when you married, it was expected you'd have children, and that was it. When my marriage was new, I just assumed I'd have children, but after that, I never regretted not having children. It's just the way it was.

While her niece takes care of her financial and personal papers, a devoted fifty-year old friend from her spiritual group helps her every week with her banking and chores. Is she ever lonely? When I asked her, she said, "Good gracious, no. There are too many things to do."

I could see what was occupying some of Lillian's time at the moment. Next to her bed was a pile of papers and books, from psychology, herbal medicine, and self-help books to *Beyond Stonehenge* and the *New York Times*.

These are just a few of the millions of women who comprised the largest generation of childless women in the history of the U.S. The majority of women, of course, still had babies in spite of the gloomy years of the Great Depression. And that generation of babies came of age in the 1940s and 1950s and made history themselves for having so *many* babies.

The 1950s: Fertility Fervor

As millions of soldiers streamed back home from World War II, the depression babies, now young women, poured out of the workplace, where they had kept the machinery going during the war. They paired up with returning soldiers and married younger than ever—from a median age of twenty-two down to twenty and dipping even into the teens.[6] The newlyweds returned to farms and cities, their only desire to put the war far behind them. Suburbs hatched, with thousands of brand-new, look-alike homes.

Fathers went to work, and the trend of mothers staying home, far from the workplace, in isolation, to take care of children, peaked. Patriotism, prosperity, and pronatalism (meaning probirth, or proparenthood) reigned.

Everyone had babies and not just one or two. Broods of three, four, five, and six children were not uncommon. The baby rate soared to record levels, expanding almost as quickly as India's. More than seventy-two million children were born from 1946 to 1964, the booming, burgeoning, post-World War II baby-making era.

By 1954, four million babies were being born each year, and that rate chugged on to 1964. Three kids was considered an ideal family; twice as many women gave birth to three or more babies in the late 1950s than twenty years prior. "The increase was most spectacular among college women; they were abandoning careers to bear four, five, and six or more children," writes historian William Manchester.[7]

Education for women began to slide. Only thirty-five percent of college students were women, compared with forty percent before the war. Proportionately fewer women in America were going to college than in any European country. Of those who did become coeds, two-thirds dropped out before graduating (like Barbara Bush), most to support their husbands through school or to head off in search of greener husband-hunting pastures.

Americans in the 1950s were obsessed with having children and raising them. The baby boomers were nurtured in a new, child-centered society, where mom devotedly made sure Bobby went to Little League and put rubber bands on his braces, and that Barbie practiced her tap dancing and found the dreamy gown she drooled over for the high-school prom. "Ozzie and Harriet" and "Father Knows Best" promoted the sugarcoated myth that raising children was fun and easy, and the only key to ultimate fulfillment for women.

Society *needed* women at home, minding the children, far from the workplace, argues psychiatrist Ann Dally, author of *Inventing Motherhood: The Consequences of An Ideal*. In order to give men their jobs back and to abolish the costly day-care facilities set up to get families through World War II, women were encouraged to leave their jobs and raise children. Motherhood was glorified and idealized as never before, and the burgeoning middle class ate it up.[8]

So women had babies and more babies—3.7 kids per mom at fertility's peak in 1957. Childlessness slumped to record lows. Only seven percent of women of childbearing age—only three percent of married women that age—did not have children.[9] Choice in those days meant either a family or a career. If you were married and had children, you only worked if you had to. The few women with lifelong commitments to their careers usually did so at the expense of marriage and children.

Older women today admit that they didn't even think about having children in those days. They just did it. They were brought up to conform, and for as long as they could remember, had assumed they would be mothers. There was no other way. Motherhood was synonymous with womanhood. You grew up, you got married, you had children. Period. That was the "American dream."

Adrienne Rich, author of *Of Woman Born*, recalls her feelings in the 1950s:

I became a mother in the family-centered, consumer-oriented, Freudian-American world of the 1950s. My husband spoke eagerly of the children we would have; my parents-in-law awaited the birth of their grandchild. I had no idea of what I wanted, what I could or could not choose. I only knew that to have a child was to assume adult womanhood to the full, to prove myself, to be "like other women."[10]

Randy, the fifty-year-old editor mentioned in Chapter One, was a student at the University of Illinois during the late 1950s:

I remember in my sorority that in January and March, the seniors who were graduating that June were in a total panic if they weren't engaged. They'd call up a guy they had maybe dated when they were sophomores and had turned down, and invited him on a date. It ended up they'd get married in June. At that time, if you weren't married by graduation, there was something very wrong with you.

Margaret, sixty-six, was living in a small city in Connecticut around that time. She was twenty-seven when she married, late for women of that era to marry. She spent the next twelve years trying to get pregnant. She had a "whopper" of a fibroid tumor and extensive endometriosis. Although surgery corrected the problems, she never conceived, and at thirty-nine, when a tumor took over her womb, she had to have a hysterectomy. She recalled:

> My friends were on their third and fourth pregnancies and here I was, thirty-five, and still not pregnant. I became acutely aware of it. We didn't know *anybody* who didn't have children. I mean everyone, *everybody* had children. We all just assumed that we'd have children. They were around in all parts of our lives.

Maybe everybody seemed to have children, but not everybody was happy about it. Grumblings were in the air; suburbia was plagued by a perplexing malaise. Homemaker-mothers discovered that their knights in shining armor hadn't carried them off into the sunset. Instead, the landscape seemed dreary and draining. Raising three or four children was a full-time job, and many housewives grew irritable and fatigued by their daily tasks. Baby boomer girls grew up watching their weary moms shuffle them off to school only to shop, cook, launder, and clean all day. The girls watched and they listened. Is this what life was all about? they wondered. Was this it?

CHAPTER THREE

Tracking the Trends of the Baby Boomers

As women on the cutting edge of social change, this group is especially well situated to illuminate the causes, contours, and likely consequences of women's changing social position. They were born into a period of rapid social change and thus had to make work and family decisions in a changing historical context. Through their choices, these women became unwitting molders of social change as well.

—KATHLEEN GERSON,
*Hard Choices: How Women Decide About
Work, Career, and Motherhood.*[1]

The story of the baby-boomer girls' control over their fertility is the story of their lives. Born to the children of the depression, the Woodstock generation grew up in the booming, prosperous postwar era. They were swooning and shrieking over the Beatles when feminist Betty Friedan struck a raw nerve in mothers throughout the land. *The Feminine Mystique* (1963) described the "problem" that didn't have a name. Something was amiss in suburbia. The "problem" was that, instead of rainbows and rhapsody from tending to hard-working husbands and three lovely children, housewives were frustrated and fatigued, despondent and depressed, but too guilty and confused to admit it. Friedan's book helped blast open every assumption and social myth women held about expecting ultimate fulfillment from being housewives and mothers.

The malaise of suburban mothers provoked a slow but steady

stream of stark realizations in the budding teenage girls about the status of women: that wives were sacrificing their own educations and vocations for their husbands'; that women labored all day at home in return for little recognition; that working women were stuck in menial jobs and paid far less than men for doing the same work; that mothers were weary, worn-out, and perplexed in a dreary, drizzly existence where Mrs. Roger Smith often didn't even use her own first name.

Yet, Mrs. Roger Smith was a devoted mother who took her task of child rearing very seriously. Her generation had grown up with so little and with the constant threat of losing what little they had. Mrs. Roger Smith was determined that her kids would have all the advantages. Education was the golden ticket in the land of JFK's Camelot. The post-Sputnik era was dedicated to preparing the children, even girls, for the coming space age. Kids growing up in the sixties were urged to compete and achieve.

Fran, fifty-four, was coming out of college then. Unlike most of her peers, she knew early on that she was not going to be like her mother, who was "perfectly miserable" as a full-time house-wife. Fran had loftier dreams, and becoming someone's wife wasn't one of them:

> I grew up in a time and era when I could either be my own person or be married, but I couldn't be both. Men were programmed to be dominant. I didn't think I could be independent in a marriage and didn't want to test it.

After college, Fran went to the Big Apple in pursuit of a mean-ingful career and landed a job at NBC. Although she excelled at her job, she couldn't break out of the secretarial ranks, so she quit and worked in public relations for a few years, then returned to school for a master's degree in finance. She worked on Wall Street, where she struggled against an all-male institution. "I was one of the first fifty female stockbrokers in the country," she said. "But to get there was insanity. Just to take the exam I had to beg." Fran paused, then she added:

> You know, in my era, there weren't any choices. You either got married and had children or you didn't get married and didn't have children. Now you can drift into those choices, but before,

you had to be very clear. I never wanted to get married, and in my day, I couldn't have had a child solo. I just didn't feel I could bring a child into this world without a husband—it would have been too rough for the child. If I were a young woman today, I still don't think I'd get married, but I probably would have had a child and a career.

Yet, it hasn't been an issue for me. I'm basically neutral about it. I'm very comfortable with my choices—probably 8.5 on a ten-point scale.

Judy Long, now fifty, was also one of those early feminist "warriors." As a child, she saw her mother grow increasingly angry and frustrated trying to raise three children alone while her husband was off at sea during World War II. Then he re-enlisted because he enjoyed the service so much. "There was nothing about [my mother's] life that looked attractive," Judy recalled. Judy's father's life, on the other hand, seemed wonderful. When he finally returned from the war, Judy was enthralled at the parades and fanfare she thought were just for him. He returned to his professorship and his radio program in rural Vermont. Judy loved tinkering with his typewriter and basking in the students' admiration for him. This was the kind of life she wanted, Judy decided; her father had it made, her mother only helped make it. So in spite of the social pressure then in the early 1960s to seek a Mrs. right after college, Judy went for a Ph.D. instead. Her first job was as an assistant professor of sociology at the University of Chicago, where she embarked on research concerning women's issues:

I had the good fortune to meet the only living feminist on the faculty. She infected me with feminism before they fired her, and I infected several others before they fired me.

It was impossible for a graduate student to get a dissertation approved if it was about women. Many outstanding students dropped out there; you can't imagine it now. It was thought it couldn't be serious if it was about women. The only reason anybody would want to do research about women, the faculty thought, was if they were totally unprofessional and spilling their guts instead of seeing a psychiatrist, as if they were acting out through their research.

But Judy persisted and landed a job at an Ivy League school, only to be denied tenure a decade later with a dozen other female faculty. They sued the university for discriminating against women and for paying women lower wages. The women lost, but Judy didn't give up. Today, she teaches in the women's studies program at Syracuse University.

In her quest to succeed in academia where "every part of it was so hard," Judy didn't even consider children. Although she married briefly at twenty-nine and remarried at thirty-seven, she said she couldn't have done both:

> I don't think I would have been willing to make the kind of sacrifice it involved. For me, I had a lack of an urge to be a mother coupled with a very strong career motivation. I have always been very independent and never thought about anybody but me taking care of me. That's all I could do, and I couldn't imagine taking care of a child, too.

By the time Fran, the stockbroker, and Judy were working their way up in their careers, the baby-boom girls were finishing high school as college-bound high achievers. But college life was no longer home economics, bobby socks, and saddle-shoed sorority teas. Student protests were flaring across campuses nationwide, upheaving the placid social landscape of American colleges. By the time Watergate shattered whatever little confidence many Americans had in the national government, the baby boomers en masse were challenging every social and political institution they encountered. The flower children doubted the validity of their parents' underlying values, roles, beliefs, relationships, and lifestyles, from work and play to housework and sex.

And then a pretty, long-haired blonde named Ellen Peck came along glamorizing the virtues of nonparenthood ("None is fun"). Her *The Baby Trap* (1971) dared women to at least *consider* the option of no children, rather than just blindly assuming they'd become mothers.

Baby Boomers Rewrite the Scripts for Womanhood

By the time the first wave of baby-boom women graduated from college, women like Professor Judy Long and Fran had cracked open a tantalizing new world. The glistening opportunities fueled the baby boomers' career aspirations while devaluing the alternative: motherhood. The boomer girls were rejecting their mothers' way; they swore they'd never grow up like them, caged in the suburban zoo of station wagons and tuna casseroles. They decided instead to follow the few feminist pioneers who had begun to cut a new path away from the well-worn one that went from college to crib and to head toward male-dominated careers. They had to work twice as hard to prove they could cut it, postponing kids for the corporate climb. *New York Times* columnist Anna Quindlen, writing in *Ms.* magazine, remembered how she felt:

> When I was growing up, motherhood was a kind of cage . . . you stayed home and felt your mind turn to the stuff that you put in little bowls and tried to spoon into little mouths and eventually wound up wiping off of little floors.
>
> By the time I was a grown-up, the answer, if you were strong and smart and wanted to be somebody, was not to be a mom. I certainly didn't want to be one . . . I wanted to climb unencumbered up to the top of whatever career ladder I managed to cling to. The women's movement was talking about new choices. Being a mom was an old one, and one that reeked of reliance on a man and loss of identity. What kind of choice was that?[2]

Choice was the buzzword. The pill, IUDs, and legalized abortion gave women real birth control for the first time in history. Many emerged from their teens with a conflicting and confusing set of values, "on the cutting edge of social change . . . collid[ing] with social institutions in flux."[3] Raised by traditional housewives and a TV diet of "Father Knows Best" and "Ozzie and Harriet," these girls had been emotionally prepared to grow up into young wives and mothers, only to be bombarded in their teens with new options. Many turned up their noses at the "tyrannical conventions of the American family,"[4] and rejected the traditional way.

The enticing world of careers and personal growth beckoned many a young woman who left Dr. Spock's baby world and "Leave It to Beaver" behind to the less adventurous and ambitious. To become a mother was now just one option among many, rather than the cultural mandate. To choose motherhood meant subjugating your needs for others, thereby thwarting success and personal fulfillment. "I either gave birth to someone else or I gave birth to myself," Gloria Steinem has been quoted as saying. "The Mary Tyler Moore Show" was one of the first shows to depict the new woman, not afraid of being single and forging through uncharted territory.

The late 1960s and early 1970s was fraught with experimentation and change. Women attended consciousness-raising workshops; communes and cooperative-living groups sprang up. Ellen Peck helped found the National Organization for Non-Parents in 1972, later renamed the National Alliance for Optional Parenthood which boasted some forty-six chapters around the country at its peak and earned national notoriety. Its slogan was: "To make non-parenthood not just a word, but an option." Although the organization disbanded ten years later for lack of interest, the term "child free" had entered the American vocabulary.

In just a decade there was a "wild swoop from the excessively domestic fifties to the fierce social unbuckling of the sixties and early seventies [leaving] confusion and wreckage. . . . Generations bared their teeth at one another," wrote Lance Morrow in *Time*.[5] Fertility plummeted to less than two children per woman in 1972 and to an all-time low of 1.74 in 1976. At the same time, education and work-force participation soared as young women ventured into the traditionally male-dominated work domain.

But then, the baby boomerang colored the 1980s. The first group of baby boomers were in their thirties. Those disillusioned with work longed for a simpler and more traditional life (for more on how job dissatisfaction is strongly linked to motherhood, see Chapter Four). The tick of their biological clocks began to sound like a thunderous and unrelenting time bomb that would render their wombs useless. So before it was too late forever, many thirtysomething and even some fortysomething women began a race against the clock. Since everything the boomer kids did made news, their having babies did, too.

Babies came back into vogue. The media's "babysell" romanticized motherhood again. On TV, Pampers and Huggies were lovingly used in soft-lit, all-white nurseries, with gurgling cherubs and lace curtains gently swaying in the breeze. In the films, *Three Men and A Baby* and *Three Men and A Young Lady*, bachelors Ted Danson and Tom Selleck went mushy over a young tot. Diane Keaton traded in her dress-for-success suits for aprons and bibs in *Baby Boom*, and Elizabeth McGovern going for a baby in *She's Having A Baby* helped sell babies back to the boomers. Even Ann Kelsey, the cool-headed lawyer on TV's "LA Law," wanted a baby. Commercials for Michelin tires preyed on parents' soft hearts. Aprica, Snugli, Fisher-Price, au pair, and nanny became household words.

With no role models ahead of them, some of these women thought they could do it all and tried to be so-called "superwomen," supposedly able to juggle a career and children. Others felt they *must* do it all; social pressure expected them to pursue challenging careers in tandem with motherhood. But many found their careers all-encompassing, and the thought of trying to squeeze in a child too seemed incompatible with their lives. Still others had waited too long. When they finally tried to take the plunge, time had rendered them, or their mates, infertile.

Infertility was the unexpected fallout of the women's revolution. Ellen, a forty-seven-year-old therapist who tried to get pregnant after she remarried at forty-two said:

> As a generation, we were very much swept away by the women's movement. We were very concerned about our rights and about being equal. I really believed you could have it all—a career, independence, sexual freedom, and so on, and that there wouldn't be negative consequences.
>
> We were all so naive. We were exploring and groping, swept away by the movement. I had to fight to have the career I wanted. I was afraid of having a family and being imprisoned. Younger women have grown up with more role models to follow. They take certain things for granted, which my generation never did. I don't know if I was able then to acknowledge the parts of me that were more traditional, that I would have liked to have a family.
>
> But you can't go back. I was the way I was. I made choices and pursued a career which I have really loved. My mother's life gave me the sense that having a family would have been very restrictive.

It seemed much better to be free and to give myself what I wanted. A lot of women around me delayed children, and I don't think we fully realized that we wouldn't be able to have them when we finally wanted to.

To help infertile couples, infertility clinics sprang up all over the country. Women who had climbed career ladders during their prime child-making years were now trekking to specialists, charting basal temperatures each morning, becoming the guinea pigs for new high-tech baby-making factories, and hiring surrogates to bear their children, thereby giving birth to a new era of child-producing alternatives.

As a generation, baby boomers have tried to keep the window of opportunity for having babies open longer and longer. Celebrities like Bette Midler, Glenn Close, Ursula Andress, Amy Irving, and Candice Bergen glamorized late motherhood. Even Connie Chung, who had broken career barriers ever since she entered broadcasting, announced in mid-1990 that, at forty-four, she was backing off her skyrocketing career to aggressively try to have a child. A few months later, scientists reported that they could produce successful pregnancies in women who had gone through menopause by using donor eggs and hormone treatments during pregnancy.

The years the baby boomers came of age were tumultuous ones with far-reaching social changes in education, work, and family patterns. These changes have exerted a powerful influence on women, marriage, and motherhood.

In education, for example, a smaller percentage of women were earning graduate degrees in the early 1960s than in the 1920s. But the 1970s and 1980s saw giant leaps for women. Education was not only key to opening career doors, but it has also been shown to correlate with shrinking fertility rates. Werner Fornos, the president of the Population Institute, has asserted that if women in the least developed countries could achieve but a seventh-grade education, worldwide fertility rates would be cut in half.[6] Such a link holds for higher education as well: the more education a woman has, the more likely it is that she will have fewer or no children. In 1980, while eleven percent of American women said they intended to have no children, seventeen percent of college-educated women said they expected to be child free.

Educational Gains for Women

• In the 1950s, women accounted for only one-fifth of college graduates; by 1989, women made up more than half the nation's crop of college grads.[7]

• In 1965–66, women accounted for thirty-four percent of the master's and twelve percent of the doctoral degrees. By 1986–87, women earned half the master's degrees, and more than one-third of the doctoral degrees.[8]

• In 1970–71, for example, only seven, eight, and nine percent of the law, veterinary medicine, and medical degrees respectively went to women;[9] by 1985–86, thirty-nine percent, forty-eight percent, and thirty-one percent went to women.[10] In 1990, thirty-six percent of medical students were female.

Better education leads to better jobs and stronger work commitments. Although fifty-nine percent of working women still work in the low-paying, pink-collar ghetto (the traditionally female, low-paying service and clerical job sectors), women continue to aggressively pursue typically male-dominated professions.

Career Gains for Women

• Ten times as many women were pursuing law in 1984 compared with twenty years earlier. In 1989, there were *twenty-four* times more female lawyers and judges (180,000) than in 1960.[11]

• By 1989, almost twenty percent of American physicians were female—almost seven times as many as in 1960. The number of female engineers rose from 7,404 in 1960 to 174,000 in 1989.[12]

• The number of women in managerial and professional jobs

nearly doubled between 1970 and 1980 and has continued to rise.[13] By 1990, thirty-two percent of computer-system analysts and almost half of all accountants and auditors were women.[14]

• In 1987, Women owned twice as many companies than ten years earlier.[15]

As women have poured into higher education and the professions, they've been able to maintain almost complete control over their baby-making functions. Widespread use of the pill and legal abortions have allowed women to choose when and if they mother. Women are staying single longer, putting off wedding vows to the record late median age of twenty-four. (That may sound young, but it means that half of all women are marrying later than age twenty-four.) And the longer they wait to marry, the harder it gets: women get more attached to their careers, more entrenched in their independent lifestyles, and have fewer unattached men to choose from. With soaring divorce rates, many married women find themselves single again.

More and more people are also living outside the bounds of traditional families; only slightly more than half the adults in 1989 (fifty-six percent) were married and living with their spouses, down from seventy-one percent in 1970.[16]

Even when they do marry, record numbers of women are postponing their first babies, which can influence whether they will end up ever having a baby.

Postponing Babies

• In the early 1970s, more than one-third (thirty-six percent) of women in their early twenties hadn't had children yet. Today, the proportion has swelled to almost half (forty-six percent) of women that age.

• In 1976, only thirteen percent of women in their thirties didn't have children. By 1988, the figure jumped to twenty percent.

Among college-educated working women, a full one-quarter of the thirty-five- to forty-five-year-olds didn't have kids.[17]
• In 1988, more than one-third (thirty-eight percent) of all women in their childbearing years (ages eighteen to forty-four) were childless, says the Census Bureau. Twenty-two percent of women in their thirties had never had children, compared with only thirteen percent in 1976.

The Baby Gap: Wanting vs. Having Babies

Although ninety percent of American women say they expect to have a baby sometime, the stark reality is that there's a big gap between expecting to have a baby "sometime" and actually having one. If they're not married, the chance that they will marry keeps shrinking as they age.[18] Even if they are married but have postponed children, the odds that divorce, career demands, infertility, and other life-changing events will steer them away from motherhood keep growing. Although about one in three marriages that break apart are childless, experts stress that childlessness is most likely not the cause. These marriages tend to be younger and, if sour, are simply less complicated to terminate.[19]

When women find themselves in fulfilling careers, they not only tend to form more permanent bonds with their careers, but they also become more financially independent and more likely to interact with other career women without children. Having a baby may eventually become a lower priority. The result: women who didn't really mean not to have children often end up without them anyway.

The Baby Busters: Having No Babies at All

The first wave of boomer women—those between the ages of forty and forty-four in 1989—are now edging out of their childbearing years.

They were the first from their generation to fully question the marriage and motherhood mystique. They were also the first to break into male-dominated professions in record numbers, to have lifelong careers out of the pink-collar ghetto, and to enjoy the exhilaration of opportunity and freedom. Their blessing—as well as their curse—has been choice.

Racial Differences in Childlessness

• White women of the baby-boom generation will have higher rates of childlessness than black women. That's a flip from the previous trend in which black women have always had higher rates. Demographers aren't sure whether improved health conditions among black women, particularly declines in venereal disease, have been responsible for higher fertility rates, or whether blacks have been making good economic strides and haven't needed to curb fertility to be upwardly mobile. According to one study, however, college-educated, high-status blacks tend to marry later and have higher rates of voluntary childlessness than high-status whites, as a strategy for upwardly mobile success.[20]

As recently as 1986, some experts projected that up to thirty percent of these women—and twenty percent of those who were married—would end up childless;[21] the experts didn't expect the pro-baby turnaround and resulting surge in later-life babies.

As a result, a "baby boomlet" is producing almost as many babies as during the 1950s peak. By 1990, the bulk of women in the gigantic baby-boom generation, those between the ages of twenty-six and forty-three, were having babies. The birth rate was up to two babies per woman, down from 1957's peak of 3.7 but up from the record low in 1976 when women had only 1.7 babies each.[22] At the same time, however, a significant chunk of these baby boomers hasn't jumped on the baby bandwagon. A full fifteen percent (fourteen percent of those born in the late 1940s and sixteen percent of women born in the 1950s) don't have children, compared with ten percent in 1976.[23] Of those women, seventy percent has always been single.

International Baby Busters

• The flight from parenthood has been even more pronounced in Europe, where most countries have fertility rates below 2.1 children per woman, the rate required to keep the population constant. In Spain and Italy, where large families used to be the tradition, the birth rate is down to 1.3 and 1.29 children per woman, respectively.[24] West Germany, with its 1.39 birth rate, anti-children sentiment has its own word, *kinderfeindlichkeit*—hostility to children. A 1985 poll in Bonn revealed that some ninety percent of West Germans considered careers and possessions more important than children.[25] That same year, about twenty percent of all marriages in West Germany were childless.[26]

• Portugal, Greece, Luxembourg, the Netherlands, Belgium, and Denmark have birth rates from 1.5 to 1.62. In Britain, the rate is 1.85 children per woman; researchers estimate that about eleven percent of thirty-five-year-olds (in 1987) were voluntarily child free (infertility accounted for only three to five percent of the childlessness).[27]

• In France, fertility is so low that the government offers generous financial incentives to couples to have more children, yet the birth rate is still a mere 1.8 children per mother.

Baby Boomers Shake Up the Family

Families and households are very different today than they were thirty years ago. It's no longer odd to live without children: in fact, for the first time in American history, the majority of households, almost two-thirds, don't have kids in them, compared with one-half in 1960. Such households include empty-nesters, the widowed, young couples, or singles. There's no "typical" American family of mom and pop and kids in tow anymore. Such families comprised less than one-third of all families in 1988, compared with forty-four percent in 1960.[28]

It's also no longer odd to live alone: one-third of American households are individuals doing just that. And for mothers, it's more likely than ever that they're raising their children alone: about one-quarter of households with children are headed by a single parent, and nine out of ten times it's a woman. That's twice as many single-mother households as in 1970, and almost three times as many as in the late 1940s.[29] (In Great Britain, things are a bit better: one in eight families with children under age eighteen are headed by a single parent, and nine out of ten are women.)[30]

Shaking Down the Trends

Women no longer assume they will marry only to stay home to raise children. In fact, a full one-third of young women from eighteen to twenty-four-years-old said in 1990 that they were not interested in staying home to raise their children, according to a *Time* magazine poll.[31] Regardless of their expectations to have a baby, new options lure modern women in unexpected directions. Today's women are more economically independent than ever and are frequently pursuing satisfying and fulfilling careers. Postponing marriage and children is common; it's also socially acceptable and easy to do in this age of efficient birth control. And then time marches on and unforeseen circumstances intervene—marriages or relationships may end, high-powered careers may become all-encompassing, infertility may blight one's system, or perhaps the desire to have children never surfaces or fades before action is taken.

A significant minority of women will never have children. Who are they? What has influenced their path away from motherhood?

CHAPTER FOUR

Who Doesn't Have Children?

'Tis fate that flings the dice, and as she flings
Of kings makes peasants, and peasants kings.
—JOHN DRYDEN,
"Jupiter Cannot Alter the Decrees of Fate"

In this chapter, we'll look at the kinds of trends some researchers have found in women's lives that seem to be linked with higher rates of childlessness. How do such factors as age at marriage, careers, a woman's orientation to traditional vs. nontraditional values, and finances play out in a woman's life in regard to having children? Which factors are most influential? What kinds of events steer women away from the baby track?

Older women say they know very few women who never had children—mostly just single women who never married and a few wives they assumed couldn't get pregnant. Many people mention an aunt, their grade-school teachers, and older, traditional college professors—especially those at women's colleges. Women under fifty, on the other hand, know scads; and the younger the women, the more they know.

Among famous people, actress Katherine Hepburn always comes to mind as the epitome of a fiercely free spirit, too independent to be bound by any man or child. Helen Gurley Brown and Gloria Steinem are thought of next: the first a magazine mogul who glamorizes the sexiness of marriage without motherhood; the other, just as glamorous herself, a crusader for women's rights.

51

Other celebrities who've never had kids include Diane Sawyer, Dolly Parton, Betty White, Marlo Thomas, Oprah Winfrey, Ann Beattie, and Elizabeth Dole. Brilliant minds and past pioneers who took the road less traveled include Jane Austen, Emily Dickinson, Georgia O'Keefe, Amelia Earhart, Beryl Markham, Lillian Hellman, Emily Brontë, George Eliot, Virginia Woolf, Simone de Beauvoir, and Anaïs Nin (who had one stillbirth pregnancy).

Researchers talk of two kinds of childless women. One-third are the "voluntary" and two-thirds are the "involuntary"—those who chose to be child free vs. those who couldn't have children for reasons beyond their control.[1]

But women's lives don't come in clear black or white packages. Take Randy, mentioned in Chapter One. She married and divorced in her twenties, and knew she didn't want children then. At thirty-seven, she remarried and quickly found herself pregnant with a baby she still wasn't ready for and so she obtained an abortion. A few years later she thought she was pregnant and felt ready, but it turned out she wasn't pregnant. She wanted a baby then, but for medical reasons had to have a hysterectomy. She is both voluntarily and involuntarily childless.

What "kind" of woman doesn't have children? Broadly speaking, marriage is the strongest link: in general, married women do and single women don't (for more on unwed mothers, see Chapter Five).

Intriguingly, though, the later a woman marries, the less likely she is to have a child. This sounds like it would be obvious, except that it holds true for women throughout their prime baby-making time. For example, a teen bride has a higher likelihood of becoming a mother compared to a woman who marries in her early twenties; and an early twentysomething bride is more likely to have a baby than a late twentysomething bride.

When Kathleen Kiernan of the Family Policy Studies Center in London looked at women born between 1936 and 1940, she found that only four percent of the teenage brides born between those years never had children. That rate doubled for women born at the same time who married between twenty and twenty-four, doubled yet again for women who married between twenty-five and twenty-nine, and doubled again for brides between thirty and thirty-four! Even though all these ages are the prime ages for childbearing, late twentysomething brides were *four* times as likely to never have children as teen brides.

Of course, fertility nose dives in the late thirties, so the pattern becomes understandable here: when women from the same cohort married for the first time between thirty-five and thirty-nine, half remained childless; of those married after forty, three out of four never had children.[2]

Kiernan found the same pattern for American, British, and Welsh women, as well as for women today who are in their thirties and seventies, and even women born in the 1860s.

What's going on here? Since fertility is still very high well into the thirties, physiological factors can generally be ruled out. Kiernan suspects that the same social and psychological factors that prompted the women to postpone marriage in the first place may be related to their higher rates of childlessness. Indeed, childless women tend to be more educated and have higher-status jobs than their "childed" counterparts. So, instead of marrying, these women were getting more education and climbing career ladders. Perhaps children eventually became a lower priority as time went on, or were unimportant in the first place. It's difficult to know which came first; it's the old chicken-and-egg conundrum.

Kiernan also found two puzzling relationships when she looked at women who had been married at least ten years. Only children were twice as likely to be childless than women with siblings. Even stranger, women who had gotten their first periods before the age of thirteen were more likely to be childless decades later. The real connection here, Kiernan suspects, is that, curiously, only children tend to get their first periods earlier. This relationship had been recognized before but not understood, and why it is so remains unexplained. Kiernan postulated that only children may have more gynecological and obstetrical problems in their family histories, which is why they were only children in the first place. Or maybe since only children are disproportionately represented among the voluntarily child free, their presence in the overall childless population skews the percent of only children among all the childless.[3]

What else distinguishes the childless/child free from others? Although childless couples tend to be much less religious than couples with children, the research on childlessness and specific religions has been conflicting. One study found that nonreligious and Protestant women had the highest childlessness rate; another study found the highest rate among Baptists and Methodists, with Catholics trailing close behind. Yet another study found no link with religion at all.[4]

Researchers have also found significantly high percentages of childless women in urban areas and in the West and Northeast, which makes sense. Careers are clustered in these areas, and alternative lifestyles are more tolerated.[5]

What else is linked to childlessness? How traditional or untraditional a woman is may play an important role. In the past, only very nontraditional women defied the overwhelming norm to marry and have children. Although some women harbored an unexpressed lack of desire to mother, most didn't really consider children a choice and became "reluctant mothers" and often resentful mothers who have felt deprived and robbed of their freedom and self-identity by motherhood. Many such women were found among the mothers of the women interviewed for this book and in other studies of childless women, including Jean Veevers' landmark study of voluntary childless couples. Hopefully, far fewer women who feel that way are becoming mothers in the freer social climate that allows choice in the realm of children.

Women with nontraditional streaks are probably more likely to remain childless. A 1987 University of Virginia analysis suggested, for example, that a woman's childbearing future is strongly connected to her traditional vs. nontraditional view of motherhood. Women don't decide about children by weighing the costs vs. benefits but rather by paying attention to their symbolic outlook. Whereas traditional women are most apt to become homemakers and mothers, "liberated" women will "strive for success, freedom, and occupational achievement," says sociologist Steven Nock. Although many of these women will eventually become mothers, too, Nock suggests that they're likely to view parenting in much the same way as fathers do; unlike traditional mothers, these women devote less of their primary time and attention to mothering.[6] Although Veevers and others have found that voluntarily child-free women don't consider themselves nontraditional, other than by deviating from the norm of having children, childless women do tend to be more nontraditional in terms of sex roles; their relationships and roles regarding housework, decision-making, finances, etc. are more egalitarian.[7] About half the women interviewed for this book generally considered themselves nontraditional.

With women facing so many more choices these days, it's no wonder that so many—especially career women—are confused and ambivalent about whether and when to have a baby. To find out how such women do decide whether or not to have children, New York University sociologist Kathleen Gerson, author of *Hard Choices: How Women Decide about Work, Career, and Motherhood* (1985) studied sixty-three career women of the baby-boom generation, ages twenty-seven to thirty-seven.

How the women felt early in life about becoming mothers had very little to do with whether they actually ended up mothers or not, Gerson found. Rather, she found four prominent interrelated factors that pulled women away from having children:

1. **Unstable marriages or relationships.** This is "one of the most powerful and disorienting events" that trigger a chain reaction away from motherhood. Gerson found that as male support falls away, women's romantic notions about having a baby quickly fade.

Sometimes, women think they've found "the" relationship that will eventually lead to a baby carriage only to find themselves single again a few years later. Feeling suddenly stranded, such women become determined to be more self-reliant, Gerson found. They may pour themselves into a career or other kinds of self-development. Plans for children get put on hold until a good relationship comes along. In the meantime, women discover new talents or hidden interests they hadn't tapped before. Time ticks on and new experiences and opportunities weave their way into women's lives. Without a relationship that lends itself to having a baby, many women's work commitments grow stronger.

Ellen, the forty-seven-year-old therapist, fits this profile. After getting her master's degree, she taught high school for five years and married at twenty-seven. The marriage was never strong enough to withstand children and Ellen knew it: "I knew I didn't want to stay in that marriage so I never tried to have children then."

By the time she divorced five years later, "everyone was having babies. I wasn't in any serious relationship, though, so I didn't really think about having children then. I always wanted to be in a good relationship rather than just have a child." So Ellen decided to pursue her dream profession and went back for another master's degree in psychotherapy. For the next decade or so, she plunged into her work. It wasn't until she remarried at forty-two that she could think about having a baby. But it was too late. After two years of a harrowing infertility experience, Ellen let go of her dreams for a child at age forty-five.

2. **Feeling that a baby would be too much of a financial strain.** This also plays an important role in moving a woman away from motherhood, even when she has a stable relationship. If having a child is viewed as a potential economic hardship, a woman may postpone a pregnancy. But that seemingly minor and temporary decision seems so inconsequential at the time, just "a mere postponement of an ultimate decision in favor of motherhood," Gerson says. "The final result, however, was often the opposite of this early expectation."[8]

For example, Diane, a forty-three-year-old middle manager at a large corporation, said:

> I always assumed as a young girl that I'd marry and have children. When I married at twenty-five, though, my husband wasn't financially ready for a child, so we decided to wait. It turned out he wasn't the right person for me anyway, and we divorced four years later.

Ever since then, although Diane has been continually in and out of relationships, even one that lasted ten years, she's never been in a situation again that would be appropriate for children.

She's grateful she wasn't burdened with being a single mother, which she knows she certainly would have been had she had a child during her first marriage. What's eerie, though, is that the unforeseen consequences of postponing a baby at twenty-six or twenty-seven resulted in permanent childlessness for Diane, a condition she never expected or planned for.

Postponement for financial reasons also motivated Dolores, now aged sixty-five, although unlike Diane, she's been married for forty-two years. She met her husband at the age of twenty-one while working as a secretary for a mail-order house. It was the late 1940s and everyone was having babies; she assumed she would, too.

> When we got married, he didn't make that much as an accountant, and we'd say, well, when he makes $100 a week, we'll have a baby. We couldn't afford it at the time, we lived in a basement apartment, but we still figured we'd have a child sometime. Then we thought we'd wait until he made $150, then $200 a week, and it kept escalating, and that was it. We kept putting it off until finally we said, we're satisfied. The feeling to have a child just faded away.

3. Turned off to staying home. Career women especially postpone children because the thought of staying home to care for them sounds boring and lonely and feels like a demotion. "Motherhood threatened to impose not only isolation, but also, and perhaps worse, personal denigration. This perceived danger prompted some respondents to reject domesticity and potentially motherhood as well," reports Gerson.[9] Janice, a forty-four-year-old married attorney, said:

> I think I'd be miserable staying home with a child; I'd miss being in the outside world, miss the excitement and challenge of my work. But if I were going to have a child, I'd want to do it right and be the best mother I could. I think it's too important to leave to a hired caregiver, at least for the first few years. But I don't really want to do it.

Such women typically view children as a trap and tend to devalue domestic life; they derive their identity and self-worth from their careers and so plunge themselves into their work. If circumstances don't switch them back to the baby track, their desire for children tends to wane somewhere in their late thirties and early forties while their careers provide for them their greatest source of self-esteem and satisfaction.

4. **Career opportunities.** Most intriguing in Gerson's work was her finding that work opportunities play a crucial role in determining a woman's childbearing decision. When career women decided to have a baby, Gerson found, it was not out of some deep-felt, abstract "mothering need," but rather as a function of two factors. First, a nurturing, stable relationship had to be in place. Second, when work became more frustrating than pleasurable, home began to look like a haven. "Many women chose motherhood not to fulfill deep-seated emotional needs, but rather as the best option among a number of unappealing alternatives."[10] In other words, when work gets boring, feels like a dead end, or just simply loses its lustre and all-important meaning in life, the thought of having a child begins to glitter. "Domestic pastures" look greener and the sanctity of home more fulfilling. The "right" time, Gerson found, was consistently linked to job dissatisfaction.[11]

Ann, for example, had already been divorced twice by age twenty-eight. That's when she went back to school for an MBA degree and worked long yet fulfilling hours as a personnel manager for a large corporation. Before she remarried at thirty-five to a man who didn't want children, she decided to have her tubes tied before the wedding:

> If I had not been sterilized then, I might have wanted to have children in my late thirties. That's about when I decided my career wasn't fulfilling and I would just as soon stay home. Having children would validate my not working.

Women given promotions or new job opportunities at critical times, on the other hand, would feel reinforced in their choice to pursue their career, thereby keeping the thought of pregnancy on a back burner.

Gerson points out that "those with declining aspirations [at work] focused on the liberating, nurturing, and fulfilling aspects of mothering, but these upwardly mobile women stressed instead its potentially negative consequences. . . ."[12]

Linda, for example, remembers always loving children, but the idea of having her own felt like a trap, and besides, she kept getting better and more exciting jobs. She started out in early education at a day-care center, and then became director of a local head-start operation. She married right after college at twenty-two and is still married to Ed seventeen years later:

> I think we assumed we'd get to having children, but every time things got real regular and predictable, one of us, usually me, did something to change it—usually a better job. I thought I'd be a good mother, but it never seemed like enough to do with my life. It was just something women were stuck with, having families and being mothers, and not anything that I considered at the time worthwhile or interesting.

At twenty-eight, she was offerred a wonderful opportunity to head up her state's cancer association in a city three hours from where Ed worked. They had a commuter marriage for a year or so, and when Linda accidentally got pregnant, their relationship was at an all-time low.

> He hated his job, it was very expensive having two residences, and my new job was really exciting. He was feeling very martyred, having to commute to see me in an old car that kept breaking down. I loved what I was doing, he hated what he was doing. We could barely talk, so we decided it wasn't the best time to have a child. I was twenty-nine. I remember feeling really disappointed but had an abortion anyway.

Ed then got a job in the same city as Linda for two years. When he got an even better job an hour away, they commuted again for a year. Then Linda got an even better job in the state capital as the director of staff development for a state agency. She now commutes three hours on weekends to their custom-built house perched on a wooded hilltop.

> I've always been back and forth about whether to have a baby or not. Then, as I got older, it seemed like it was getting too late to get started. The last time we talked about it seriously, a few years ago, we both realized we were happy with what we were doing.

The connection between work dissatisfaction and dropping out to have a baby is perhaps highlighted best by Lisa's story. She remembers always loving children. She babysat for years and worked with children in camps, hospitals, and adoption agencies. At twenty-four, she married and worked full time at an adoption/foster-care agency. At twenty-six, she decided to have a baby.

I thought I really wanted a baby. I worked with babies, I adored babies, and I always imagined I was going to have six children. When my husband and I got involved, we assumed we'd have children. He was the first man I met who seemed interested in settling down and having a family, and that was important to me.

After two years, I announced I wanted a baby. Work was draining and putting a strain on us. I'll never forget what he said: "Do you want a baby or do you just want to stop working?"

It had never occurred to me to stop working for no reason. I was brought up to think you stopped working if you had a baby, but otherwise you worked. Yes, I wanted to stop working and thought that the way to do it was to have a baby.

Lisa quit working, started painting, and put off getting pregnant temporarily. Two years passed, and she felt very content painting, housekeeping, camping every weekend, and traveling all summer. People kept asking her, "Well, aren't you going to have your baby now?"

And I thought, I like this too much to have a baby. I no longer had a need to have a child. I don't know what those needs were that fostered wanting one. I suspect they were wanting this loving creature who adores you back, and it's a very warm, wonderful, responsive relationship. But I had that with my husband and didn't need it from a child.

Lisa, now forty-six, has not worked at a paying job since. She would have had a baby to quit her job had her husband not suggested that she merely quit first and "wait and see." She had a tubal ligation at thirty-five and has never regretted it.

So who doesn't have babies? Obviously, women who feel they don't have the right relationship as well as women who clearly know they don't want to mother. But many women don't have children because of the consequences of decisions made long ago.

"Neither chance circumstances nor individual personalities determined the paths these women took as they made decisions that shaped the direction of their lives," Gerson points out. Women make decisions based on information they have at the time. They can only guess what the future consequences of those decisions will be.

Says Gerson: "Even the most carefully calculated choices often had unintended consequences that led to unanticipated directions. Change occurred not simply because people wished it to, but more fundamentally because seemingly static, discrete, inconsequential decisions had only dimly perceived long-term consequences."[13]

In other words, some women don't have children because of fate and fortune. As their life histories unfold, they face critical turning points of choice and action. They make decisions—however minor, ambiguous, or conflicted—the best way they can, with the information at hand. Some choices, however, may lead women unknowingly down paths with unexpected consequences, of which never having children may be one.

CHAPTER FIVE

The Never Married

How dare I fail to marry? How peculiar. How brazen.
How sad. Or so many believe. Were I weak in the knees,
I might believe that, too. But fortunately, my knees are
steady and hold me up fine when people give me those
patronizing looks and commiserating tones.
—EIGHTY-TWO-YEAR-OLD WOMAN[1]

They are not halves, needing complements, as are the
masses of women; but evenly balanced well-rounded
characters; therefore . . . models to be reached by the
average women we everyday meet.
—SUSAN B. ANTHONY, 1877[2]

The old maid is dead. Thank God. Mary Tyler Moore and Marlo
Thomas in "The Mary Tyler Moore Show" and "That Girl" began
breaking the stigma barrier in the 1960s and 1970s. They were
charming, vulnerable working women trying to get free, and we
all fell in love with their humor and spirit. Candice Bergen's
"Murphy Brown" is the 1990s super single woman—smart, gor-
geous, and funny—light-years beyond the not-too-distant image
of the never-married woman: a prim and peculiar, past-her-prime,
prudish soul like the ones who visit the vicarage in Barbara Pym's
novels.

Today's "old maids" are some of our most glamorous women,
moving through their forties with a panache we can admire:
Donna Mills (TV's "Knot's Landing" star), Jacqueline Bisset, Lauren Hutton, Julie Christie, Linda Ronstadt, Teri Garr, Bernadette
Peters, Betty Thomas, and Brooke Adams, to name but a few.

But never-married women are still a small minority in this pro-couple, pro-family culture. Most of us marry at least once, even if we bail out later. Less than ten percent of women never get married. And stereotypes still abound.

One older version of the stereotyped spinster is the aging, sex-ually repressed woman who is stubborn but hard-working, devot-ing her life to helping others, like Katherine Hepburn's character in *The African Queen*, Jane Fonda in *Old Gringo*, and Maggie Smith in *The Prime of Miss Jean Brodie*. Another is Agatha Chris-tie's elderly detective, Miss Marple, so bland and invisible, she can snoop in corners and go totally unnoticed.

A more modern stereotype is the beautiful career woman totally dedicated to her career such as the famous prima ballerina played by Anne Bancroft in *The Turning Point* and Cagney in "Cagney and Lacey." But why does Bancroft's character have to be the one who's emotionally aching and Cagney the one with problems with alcohol and rape?

And though we've got some bright, funny, and attractive role models in Murphy Brown and Molly Dodd in "The Days and Nights of Molly Dodd" (although Molly Dodd is divorced after an early, brief marriage and is now a single mother), many still view the unmarried woman as desperate and/or neurotic, like Diane Keaton's character in *Looking for Mr. Goodbar*, or as dual-edged swords: sexually enticing but possessed by a neurotic or psychotic streak, like Blanche in *A Streetcar Named Desire*, Glenn Close's character in *Fatal Attraction*, or the female villains in Raymond Chandler's Philip Marlowe detective stories.

And our language still reeks of sexism and an unflattering view of single femalehood: a never-married man is an enviable "bache-lor" (though research tells us that bachelors are the unhappiest and shortest-lived among men and women), but no word has yet replaced "old maid" and "spinster"; the closest we've got is "permanently single woman."

In colonial times, few women remained permanently single. By the late 1800s, their ranks swelled to an all-time high: eleven per-cent of women born between 1865 and 1875 never married.[3] Around this time, white middle and upper class never-married women upgraded the view of female singlehood, forming the "Cult of Single Blessedness." The movement tried to emphasize that remaining single was a choice. But then the status of never-married women slipped again; female singlehood, once more, was "devalued and considered a personal failure."[4] Fewer women remained single. Less than five percent of the women born during World War I, for example, never married.

As I said in Chapter Two, working-class women who never married typically were doomed for life as a domestic—a nanny, maid, or housekeeper for the upper classes. If middle class and educated, a woman typically served humankind as a teacher, nun, nurse, librarian, or secretary. Especially studious women might become scholars who were the intellectual fuel at women's colleges.

By 1987, almost seven percent of women ages thirty-five to forty-four were still never-married, though almost twenty-three percent were unmarried at the time.[5] Whereas women who divorce are fairly likely to remarry again, the odds of never-married women marrying seem to drop precipitously as they grow older.

A controversial Harvard-Yale study of the mid-1980s claimed that if a woman were still unmarried by the age of thirty-five, her chances of ever marrying drops to five percent; by forty, her chances fall to one percent. These experts predicted in 1986 that twenty-two percent of the college-educated women born in the mid-1950s would never marry, compared with only nine percent of the college-educated born two decades earlier.[6] After much criticism, however, the economist and sociologist team revised their figures to state that 11.5 percent of white women with a high-school education or more, born in the mid-1950s, would never marry.[7]

Other researchers, however, claim the odds are much less grim. Using different data, a Census Bureau demographer found that a thirty-five-year-old female single college graduate's odds of marrying were between thirty-two and forty-one percent; a forty-year-old's odds were seventeen to twenty-three percent.[8]

In any case, although about one-third of American adults are single, only five percent of women over the age of thirty-five have never been married. But that's changing: the National Center for Health Statistics predicted in 1988 that up to thirty percent of American women may end up never marrying, compared to only thirteen percent in 1972. More women may remain single now and in the future because many of the past benefits of marriage, such as sex, financial security, and even children, are now readily available to single women.

Julie, fifty-five, a nurse, never married for the most common reason: she never found Mr. Right and felt that marrying anybody else would invite disaster. She couldn't compromise, and she was confident that it was far better to stay single if she had strong doubts. Julie said:

> I didn't have children because I didn't meet a man I really liked enough to marry. I wanted to be happily married or happily single. I believe that a happy marriage is the happiest state. However, from what I hear, an unhappy marriage is probably the unhappiest state. And I would not want to be unmarried and trying to raise a child.

Although Julie is right when she says that marriage is the happiest state—married people continue to report higher levels of happiness than the unmarried—the gap between the two seems to be closing. In the early 1970s, for example, there was a thirty percent difference in how many married women (ages twenty-five to thirty-nine) said they were "very happy" vs. never-married women. By the early 1980s, the gap had shrunk to twelve percent.[9]

In Julie's case, she's "quite" happy; she has a steady boyfriend she's been seeing for nine years, and she has no regrets about never marrying.

Hilda, sixty-nine, also never met a man she wanted to marry so she stayed home with her mother until she was fifty. Money was always tight. When Hilda, the eldest child, was twelve, her father died. Her mother was pregnant with her fourth child. Throughout the 1920s and 1930s, the family lived on public assistance. Hilda earned scholarships for college and ended up working for the welfare agency that had supported her family years before, becoming their success story. On the subject of dating and marriage, she said:

Oh, I had a few opportunities to date in college, and then after that, my friends would fix me up with this one or that one. But I just never related well to any of them, and by my thirties, I realized I just wasn't going to get married.

Hilda was also overwhelmed by a controlling, dominant mother. "I had no privacy," she told me. "My mother was always involved in what I was doing. I didn't finally leave home until I was 50!" Hilda would have loved to have had children and was glad for the opportunity to help raise her niece and nephew for nine years after her sister-in-law ran out on her family. She thinks that had she been born a few decades later, though, she would have had children whether she had been married or not.

> I think I still have some regrets for not having children. I think I would have been a very good mother. As I've gotten older, though, I'm very content with the way things have gone. I sometimes get twinges when my friends talk about their sons and daughters, and although I talk about my niece and nephew, who to me are my kids, I know they are not.
>
> Periodically I wish that I had had children, but it never happened and you accept that. I've had a very rich and fulfilled life and still concentrate on my profession.

Hilda derives an enormous amount of satisfaction and fulfillment through her work as a social worker; she's been named by her governor as "Social Worker of the Year," and she continues to write grants for teen pregnancy intervention programs and helps institute such programs around her state. She thinks, in hindsight, that if she had to live her life again, "I would have gotten away from my mother a lot earlier. I know my life would have been different." She regrets not having gone into therapy earlier in her life to develop the confidence and courage she needed to defy her mother's control.

For many never-married women, the issue of children seems dormant since so many other factors aren't in place. Laura, a never-married forty-five-year-old city planner, described the context in which she has always envisioned children:

> I always couched having a baby in a long series of qualifications. I have always thought about it like this: If I meet somebody who I love and love living with, and if he is really, really serious about

wanting children, and if he's clearly somebody who, with his behavior as well as his words, is really committed to having children, and if there's enough money, and the phase of the moon is right—you get the drift. And that's the closest I ever got to the topic with any enthusiasm. I think I let go of the possibility at forty. That was a turning point, given that I wasn't relating sexually to any men at that time.

Laura's long list of qualifications isn't even complete. To be completely accurate, she'd have to add: "and if I could get pregnant and carry the child to term, and if I could leave my job or get good child care," and so on.

Pamela, an elegant sixty-one-year-old retired dancer, on the other hand, never married because she's always been one of the "never wanna be's." She rejected the institution in favor of an independent, untethered life. As Susan B. Anthony wrote: "The woman who will not be *ruled* must live without marriage."[10] Likewise, actress Julie Christie told *Cosmopolitan*: "From the time I grew up, I said I had no intention of ever marrying anyone. What I wanted most out of life was to be a . . . free soul with no strings of any kind. That has never changed." (August, 1988, p. 131.)

Pamela has long brown-silver hair twirled in a casual bun and wore Birkenstock sandals on her feet the day we spoke. Pamela talked with her hands, gesturing gracefully, as only a dancer would, to emphasize her feelings. Living in a knotty pine-paneled handmade house she helped build twenty years ago in the back woods of rural Vermont, Pamela talked of her years as a professional dancer and then as a dance instructor at a large university. At fifty, she had "barnstormed" for a year around the country, raising interest for her dance performances in each town she visited.

> I grew up in New Orleans and from a very early age, I had my own ideas about what I was going to do. I guess I always assumed that I would be married and have children, but at the same time, I think I was having very strong ideas about who I was and what I wanted to do.

After college, she taught briefly, toured with a modern dance company for four years in the 1950s, danced in New York City for several years, went back to school for a master's in dance, and then went to the university to teach dance when she was thirty-six. "I was very independent," she told me. "My father always encouraged me to be that way, and then in the dance world, people don't live traditional lives."

She remembers that when she got to the university, she sensed that men who were looking for wives instinctively knew to rule her out. Although Pamela got very close to marrying several times, she always backed off when she got *too* close.

> I think I never wanted to be told what to do and that had something to do with not ever getting married. Every time I got close, which was quite a few times, I'd say "Ahhhh, wait!" These days it's probably easier to get married and not have that sense of panic about it. My ideal is to have this permanent but not constant companion. There aren't a lot of men who'll put up with that.

These days, Pamela has relationships with younger men. She knows they'll eventually need a younger woman to settle down with, but in the meantime, she enjoys their companionship. And as far as children are concerned?

> Oh, I get occasional pangs. I'm sure that the bond one establishes is a very special thing, if you do manage to establish a good relationship, which isn't the majority, but I've seen a few cases and have recognized it. But those feelings aren't as strong or as much of an emotional issue for me as having someone, a mate, close to me.

Fran, the fifty-four-year-old stockbroker first mentioned in Chapter Three, also never married because she didn't believe she could marry and still be her own person.

> Truth is, if I wanted to be married, I'd be married. All along, I knew I didn't want to get married. In my era, the man was programmed to be dominant and I didn't think I could be independent in a marriage. And I hadn't grown up in a time when it was acceptable to have a child without a husband. If I had been born ten or fifteen years later, though, I would have had a child by myself.

Fran says she gets pangs about not having any children every now and then, but as many women who never have children find, she became a very important person to her niece and nephew.

Her sister decided she didn't want her son around once he became a belligerent teenager, so he moved in with Aunt Fran from the age of twelve until he was twenty-two. His sister joined them for much of that time, too.

In spite of record numbers of never-married women having and rearing children without fathers in the home (2.6 million in 1989),[11] more than ninety percent of women who never marry never become mothers.[12] Yet, this trend is changing quickly. In 1985, twenty-two percent of all births (sixty percent of black births) were to never-married women, compared with five percent (twenty-two percent of black births) in 1960.[13] By 1988, seventy percent of never-married women in their early forties had no children: eighty-three percent of white women and thirty-three percent of black women.[14]

Yet, most middle-class women who don't marry do not have children. Many say they'd love a baby, but only in a loving, supportive marriage. While they remain single, the idea of children stays distant and often doesn't seem to surface as an issue. That's how Phyllis, seventy-six, always felt. Born in 1913 in upstate New York, the eighth of nine children, she worked for years as a hospital dietitian. Had she married, she would have had children; but since she never did marry, she never got very close to thinking about having children.

> I never felt any stigma involved in not having children. I think it was more of a question as to why I hadn't married. That was the thing. I've never felt it was important to have a child, but I would have liked to marry.

Janet, a forty-five-year-old college administrator, never dated all that much, and always assumed she'd remain single.

> I never thought I'd get married and because of that, children didn't play into my thoughts. It wasn't that I didn't want to get married, I just didn't assume it like most women do. I was always very studious and that was my priority.

Both women are very independent, and although they have some interaction with friends' and relatives' children, they have no sense of regret about not having their own.

Although little research has looked at older, never-married women to glean their feelings about never having children, a small study published in 1989 found a split down the middle, though slightly in favor of no regrets. Of fifteen women born in 1910, eight regretted neither their singlehood nor lack of motherhood; they said they had the best of both worlds. Three were ambivalent; they missed having their own children but didn't regret never marrying, and four were disappointed about both. Two out of three took pride in their role as "surrogate mothers" to nieces and nephews.[15]

In another study of eighty never-married women, ranging in ages from the twenties to seventy-eight, only a few had regrets about not marrying. The researchers discerned, however, a "thread of regret . . . with some regularity" among elderly women about never having children. "Certainly not all older women feel this way, but for those who wanted children, the persistence of this desire deep into old age seems both striking and touching."[16]

In yet another study of fifty older women, ages sixty-six to one hundred one in 1987, of which thirty-five percent had professional jobs, professor of social work Barbara Simon found that seventy-five percent chose to stay single. Most cited financial and emotional independence as well as devotion to a career as motivations; seven wouldn't marry because they didn't want children. Although Simon found that "most" took pivotal roles in helping to raise their siblings' children and took their role of aunt most seriously, she makes no mention of how the women felt about not having their own.

Today, unmarried women who feel strong maternal pulls can have children without facing the strong societal stigmas of the past. Yet, many feel that parenting is so difficult as it is, that to parent solo would be too overwhelming. One blessing in disguise, however, is that there's no social pressure to have children the way there is for married couples. Unmarried women aren't expected to bear or adopt children.

In the group of never-married women interviewed for this book, many expressed their strongest regrets about not having a lifelong mate with whom to share their lives. Even if they'd always assumed they'd have children, since they weren't married, the regrets were only occasional pangs, especially when their married friends brought out "their brag books." As they grow into middle age, however, they have come to accept their childlessness just as they'd accepted their singleness: as part of their lives. But they have also learned to appreciate their advantages. Said fifty-five-year-old Julie:

> I think I would have loved to have had children and grandchildren and experienced all the joys that come with them. However, I know that I've also been spared the heartache I have seen some mothers experience over their children. I've enjoyed my life and don't think I would have changed it, had I to do it over again.

Another group that fully appreciates their advantages has very consciously chosen to not have children. We'll look at them next.

CHAPTER SIX

Choosing to Be Child Free

My reasons for not having children are freedom, stability, and never having strong maternal feelings. We married sixteen years ago and we're very, very close. At the beginning, the thought of having children was a remote possibility. But as I watched my peers, co-workers, and my best friends and relatives bring up their children, I never felt a strong desire.

I have always loved the challenge of going out into the corporate world every day in New York City. I never entertained the idea of staying home to play wife and mother. I had the freedom to do as I pleased, travel and enjoy myself without being tied down. Although we are both loving, good people, we both never felt up to the difficult challenge of a lifetime commitment to children.

I live my entire life however I feel comfortable. I have total freedom in my mind and heart.

—LOUISE, 42

Like forty-two-year-old Louise, quoted above, many women who don't have children would have it no other way. They made the thoughtful, conscious decision to have no children. Why? Freedom. Freedom rings loud and clear as the most cited reason as to why women choose to be child free—free from child-care responsibilities, to pursue personal goals and self-fulfillment, from financial hassles, from the worries and strains of bringing up children in a difficult and complex society.

Basically, two kinds of women fall into the "voluntarily childless." The first are women who made the decision early on in their lives that there would be no children; researchers call them "early

72

articulators." The second are women who keep postponing children; they never feel ready to make *the* decision, so the decision is made passively, by *not* making the decision to have a baby. Although some might argue that these "postponers" should be included with women for whom the time for having a baby never seemed right (See Chapter Seven), researchers include postponers with the voluntarily childless because they are women with long-term committed relationships who voluntarily put off the decision and drift into childlessness. The primary factor that prevents them from having children is their own will to put it off.

Helen Brooks, now sixty-six, is an "early articulator." She knew from the time she was a teenager that she didn't want children. Born in the heart of middle America, the Kansas girl rejected motherhood despite the baby-making era of the 1950s around her. Like many women who decide against children, she didn't want to repeat the strife of her mother's life.

> My mother was a city girl and wanted to be a nurse, but her wealthy father refused to hear of it. So she took teacher's training, and in the meantime, acquired a stepmother. My mother viewed her father's new wife as all that the "wicked stepmother" implies, and she rebelled. Mother, a straight-A college student, married a sixth-grade dropout, a farmer-rancher and lived an average rural life in the early 1920s. After three children—I was second born—she was persuaded that my father was not a good provider so she took us back to her father's. But going back to her "wicked stepmother" was the greater of two evils, so she returned to my father, and then had four more children.
>
> By the time I was a teenager, my awareness of the grinding work, monotony, the monopoly of my mother's mind by the mundane, and trying times of feeding, clothing, and molding children became the underlying reasons I chose not to have children. Children stifled my mother's life.

Helen decided early to be child free as a way of rejecting her mother's life of "quiet desperation." Jean Veevers, author of *Childless by Choice*—one of the first and most authoritative studies of voluntarily childlessness—found profiles like Helen's to be quite typical. Like Helen, about one-third of her interviewees decided before marriage not to have children. Another study found that nine out of ten voluntarily child-free couples, like Helen and her husband, make an active decision to forego children. That's quite contrary to the statistics on parents: two-thirds have children as the result of a deliberate decision, but one-third become parents by passive default; they don't really think about having children as a choice, but rather *assume* children without actively deciding to have them.[1]

Veevers found that some women like Helen viewed their mothers as martyrs *because* they had children. The sacrifices they felt their mothers made for children were just too great, and they could not see themselves making them.[2] Some child-free women also felt that their mothers had lost control over their lives because of children.[3]

Although studies have conflicted over the issue of whether the childhoods of child-free women are any different from those of women who became parents, about half of the women who chose to be child free interviewed for this book, including Helen, pointed to their childhoods as influencing their decision.

Helen wasn't "violently opposed" to children, but she didn't really want them and was glad that her husband felt the same way. She's been married happily for thirty-eight years. She enjoyed working as an office clerk for the U.S. Department of Agriculture and then as a county supervisor, but horses have always been her passion. Living in rural Texas has allowed her to pursue that love:

> I have loved horses all my life, and I wanted the freedom, money, and time it involved to show and ride them. I've always had pets—many calves and colts, puppies and kittens—so I have always had plenty to nurture, but I don't think I've got a lot of maternal nurturing instincts.
>
> I also don't think I would have been a good mother. I'd probably have been too protective and demanding. I have been able to control my own life. My husband has always been supportive in anything I chose to do. Our relationship has always been very close. Intimacy, sex, and spontaneity have always been very important to us.
>
> But mostly I value the freedom from responsibility for another

person's life. Freedom to live my life without the demands and pulls that children make. I've many hobbies and had my first novel published last year. I still ride and compete in barrel racing, and traveled 5,000 miles this summer seeing the country.

There isn't anything I dislike about not having children. I am totally comfortable with my choices—I would do it the same yesterday, today, and tomorrow.

Although Helen and most child-free persons cite freedom as a primary reason for not having children, reviewers of the literature have not been able to really rank how significant different reasons given for not having children are across the board. That's because studies use different samples—such as just women or couples— or different methodologies. Nevertheless, when Sharon Houseknecht of Ohio State University, a researcher on voluntary childlessness, examined twenty-nine studies in 1988, she found that four out of five women who never had children cited freedom as a primary reason for not having children. Two out of three cited protecting an intimate marriage from the strains and stresses of raising children. About half claimed that the women's careers (compared to three-quarters of the studies that only asked women) and financial freedom were very important reasons. One out of three say there are already too many people in this world, that they don't like children, and/or they don't think they would have been good parents. One in four is terrified of giving birth, and one in five doesn't want to bring a child into a world so overwhelmed with crises, pollution, war, and so on.[4]

Hope, fifty, was an early articulator who mentioned many of these factors. Born the second eldest in a family of seven, she didn't feel close to either parent—they were both always too ill or tired to give her much attention:

My childhood was not very happy. We were a burden to my mother, a lot of hard work, and my mother was ill a lot of the time, first with pneumonia, then ulcers and other things, and my father had emphysema. I saw that they did not enjoy their kids. They were always too tired, too busy, and too worried about money. I never saw children as something that were fun to have around.

So I grew up thinking that children were a problem and that my mother was tired all the time—that's what I remember. She never had time for herself and felt she deserved a lot better in life. She had been a private nurse, and when she married at thirty-three, it all ended.

Even as a young child, I knew I would never have children. I just knew I wouldn't. I could see they were never in my future, and I even broke up my second engagement because I could see he really wanted a family.

When I met Bart, I didn't have to persuade him about not having children. I think he could have gone either way.

Hope, a fourth-grade teacher, has been married for twenty-two years and knows that for her, she made the right decision. She said, "I could just never see myself as a mother, ever."

Another common thread among the child free, including Helen and Hope and many of Veevers' interviewees, is that many had either spent much of their childhood taking care of younger siblings or having no siblings at all. One study found, for example, that three-quarters of the child free had been burdened with taking care of youngsters while they were young, compared with only one-third of the adults in the study who became parents.[5]

Firstborns and only children are disproportionately represented among the voluntarily child free. In fact, about half the husbands and wives in Veevers' study who chose to forego children were either firstborn and/or only children, compared with about one-third in the general population.[6] (Although Helen and Hope were both second born, they both had many younger siblings for whom they took a lot of child-care responsibility.) One in five were only children vs. one in twenty in the general population.[7] The now defunct National Organization for Non-Parents found a similar pattern: fifty-three percent of their members were either firstborns and/or only children.[8] And yet another study of 1,000 working women, published in The Biological Clock, found that while two-thirds of women who were the middle or youngest child in their families wanted a child "very much," only half of the only children and fifty-five percent of the eldest children wanted a child that much.[9]

Why the difference? Typically, firstborns and only children are high achievers because of so much parental attention, and as such, they tend to pursue higher levels of education and professional status than children of descending birth orders. These factors, we've seen, play into postponing children or not having them at all.

Some experts suggest that only children shrug off having children because of their lack of experience in taking care of youngsters or in observing their mothers and fathers parenting other children. Others speculate (although some research on only children disputes this) that only children may be less willing to sacrifice for children because they're unused to giving up their needs or putting their needs aside for younger siblings.

Forty-three-year-old Candice, for example, was the only child of an upwardly mobile black family in western Virginia.

> I grew up entirely around adults. I think my parents were married well over a decade before I was born. I was very independent and did not like to have the routine that I established for myself disturbed. I've always wanted a life of my own to do as I wished, without anyone telling me what to do. This has expanded, even from a very early age, to not wanting anyone involved in my life whose well-being and preferences had to be considered.
>
> I have always disliked family life and children per se. I always wanted to have my own household of which I would be the undisputed head. I have from time to time thought that there could possibly be a man that I'd really want in my life but very sadly, I've never met him.
>
> In visualizing a future with "Mr. Right," though, it was only the two of us—no children. No matter what has happened, I have never, not even for a second, ever wanted to have a child.

Candice has been so certain in her convictions to never mother that she was sterilized at the age of twenty-three, just before her divorce. Her only regret, or sadness in this matter, is that she has lost men she may have wanted because of her adamancy to not have children.

Fifty-year-old professor of women's studies Judy Long, on the other hand, represents another profile not uncommon among the child free: she always identified more strongly with her father and became achievement-oriented as a result. At the same time, she rejected her mother's life.

> My strong impression is that my mother was a very angry and frustrated woman. She was poor after marriage and unprepared for the hardship of raising three kids basically by herself when World War II came and my father enlisted.

Judy decided to grow up like him. Recall from Chapter Three how she was enamoured with his lifestyle as a war hero and as a college professor. She decided by age twelve that she would not be like her mother but would have two other priorities—education and career. Interestingly, her two sisters are also child-free, high-level professionals: one is a physician and the other a high-ranking hospital administrator.

Researchers have also found that some women who come from "empty-shell" families or broken or abusive homes may also shy away from motherhood. Jill Layton, now forty, grew up in Salt Lake City and swore off children before she was ten. Although her father made good money as an airplane mechanic, he hoarded it, and his four children grew up poor. Jill remembers that she always slept on the sofa in the front room of her parents' two-bedroom house. Her mother slept in a chair.

> My mother spent her time saving unusable junk and filling up any available space in the house. My father eventually moved out of his bedroom and into a trailer for fear that the junk piled up along the sides of his bed would fall on him and no one would be able to find him. Anyway, that's the excuse I remember. After Dad moved out, she filled up his space, too. I had no privacy—the house was always such a mess I was reluctant to bring my friends over. The bills were always late and mother had me answer the phone to tell them her latest lie. She was very good at lying. She also had a bad temper and used to throw things at me. My mother was miserable being a mother. I haven't wanted children since I was about nine years old.

Jill married at twenty-one, and when she became pregnant three years later, she had an abortion without any doubts. She also found a doctor to perform a tubal ligation. Around that time, she had a falling-out with her mother:

My mom told me never to darken her door again. It's been at least seventeen years since I've seen her, although she just lives across town.

I can't say I had a bad childhood, but it wasn't a good basis to learn how to raise children. I know a lot of people go ahead and have children with an even worse background, but when you're dealing with a human life, shouldn't he/she deserve better?

Jill believes that her decision was a blessing in disguise: ten years ago she was diagnosed with multiple sclerosis and today, can't get around without a wheelchair. Costly acupuncture treatments that she says she'd never be able to afford if she had had children, keep her out of pain. "I can't imagine having children *and* this disease," she said.

No Maternal Drive

Some women who articulated early their desire to remain child free came from very happy childhoods, full of warmth and joy. There was just one thing missing, though: a maternal desire. Thirty-eight-year-old Natalie, for example, grew up in a warm, loving family. Her younger sister played with dolls, but Natalie always preferred stuffed animals. She babysat, just like all the other girls in her neighborhood, but never really enjoyed it. She was married for ten years in her twenties, and now has been living with a man for five years. An unplanned pregnancy ten years ago ended with an abortion; for Natalie, this was the only option. Having children just never held any interest for her and she's always felt that way:

I don't feel like this was ever a decision. I never struggled over it or agonized about it, or ever really talked about it much with anybody. It's just never been an issue with me. I never felt the need to have children. I consider myself a very nurturant person—I give a lot to my relationships—but that feeling has never carried over to kids. I've never had a doubt and I'd say I've felt this way since I was about twelve.

There are a lot of things about kids that I think are really neat, but I just somehow lack whatever it is that's supposed to be the maternal instinct. It just seems to be missing.

Tammy, a forty-one-year-old advertising copywriter, also mentioned her lack of a maternal pang:

> Sometimes I wonder if I *am* missing some maternal instinct. I *know* I'm missing the desire to take responsibility for kids and for committing all my time and energy to raising them. But I wonder, too, what I'm missing in terms of love, joy, commitment, and even the worrying and hassling. I might like it if I suddenly woke up with an overpowering urge to have a child—so far, it hasn't happened.

For some, the lack of maternal desire comes from a downright disinterest in or an intense dislike of children. Said Jill Layton:

> I assumed children were messy, noisy, demanding, selfish, and delicate. I still find that to be true. I also don't feel comfortable around children; I don't know how to talk to them or feel that they'd care to talk to me.

Candice, who earlier spoke of her visualization of marriage with no children, said she thought children to be "a bore and a nuisance." Lynn, a fifty-four-year-old divorced college professor who swore she would never remarry, was even more negative:

> Actually, I just don't like children. I'm sorry, I know you're supposed to like children, but actually, I really hate them. In fact, I always thought as a child—an only child—that kids who had siblings were disadvantaged. It never occurred to me to *want* to have children—they were just something that had to be done when you got married.

Although some of the women interviewed feared that their lack of desire to have children was a reflection of "something wrong" with them, researchers who have studied voluntary child-free couples say there's no evidence of any deficiency or deviance in terms of social adjustment, mental health, or sexual identification.[10] Rather, the decision to remain child free stems from an interaction of lifestyle characteristics, and personal and family makeup, attitudes, and values. The voluntarily child free have not been found to be particularly selfish or abnormal in any way, either. Rather, women and couples who intentionally do not have children tend to either strive to avoid the "penalties of parent-hood," i.e., the costs in money, time, and on marriage, or they want to "reap the rewards" of child-free living; to have the free-dom to pursue a career, be spontaneous, to travel, to be free from the stress and responsibility of raising children, to preserve marital harmony, equality, and closeness, etc.[11] When women don't feel particularly maternal and have fulfilling, enriching careers—in-cluding celebrities such as Sandy Dennis, Donna Mills, Loretta Swit, who told *Cosmo* they never wanted children, as well as thousands of successful career women—life already seems so full, and it would feel too disruptive to have a child.

Some happily married couples, for example, fear—and justifi-ably so—that the pressures, unpredictability, and financial strain of having children would disrupt their marital harmony. Research bears them out: parenthood, in fact, tends to wreak havoc on a marriage. Babies, bottles, babysitting and Bobby's problems can be a shocking "crisis" and "trauma" for a married couple. Study after study confirms that the negative impact of children on mari-tal happiness is pervasive, regardless of race, religion, education, and wives' employment.[12]

Young women are rarely prepared for the sleepless nights, the noise, exhaustion, worry, and responsibility that come with chil-dren. Louis Genevie and Eva Margolies, authors of *The Mother-hood Report* and researchers who looked at 1,100 mothers of all ages, found mothers frazzled, frustrated, and furious by the day-to-day grind of raising children. Said one twenty-seven-year-old mom of two children:

> Twenty-four hours a day, 365 days a year . . . the children's con-stant demand for attention . . . there are times when I am so tired but must push on for them, while their crying, fighting, and disobe-dience tears at my nerves. Sometimes I feel like screaming if any-body says "Mommy" one more time . . . . The demands are endless.[13]

Said others: "This is not what I bargained for." "Your life is not yours. You have to put your children first. Your emotions and needs come last."

> There are times I feel like a "prisoner" in my home—really tied down—unappreciated. I often feel that I am losing myself—my own time no longer exists. I did not realize how my whole life would center around the children.

A staggering seventy percent were "extraordinarily illusionistic" in their visions of what motherhood would be like, said the coauthors. "Their unrealistic fantasies ran the gamut from slightly romanticized notions to fantasies of perfections: perfect children, perfect mothers, and perfect families."[14] Almost half—forty-five percent—said that the day-to-day chores of childrearing were more drudgery than pleasure,[15] and that few were prepared for how often and easily mothering would drive them up against a wall, angry and enraged and sometimes out of control.

The *New York Times* reported in 1989 that several recent studies "have documented in greater depth than ever before the astonishingly stressful social and emotional consequences of parenthood." Half the couples studied said that their marital happiness had dropped since they had children: they argued more; showed and received less affection from their mates; doubted their feelings for each other more often; felt more ambivalent about the marriage; and many, especially women, had lost interest in sex.[16]

Joan, forty, a former child actress/model, is now a pediatric nurse who helps children and their families cope not only with illness, but also with the devastating effects of child abuse. Every day she sees children suffering because their parents could not cope with the stress, worries, and financial strains of bringing them up. As she's seen her friends become parents, too, she's noted how so many suffer from emotional and financial strains. She and her husband, on the other hand, have been free to return to school and change careers. On the subject of parenting, she said:

> Parenting is *the* most important responsibility possible. A person who masters that skill is incredibly talented and important to society.
> Motherhood is clearly underrated by society—evidenced by how many people do it without really considering what they're getting

themselves into. People spend more time picking a house or a car than they do deciding whether or not to become a parent.

Joan knows how stressful raising children can be. So she has chosen to preserve the magic of her marriage without risking it:

> My marriage is very fulfilling. Children are not necessary to "bond" us. Our love will last forever. We don't need to reproduce to give our marriage meaning.

For Jackie, a forty-year-old only child married for nineteen years, not having children probably saved the marriage.

> Although I've been married for almost two decades, it's been tumultuous—up and down. We've been separated, and when the marriage was bad, the last thing I wanted on earth was children. I felt that would cause additional pressure on us and certainly would not be good for a child. When we were finally able to work things out, I didn't want to mess up a good thing.

Another deterrant to having children for some of the "early articulators" was their fear that they'd be "bad, abusive" parents. Jill, for example, knew she had a volatile temper. She remembers when she was a young girl and a five-year-old neighbor would stare at her:

> I'd yell at her to stop, but she wouldn't, which would make me mad and I'd hit her. This made me feel that the possibility of me being a potential child abuser was very real. I was about nine when I thought, "This is no way to treat a child." The fear of inflicting similar childhood experiences on children of my own brought me to the decision of remaining childless.

Lynn, the divorced college professor, thinks she would have been a mentally abusive parent:

> I think I'd have been abusive, not because I'm cruel or physical, but I've got a friend with two children who I like, but after four hours, I know if I don't walk away, I'm going to say terrible things. I can't imagine having children in my home twenty-four hours a day.

Other kinds of fears sometimes influenced women from becoming mothers, such as fear of pregnancy, childbirth, or of bearing a defective child. Susan Jeffries, a forty-two-year-old aide in an adult care foster home in Michigan, said:

> When I was younger I didn't want children because I thought the pain would be too awful and I'd die. In fact, until I was a teenager, I never understood why women didn't die when they had a baby.

Susan is also an Afro-American who has observed too many unwed mothers and their children living in poverty. "Seeing that, I thought I'd be an absolute fool to even think of having a child," she said. As the eldest of five children, with her little brother 19 years younger, Susan also had years of raising children and never longed to have her own.

Karen, a forty-five-year-old married college professor who has never wanted children, remembers the devastating effects a handicapped child had on her cousins' family:

> I had an aunt, a terrific person, who had four children. Her youngest got the mumps, which fried his brains, and he became a hopelessly retarded person forever. He's always lived at home, has never been able to speak, and has had to be cared for like an infant his whole life. He's now in his late twenties and my aunt's getting on and she's still taking care of him.
>
> Since I had minimal interest in having children to begin with, seeing something like that, which seemed insurmountable, certainly didn't help any.

Usually, women are the ones who first bring up not having children. Often, men don't even think about it the way women do, and about half the married men in one voluntarily childless study said they'd change their minds if their wives decided to have children, whereas none of the wives said they'd change their minds if their husbands did.[17]

Women Who Postpone Children

About two-thirds of women who choose not to have children are not early articulators but postponers—women who end up living in an ambivalent limbo about having children until time makes the decision for them. Like many women of the baby boom generation, Tammy, the forty-one-year-old advertising copywriter, was ambivalent about children for years so she did nothing about them. As mentioned earlier, Tammy felt she lacked a strong maternal drive. She kept waiting for her vague desire to have children to grow into a hungry baby craving. But it never did:

> As a child growing up in the "Ozzie and Harriet"/"Father Knows Best"/"Donna Reed Show" era, I always took it for granted that I'd have kids. I don't think I ever suddenly "realized" I wouldn't have children. The idea of having children, even when I took for granted that I *would* have them, always seemed like something I would do in the future. I think I was waiting to really want to do it, figuring that suddenly it would seem right to me—that there'd be an irresistible urge, some kind of push or motivation from my husband, or the perfect circumstances.
>
> Really, I was waiting for the desire to make the decision for me, I guess. But it didn't. I don't *not* want to have children. I simply don't want to do it badly enough to make the commitment and change my entire life. For most of my life, I've just been kind of ambivalently in neutral.
>
> Since my second marriage (at thirty-five), it has started to look as though not making the decision to *have* kids was the same as making the decision *not* to.

Raised in such a pronatalist culture as ours, postponers like Tammy often have strong career drives that put them in traditional male-structured workplaces that are inflexible about taking time off for childrearing and provide few, if any, day-care opportunities. To integrate a child into such a lifestyle requires an enormous effort, which many women who have endlessly postponed the decision to have children eventually make with a last-minute baby before it's too late. Yet, as Marian Faux, author of *Childless by Choice*, a popularly written 1984 book (not to be confused with Jean Veevers' more academic 1980 study by the same title), observes, such women often end up "in a kind of ambivalent motherhood, a motherhood by default":

A last-minute resolution of maternal ambivalence by deciding to have a child may look like a good and even natural solution, especially when time is running out, but too often it is not any better a solution than choosing childlessness . . . The very fact that a woman has been postponing motherhood for ten or fifteen years is often testimony to how deep-seated her maternal ambivalence is—and how unlikely it is to be erased by a last-minute leap into motherhood.[18]

Faux found that many such mothers remained ambivalent; they loved their children but continued to question whether they made the right decision. In fact, ambivalence describes how the majority—fifty-five percent—of mothers feel about motherhood, according to *The Motherhood Report*.[19]

It's no wonder, therefore, that many women like Tammy "drift" into childlessness. They start out believing they're just postponing children for a definite period of time. The second stage occurs when the postponement becomes indefinite, according to Veevers' analysis. The third stage is marked by a woman acknowledging to herself that there's a distinct possibility she won't get around to having children. The fourth and final stage for postponers is reaching the conclusion at some point that this has now become a permanent decision.[20]

Nevertheless, Tammy is haunted by the fear that she may be making a big mistake:

A lot of times I feel pressured to have a child because I *should*, according to the way I was raised and, I think, social pressures in general. I'd resist having a child even when some inner voice told me I "should" do it. Still, coming close as I am to a definite limit that tells me I no longer have the option, no longer can choose to have children . . . well, it's a scary kind of pressure.

Am I making a mistake? Will I come to regret this more over the years? That's what I wonder. So I suppose I'm having more and greater internal conflicts about the decision or *lack* of decision as I get closer to the point of no return.

Postponing children doesn't always cause so much dissonance, though. Linda, the thirty-nine-year-old staff development director (from Chapter Four) who kept getting promotions that steered her away from the baby track, has been married for seventeen years, ever since college graduation. She also kept waiting for the right time, but it never came, and she devoted all her energies into an enriching career that kept getting better. She's not tormented, however, by the outcome:

> I've always loved children and even got my degree in early child-hood education. We talked about having kids, but throughout my twenties we kept postponing it. In my mid-thirties I guess there was a turning point. We realized that we were happy with what we have now—our careers, the freedom to travel, to afford things because we don't have children. It's never been an absolute decision, and I don't really know when I started to think it was too late to get started.

As might be expected, ambivalence tends to grow with age. In *The Biological Clock* (1987), Molly McKaughan studied the attitudes of 1,000 readers of *Working Woman* magazine. She found that while only forty percent of women in their early thirties weren't sure they wanted to have children, seventy percent of women in their late thirties felt that way. "Thus, postponing having babies for a few years may turn out to be postponing it forever," writes McKaughan.[21]

Compared to other groups of women without children, women who are voluntarily childless, or child free—and both early articulators and postponers are always included together—have been studied the most. Researchers have tried to tease out whether women who choose not to have children are different in any ways than other women.

Careers

One of the strongest links to voluntary childlessness is work: while nine out of ten women work outside the home, up to two-thirds of child-free women are particularly dedicated to their careers, which tend to be high-status and well-paying jobs.[22] Women who choose not to have children tend to not only derive much of their self-identity and self-esteem from their work, but several studies suggest that half to two-thirds also considered their work as important as marriage and family.[23] Accordingly, educational levels and incomes of women without children are far above average.

Whether such women decide early on that children are a lower priority than their education, or decide later on after they've attained their costly education and high-status careers that having children would be too difficult to integrate into a busy and demanding schedule, is not known. Veevers found that about half the women she interviewed felt that "Being childless was . . . an important if not also a necessary condition of excellence. . . . Their levels of achievement were high, but their aspirations for achievement were higher still. . . . being child free meant being free to achieve to their full capacity."[24]

In other words, women who choose not to have children, or who endlessly put off the commitment to have children, tend to be preoccupied with their careers, which are important to them, are highly fulfilling, and in many cases, very demanding.

Janice, forty-four, works twelve- to fourteen-hour days as an attorney, trying to make it to partner. She loves her work and feels that being child free empowers her by allowing her to pursue personal growth and fulfillment through her work and creative activities.

> I know how much I love my job and I feel very fulfilled in being able to do the best job possible because I can devote all my attention to it when I need to. I think having a child would cost too much in terms of my career, and would constantly pull me in two opposing directions. I know I could never be a full-time, at-home mom, and so I think I'd become only mediocre in both roles instead of excelling in one.

As Kathleen Gerson found in her study published as *Hard Choices*, women like Janice, highly motivated, ambitious baby boomers with high standards, saw the overwhelming job of raising a child "as a formula for failure." These women, says Gerson, adhered to the highest standards in everything they did, "including their approach to mothering. . . . These high standards were in fact their undoing, for they could find no way to do both tasks well."[25]

Gail, forty-three, had no career objectives when she went to college in the mid-1960s. When she married her husband in her early twenties, they didn't discuss children as he launched his career. She had started working as a secretary for a large corporation, and by her late twenties, was promoted into the administrative ranks and then up into management.

> I felt my identity changing then. The job became very important. I was entertaining a lot on the job, my husband was working hard to get his business going. Life was pretty full and I didn't feel anything was missing.
>
> Will had also been an only child. His father was a self-made man, strong willed and prone to violence. Will was under a lot of pressure to succeed. His father had had polio and walked with a limp. His son had to do everything, win every award. You mention Little League to Will now and he practically has to leave the room. When his parents divorced while Will was in college, his father made him choose between being his son or his mother's son. He couldn't be both. (He chose his mother.)
>
> As far as kids were concerned, we hadn't really talked about children before we got married. I had assumptions—I had bought a bunch of A.A. Milne books. But between paying off debts, building the house, plunging myself into a career for the first time, and my husband building up his law practice, kids weren't an issue.
>
> We just didn't talk about having kids. He was operating on the assumption that we wouldn't have them and I wasn't thinking about it much. I think I just drifted toward the assumption that it wasn't something he wanted. He was an unhappy, only child who now doesn't like children. Other people's children was all he could stand, and they would drive him up a wall. I knew that he wouldn't be that involved as a parent. I think I would have resented that.
>
> I think having children would have affected our marriage, putting a great deal of stress on it. I don't know if we would have worked it out. Plus, I wasn't driven strongly to do it. We were both in career situations that appeared to be improving and were becoming more demanding.

When Gail turned thirty-four, her gynecologist started pressuring her to make a decision one way or another about children:

> We talked about whether Will or I should be sterilized. I was coming to a point in *my* life where I was making decisions and feeling very good about making decisions and taking responsibility. I think I viewed this as *my* problem and that I'd take care of it. I had the operation but came out of it very depressed. I felt a real sense of loss.

But about that time, Gail's boss retired and she was promoted to director of a department, supervising more than fifty employees. She became too busy to think much about her surgery, and within five years, she exceeded by several million dollars the sales goals her corporation had set out for her. She quit and now runs her own bustling consulting business for which she travels about half the time.

> I guess I'd have to say that there's a sense of regret, although I don't know if I could have balanced it all or not. Women my age came to the notion late regarding careers and we placed demands on ourselves. It meant a real focus. We had to simplify our lives, whatever that means, to get to it.

Although Gail had a happy, normal childhood, her husband's unhappy childhood influenced their decision away from children. By not having children, Gail was free to devote all her energy to her career without bearing the strain of compromising either the children or the job. So was Judy Long, the fifty-year-old professor of women's studies, who knew she could never get her Ph.D. and raise a family at the same time. "I just don't think I could have managed with a child the way that I worked," she said. She needed all her time and energy to pursue her doctoral degree and then to devote herself to teaching and research.

> I was lucky that I knew early what I wanted to do. I don't see how women who do work that takes a lot of concentration and where there's a very long-term investment with a long payoff do both. I can't imagine doing the kind of work that I do and also having that responsibility which never quits.

Other women, on the other hand, use their freedom to allow themselves or their husbands to take their work less seriously, to stop working, to change jobs frequently if they're not completely happy, or to completely "quit the system" if they want.[26]

Ilene, fifty, has taken advantage of the freedom to change jobs. She worked first as a secretary, then as an insurance saleswoman, and then as the manager of an insurance office.

> I'd work a year and then take six months off; then I'd work again and take a year off. I've lived in Sydney and London for a year, in New York and Los Angeles. My job in Los Angeles required two to three weeks of traveling at a time. About three years ago, I realized I hated what I was doing and chose to semi-retire.

Ilene now works part time in a bookstore and runs a small catering operation in her town. She lives on the coast in Oregon and has the freedom to work when she wants and to travel when she wants.

Values and Attitudes

In comparing values, child-free couples tend to have less religious affiliations than couples who parent. They also put more emphasis on individuality, autonomy, travel, attaining personal goals, equality in their marriage and gender roles, flexible lifestyles, freedom to pursue a career, and companionship.[27] The child free tend to have higher self-esteem than parents do and to be just as empathic as parents.[28]

Child-free couples also tend to make decisions and do the housework more equally, live less conventionally, and have happier marriages.

The highest rate of voluntary childlessness is 7.7 percent among American Asians and whites. The rate for American Indians is six percent; and for blacks, almost three percent.[29] Hispanics have the lowest rate: only 1.6 percent choose to forego children.

Understandably, childless couples tend to live in cities where more work and educational opportunities flourish and family life is less prominent. Urban childless people lead adult-centered lifestyles much more than those in suburbs and small and rural towns. They're also more apt to work and live among others without children, thereby finding more social support and role models.[30]

Fran, the financial consultant who became one of the first women stockbrokers in the country, lived and worked in Manhattan for years. Family life and children were never part of her daily life. Her colleagues were all in the financial world, and families were never part of the office scene. Children and families were hardly evident in the restaurants, concerts, and theaters which Fran frequented. "I never felt different," she said. "I don't inhabit that world focused on children. I don't know many people, in fact, with a typical middle American mentality."

In fact, women without children who live in smaller towns tend to feel more "out of it." Hope, the fifty-year-old fourth-grade teacher, has always lived in a small, family-centered city. For the first few decades of their marriage, Hope and her husband lived in townhouses or apartments. Some families had children, but many did not, and her childless status was never an issue.

But last year, the couple designed and built their dream house—a beautiful contemporary, decorated in stark white, nestled in the trees of a small neighborhood of about twenty-five houses in a small hollow outside of town.

When we moved in here, the first question everybody we met—and I mean everyone—asked was whether we had children. I know they meant no harm by it; I guess they were looking for playmates for their kids, but it was the very first question they asked. And because we don't have children, it's hard to make friends here. It's a good thing we already had our friendship network in town, because I think it'd be a lot harder to connect and make friends here because everybody has kids.

Sometimes I feel a bit like a social outcast—you don't really fit in. It's kind of hard to function in society—you're sort of left out in a lot of social gatherings that are based on families.

Yet, Hope knows her decision was right for her. Having children just never seemed to be the right route.

Other women, however, always assumed they'd have children, and always wanted them. But the times of their lives ticked out of beat with a baby's. Next, we'll look at some women for whom there never was a time when love and marriage and a baby carriage could all come together.

CHAPTER SEVEN

No Time Was the Right Time

To every thing there is a season, and a time to every purpose under the heaven: A time to be born, and a time to die . . . A time to weep, and a time to laugh; a time to mourn, and a time to dance; a time to cast away stones, and a time to gather stones together; a time to embrace, and a time to refrain from embracing. . . .
—OLD TESTAMENT,
Ecclesiastes, 3, 1–8

Women can have children for roughly the middle season of their lives. But sometimes, that season is out of sync with their loves, their lives, and their desires.

As Diane said in Chapter Four, she always assumed that she'd marry and have children. She is surprised at herself that at forty-three, there will be no children of her own in her life. It's not because of her career, either. Diane is not a career woman although she's always been a working woman with an interesting string of assorted jobs, including being a dietitian, gift boutique owner, sales manager, operator services executive, and personnel trainer. Right after college, she had a healthy dose of the psychedelic singles scene in the late 1960s, before it became too dangerous. By twenty-five, though, she was ready to settle down, so she married.

But like half of all the marriages that have been formed in the past fifteen years, Diane's fell apart. She only feels grateful that they never had a child. The relationship would never have survived, and Diane would never have wanted to be a single mother. She thinks it would have been too stressful to manage the unre-

94

lenting strains of trying to stretch money and quality mothering time, exacerbated by job pressures and day-care problems.

And although she's never been without an interesting relationship for very long, she's also never remarried.

There was always something wrong with the men I was with—one had diabetes and was really deteriorating, another just left the relationship abruptly after ten years—I never really knew why. By that point, I was thirty-six or thirty-seven, and I got really depressed because I thought I'd never have a child.

I was really upset for a couple of weeks. I had a really good cry and was quite unhappy. I think it was a mourning period. And then I said, "Okay, I'll never have children; I'm not getting married and that's just the way life is going to be." When I realized I had no choice about it anymore, I figured I'd better look at the bright side. So I worked to readjust my priorities.

Diane feels relieved that the hunt for a man to father a child is over. The pressure is behind her, and there's never really ever a lack of men in Philadelphia. Someone interesting always shows up eventually. She isn't lonely; she has her girlfriends who, ironically or unconsciously chosen intentionally, also don't have children. She's free now to pursue other goals.

I have a more positive outlook; I don't feel needy; I don't have to search out a man; I can feel more relaxed about it now. It was such a tremendous burden unconsciously for me to find the right one to get married and have a child. Now I can let relationships into my life not because I want to get married, but because there's a nice friendship and a sense of sexual excitement. It's much more casual and relaxed.

As far as a child, it just feels like I really missed my time. I was blinded by the fact that time goes so quickly.

Diane had a fibroid tumor removed a few years ago and thinks that she might have had a fertility problem anyway. Ironically, Diane's current boyfriend would love to settle down and have a child. But Diane feels it's too late.

I really don't think I want a child at this point. I'd be forty-five by the time I'd get pregnant, and I just think I don't have the energy anymore.

This is just my evolution. Regrets? No, I was too young and naive then. I just wasn't ready.

Of the women interviewed for this book, about one-third had been divorced at least once. In every case, it was a relief for them to be free from the chains of a sour marriage. But women felt sad about it too: high hopes and childhood dreams were shattered, rattling their self-images and planned futures. They had married because they were at that time in their lives when everyone was marrying, but they soon learned they'd been too young. Having a child would have been disastrous. They all knew tragic stories of friends who divorced with young children for whom the effects were devastating. Children of divorce, research has shown, are wounded in their hearts and minds; the emotional pain leaves them aching for years to come. It takes years for them to try to recover their emotional and psychological well-being.

Elizabeth divorced young and finds herself at forty-three unattached and childless, although this had never been her plan. During her stormy childhood, in which she "grew up between an iceberg (my mother) and a volcano (my father)," Elizabeth had planned to "get the hell out as fast as I could" and have a family.

"When I was a child, I assumed I would have children. It was one of those 'of course' kinds of things: of course I would go to college, of course I would get married, or of course I would have kids," said the California editor. "In fact, I had planned to start having kids at twenty-five—old enough to know what I was doing, young enough to have plenty of stamina."

After college, Elizabeth became very insecure about her future and felt compelled to get married to put some backbone, some structure, and some purpose into her future. "I was so scared and desperate, it was inevitable that I would marry someone as quickly as I could find one," she said. She married within two years of graduating, but at twenty-five, instead of having a baby, Elizabeth was having serious doubts about her marriage and was divorced by the next year.

Now almost forty-four, Elizabeth's still trying to come to terms with being single and letting go of the childbearing season of her life:

I have been gradually realizing over the past three to five years that I probably won't have kids. I haven't quite ruled it out, but it seems very unlikely that I'll find a man in the next few years with whom to share my life and raise a child.

Elizabeth sometimes thinks about the abortion she had at nineteen, but never regrets it. Only recently has she felt finally mature and capable enough to handle the challenges of motherhood, though Elizabeth, like Diane, felt weary even thinking about it: "I'm not sure I want to anymore."

As she gets older, Elizabeth thinks it'd be harder and harder to put her child first, something her parents never did. "I fear I'd do to the kid what was done to me and that's very sobering," she said. "It wouldn't have been deliberate, but I've been so screwed up myself, I'd screw the kid up, too."

Unlike Diane, who seems to flow from one relationship to another, Elizabeth has found it painfully difficult to find intimate, loving relationships. In fact, she's been celibate for most of the past decade. About ten years ago, after a few unsatisfying relationships with men, Elizabeth had one with a woman. It ended "disastrously," and Elizabeth hasn't been intimate with anyone since.

Every time I meet a man who looks intriguing and laughs at my jokes, I think, "Hmmmmm, maybe this one?" Visions of a cottage by the sea with children playing on the hearth float like sugarplums through my mind. Cinderella, Snow White, and Sleeping Beauty whisper in my ear. On one level, I know I'm in love with a fantasy. On another, I refuse to admit that finding a man who listens and cares is an impossible dream.

These days, though, she tries to approach men differently, not necessarily letting go of her cherished fairy-tale fantasy, but looking instead for other kinds of attachments that may or may not ripen over time.

I've said, the heck with sex, let's see if I can find a few (male) friends. So I've tossed all my wishes and expectations out the window and gone exploring, just like an anthropologist in foreign lands. Who are these guys? What do they want? What do they care about? How do they feel? Thus far, I've found two friends, and a recent possible third.

Nevertheless, realizing she'll never be a mother pains her.

I did want to be a mother, though not in a soul-searing way. If I had, I'd have gone to a sperm bank several years ago. But the hardest parts about not having kids have been recently. I had a lovely fantasy of getting married and having a family, and I'm having to give that up inch by painful inch. Realizing that I enjoy my life the way it is has helped, but that Cinderella fantasy is very slow to die.

My greatest wish is that I hadn't been so scared and so desperate that I married a thoroughly incompatible man who I didn't even like and wasted five years. But mostly I wish I'd had enough courage to go off into the world on my own, exploring things, and being adventurous. But wishes aren't horses, and beggars don't ride. In fact, I've done the best I could just about every day to manage my own life, and I don't see how I'd have done anything differently, given the choices I felt I had. And I'm still struggling to go off into the world on my own, explore things, and be adventurous. It would be very exciting to find a man I can walk along the beach with, laugh with, and maybe even raise some kids with—but I'm not holding my breath.

Tick tock, tick tock. Time is forcing me to make this transition from thinking I would have kids to realizing that I probably won't. What helps me is discovering that I like my life the way it is. With kids, I would have been pressured—and so overwhelmed—in so many ways. Without them, I've had the time and the freedom I needed to grow, and to grow up.

The fantasy still lives, but I'm finding out what reality is like, too, and who knows? Maybe one of these days, I'll find someone who likes to walk on the same patch of beach that I enjoy. Maybe he'll have some kids of his own, or want to adopt a few new ones. Or maybe he won't want kids; and maybe he doesn't exist. In the meantime, I still get to walk along my patch of beach, write my books, enjoy the sunset, make love to myself, talk with my friends, and hug my dog. Life could be a lot worse. It once was.

Neither Diane nor Elizabeth feel they could have coped with being a successful single mother. And neither of them has remarried either, although the odds are in their favor: most divorced women eventually remarry (about seventy-five percent of whites and sixty-seven percent of blacks[1]). Nancy Lucas Hampton, who lives on the Kentucky side of Cincinnati's urban sprawl, did remarry, but her timing was too off. said:

> I never planned to have or not have children. I divorced my first husband at twenty-eight and remained single until forty, missing the prime childbearing years. By then, we decided we were a bit old to chase after a toddler.

Nancy acknowledges, as many women did, that her lingering feelings of regret and relief are a mixed bag. As we'll see in Chapter Eleven, which discusses emotional issues relating to childlessness, although women may appreciate the positive sides of their circumstances, they may mourn the loss of never having a child as they move through their forties.

But Tammy, the forty-one-year-old advertising copywriter who divorced at twenty-nine and remarried at thirty-five, summarized how many women felt:

> In the same time frame, I wouldn't have done anything differently. My first marriage was terrible. Bringing a child into it would have been awful. Then I was single and not at all the type to opt for single motherhood. Right now, my present husband and I have a pretty idyllic life—not perfect, that's for sure, but we're indulging ourselves a lot, not working too hard, not earning too much, but living well and playing a lot. I still feel I have a lot of possibilities in my future and I love my freedom.

Vickie Riggan, thirty-five, is a Tennessee woman who has tried marriage three times, but still hasn't given up hope on the institution. Her checkered history includes an earnest effort to get pregnant during her second marriage. She was twenty-one, and she hoped a baby might save the marriage. Her husband's large Catholic family hungered for a child, and Vickie hoped her mother-in-law might come to like her if she gave her that grandchild.

> When I didn't get pregnant, it was viewed as a reflection of my husband's masculinity and made me feel that I was not a person, but a baby-maker, or rather as not a baby-maker.

For that reason and others, the marriage soon fell apart. Like the other women who divorced, Vickie was also grateful to be able to bale out of a lousy marriage unfettered: "Thank goodness I never got pregnant."

Within a year, Vickie was involved with a married man, a father of two, and when she became pregnant, she had to battle with her ambivalence and tumultuous feelings:

> He wanted the baby, but I knew he probably wouldn't leave his wife and if he did, I thought, when would he leave me stranded for somebody else? I knew I'd end up with the ultimate responsibility for the child. And as a single mother, would I be able to take care of both of us? And what if the child weren't normal? How would I ever afford medical care?

After a lot of soul-searching, Vickie decided that she not only didn't want this baby, but never wanted the responsibility for a child. She thought about her own childhood which had been dominated by her father's constant drinking and her mother's "bitchiness." She didn't think she had the makeup to raise a child right, and she never felt possessed by a maternal longing. So Vickie had an abortion and then hunted for months to find a doctor to tie her tubes. She was twenty-four when she had the surgery. Then, at the age of thirty, she had to have a hysterectomy. Now thirty-five, she's happily involved with a divorced man twenty years older who has three grown children. In fact, his oldest daughter is Vickie's age. Vickie feels good about being a part of their family and enjoys his two grandchildren. She hadn't known how she felt about having children until she was pregnant. So far, she has no regrets about it.

Like Vickie, Lynn (first mentioned in Chapter Six) never felt maternal longings and didn't realize until after she became pregnant that she didn't want to go through with it. But unlike Vickie, she also didn't know she hated the institution of marriage as well. As a young girl, she was desperate to be liked and hungry to get married; she assumed children would be part of the package. She was doing clerical rewrites for the "Today" show in New York, when a dentist she was dating asked her to marry him. She eagerly accepted.

> I was nineteen, after all—that was the time to get married then. He was a professional, and I thought I'd better get married because no one else will ever want me. I'm fat, ugly, and not very bright, or so I thought.

Frank was a hardworking, plain man with simple aspirations: he wanted a home, children, and a white-picket-fence kind of life. Lynn's mother was thrilled that someone should want her only child, who she always found difficult and feared would never find a man to marry; she gave Frank $30,000 to start his dental practice and threw a wedding bash for 500 people.

Six months into the marriage, Lynn knew she'd made a terrible mistake but didn't know what to do about it.

> I realized what a stupid thing I had done. This was the nicest human being that walked the face of the earth, but of all the things I didn't want in this world, one was to be tied to one human being, and most of all, the last thing I wanted on God's earth was children. That really frightened me because that was what life was supposed to be all about—you get married and have children. But all I wanted to do was to explore, meet new people, and hang out.
>
> I decided I had to stay married. No one else would ever want me, and what would I do if I weren't married because *everybody* who's *anybody* got married. So I said, okay, before Frank finds out, I'll have a child. He's chomping at the bit for these lousy children, so I better have one. I'm a good girl, so I got pregnant.

Lynn recalls viewing her pregnancy as something that had to be done. Her intentions to be a good mother were sincere and she was determined to do her best. But six months into the pregnancy, she suddenly miscarried.

> Frank's mother, father, sister, and his brother- and sister-in-law, and my mother, father, Aunt Gertrude and her husband Sam, and my cousin Ellen all came to the hospital. I don't think there was a dry eye among them but one—mine. I was so happy, and I was so ashamed of myself.

But so relieved. Lynn went back to the marriage but things eventually got worse. When Lynn suggested to Frank one night that they divorce, he answered without a pause, "Please." He paid her mother back, she gave back his family's diamonds, and introduced him to his next wife. Their first child was named after Lynn.

Although three out of four divorced women will remarry, Lynn at fifty-four vows she'll never be one of them. But she still loved men and loved loving them. After the divorce, she lived platonically with a male friend, scandalizing her family but not caring anymore. When she went to Europe for a vacation, she didn't come back for twelve years. There, she lived with a widower, helping him with his two teenagers for several years, opened an art gallery, and then returned to New York to help out her widowed mother. While working at a university, she figured she might as well take courses. She ended up with a Ph.D. and became a college professor.

At forty, she fell in love with the love of her life, and they planned a future together. He retired to California, and they visited each other during every vacation she had. It was Lynn's dream commitment. She was at her happiest, and it lasted ten years.

But then time and circumstance intervened, and her lover died unexpectedly of a heart attack.

It's been four years since his death. Lynn continues to teach and keeps looking for new job opportunities somewhere else. Though bored with her life, she believes she's now paying her dues for the years she "lived like a princess," traveling and thoroughly enjoying her life. Most of her friends are also single women free of childrearing responsibilities.

Most of the women interviewed for this book nurtured and valued their family networks. Lynn, however, is fiercely independent and maintains very few family connections. Yet she recognizes that her isolation is of her own choosing, because she often turns down social invitations. As far as children are concerned, she's still "ever so grateful" that she miscarried her one pregnancy. She laughed when I asked her if she had any concerns about growing older without children. Although she currently didn't have a love in her life, she loved herself and did just what she pleased. Living alone was the only way she ever wanted it to be. No, she had no concerns, she said, and certainly no regrets.

So far, the women in this chapter married young and then divorced. Some went on to remarry, others are still looking, and Lynn, for one, doesn't care to remarry. The flip side of these lives, however, is the woman who marries too late for children.

Alone No Longer

Too late for children. Too old to get pregnant, too old to change their ways. Like Elizabeth Dole and Ann-Margret, some women don't find Mr. Right until after their prime time for bearing children has slipped away. Sometimes, he's got grown children like Senator Dole and Ann-Margret's husband (former actor Roger Smith) did; many times he doesn't. In either event, it's too late for children of their own.

Mary, now seventy, had a high school sweetheart she planned on marrying. But a few years later, he deserted her before they married for someone else. It broke Mary's heart and took years for her to trust again. In the meantime, most of the men her age went off to fight in World War II.

On weekends, Mary would take the bus to her parents' house to help out her sister, who lived there with her children. All her co-workers were single, too; in those days, only unmarried women were hired for the few jobs available, and women who got married had to quit.

At the age of thirty-three, Mary experienced a turning point in her life: she had a hysterectomy.

> That was my one and only operation. It was a cut-off point and a crisis for me. Ever since I had been hurt when I was young, I remained a loner. But with that operation, the walls just came tumbling down and I knew that was it.

It wasn't until her early forties that she started dating a co-worker who was a widower. They married when she was forty-five and his two children were grown. "I would have wanted children, but I married too late," she said. Period. Today, her husband has five grandchildren, and although she feels awkward with youngsters and babies, she's trying hard to be a grandmother, although she recognizes she's a very reserved one.

> I still think that the most important thing a woman can do is to have children, but you can have a full life without them. I would have wanted children, but as you get older, you learn that everyone doesn't always get what they want, and sometimes if you have chil-

dren, you lose them. And besides, who knows, I might have been a disastrous mother.

I was hurt for a long time, but I never brooded about not having children. I've no lingering sadness. I just don't dwell on it. I've got a full life and take advantage of my good health and quick mind and am thankful for that.

Grace Downs, seventy-four, is another woman who married too late to consider children. For years, Grace stayed single, working in Manhattan for the phone company. "It was difficult not being married," she said. "All my friends were married and had children. They weren't interested in my office problems and they had their friends to discuss children with."

But Grace took advantage of her freedom and financial security. She was making good money and traveled often. She's been to China, South America, and Europe many times. At forty, she met her future husband on one of those vacations. They married later that year.

If I had married earlier, I would have had children. When I was forty-one, I thought I was pregnant, and I had really mixed feelings. It would have been a problem—what would I do? I was so old, and my husband was in the middle of changing jobs and all. It turned out I wasn't pregnant, and we discussed adopting then. We thought about an older child, ten or eleven years old, but that's a hard age for kids. We made a few inquiries, but it never happened.

But having thought about children made Grace and her husband decide to incorporate young people into their life. They began housing college students in their large farmhouse, and they became very attached to several. But tragedy followed: one young man they were particularly fond of was killed in Vietnam. Grace said that it was a "terrible blow." Then, a few years later, another young man who used to live with them died in a car accident. Yet the Downs continued to have college students live with them. Over the years, Grace estimates that some sixteen students probably have lived in her home. She's enjoyed opening her home to students and continues to host one or two a year. But how does she feel about not having her own?

It just wasn't a priority. But in some ways, my feelings have changed as I've grown older. I love my nieces and nephews and see some of them all the time, with my brother living next door, but it's not the same as if they were my grandchildren.

But Grace, who has been widowed now for nineteen years, feels satisfied most of the time and keeps busy taking care of the farmhouse. She still mows the grass and does most of the upkeep on the sixteen acres.

I think sometimes about how it'd be nice to have the feeling of closeness with a child, but I don't dwell on it. I have enough to do. I belong to myself, and I don't have to consider anyone else. Since I broke my arm last year, though, falling off a ladder, my brother's been nagging me about not doing this and that and it's really annoying. I think children as they get older might try to push you around like that.

I think from time to time about the future, but I don't worry about it. It's wise to do some planning and I am. Most of the time, I'm a very happy person. Now, also, more and more of my friends are widows and they're free, too.

I guess I have occasional regrets about not having children. It's natural to sometimes feel down in the dumps; it'd be nice to get calls from someone concerned and interested in what you're doing, but children nowadays are so much more independent, and I don't think always as concerned as we were, so who knows.

Besides, I'm busy and happy: my niece is moving in this fall to go to college locally; I've got season hockey tickets; I love watching sports on TV; I sew, read, and paint china; I work on the house; and I'm always busy with the church.

Iris, a seventy-seven-year-old widow, also married too late for children but gives it even less thought than Mary and Grace. It's as if she went through one door of life by marrying late and never looked back. She married late, she thinks, because she didn't find men particularly appealing until later in life. Her father left the family when she was very young and she grew up with her mom, sister, and childless aunt and uncle.

Mother kept house for them and helped them with their business. There were five aunts and uncles altogether, and I remember the men were all very weak. My aunt was very devoted to us; I always said she was my second mother.

Iris went to college but didn't date much. She was "not especially interested in marrying" in her twenties and thirties. She was
busy teaching high school and actively involved in social and
political organizations. By the time she married at forty-six, the
thought of having children was an image that had faded long ago.

I was very fond of children and had a reputation of being very
good with little ones, but I didn't have any strong maternal instinct.
We talked about adoption after we married, but it wasn't a very
strong urge. Had I married earlier, I suppose I would have had
children—it was the thing to do—but I don't think about it.

With three sisters-in-law and three cousins, and my teaching,
I was surrounded by children all the time. They were wonderful
children, but I was very glad to give them back to their mothers.
I've never felt any regret, never, about not having my own. I'm sure
I've missed something—there would have been certain pleasures,
ecstasies maybe—but it doesn't distress me. I've had other things.
Women who have had children have been denied what they thought
they'd like to do and have missed all that I've had.

Having or not having children has just never been a strong interest or concern of mine. I never think about it.

The stories of these women don't embrace all the issues that a
woman who has "missed her time" may encounter, but they do
capture the major themes. Regardless of what plans or assumptions these women had while younger, the thought of having
children couldn't surface until they had a stable relationship at
the right time of life. But none of them did, and they are grateful
not to have gone through the heartache of divorce with young
children.

Unlike these women, however, others find Mr. Right during
the right season in their lives. There's only one problem: it's the
wrong season for their mates.

CHAPTER EIGHT

When Men Don't Want to Father

Inside of this woman there is . . . still the ghost of a little girl forever wailing inside, wailing the loss of a father. . . . It would be better to die than to be abandoned, for you would spend your life haunting the world for this lost father, this fragment of your body and soul, this lost fragment of your very self.[1]

—ANAÏS NIN,
*writing to her unborn, to be stillborn, child during her
only pregnancy*

When it comes to children, men are too often the problem. Even if they're committed to a relationship, they may not be committed to becoming a parent. Many women don't want to bring a child into this world with only a halfhearted father. The risks are too high, not only for the child, but also for the mothers themselves.

Paula, for example, knew from the very beginning that Gregory didn't want children. She was eighteen when she fled to the army to get away from an abusive father. She met Gregory at nineteen and they married the next year. Paula didn't think much about Gregory's aversion to having children at the time. She was young and assumed he'd change his mind later on; besides, she had years to think about having children. They didn't talk about it much in the early years; they moved and changed jobs often. When Gregory went to graduate school, Paula helped support him.

By her early thirties, Paula had developed a circle of close female friends, many of whom were starting to grapple with whether to have children or not.

We used to spend hours and hours and hours talking about it. I didn't see myself going through this the way my friends did. It was a compelling issue for them. They were very high-powered women committed to their careers, very focused on their jobs. They were asserting themselves about work and all and I went along with their sentiments for awhile, but then I began to realize how I really felt. "I'm domestic," a little voice peeped out in this group. "I like to nest, cook, weave." But the thought of having babies had been given up because I was still with Gregory.

But not totally given up; Paula would mention children to Gregory every now and then. But the issue was sealed shut for him.

It wasn't even something that was allowed to be discussed—he'd just walk out of the room if I wanted to talk about it. You know, you can't compromise on something like this, you just can't. You either do or you don't have kids—there's no ground in between. If someone gives in, it has to be okay—it has to be more than okay. And with Gregory, it wasn't.

Paula felt that to have a child with Gregory would invite disaster. She knew that even men who are eager to become parents are all too often inattentive, uncommitted fathers. American fathers spend an average of only thirty-eight seconds a day with their babies, twenty-six minutes with their preschoolers, and sixteen minutes a day with their school-age kids. About half have never changed a diaper, and three out of four fathers take no responsibility for the care of their children.[2]

For all the talk about "the new father," the old father still reigns. When 1,100 mothers in one study assessed their husbands as fathers, a whopping fifty percent rated them as lousy—uninvolved and/or too critical. Three out of four wanted more support from them in parenting. One in five said that their husbands gave them so little help and support in raising their children that they felt like single moms. Only one-quarter of the mothers thought their husbands were good, nurturant fathers and gave them enough support in parenting.[3]

If the majority of so-called "committed" fathers were failing to live up to their roles as parents, what would an uncommitted father like Gregory be like? Paula knew that having a child would destroy the marriage, and when marriages fail—even with committed fathers—men quickly lose their parental closeness. "The phenomenon of the disappearing father [is] alarmingly wide-spread," the *New York Times* reported in an article on divorce. Studies show that many men's commitment to fatherhood lasts only as long as the marriage is intact. "When that relationship ends, the paternal bond usually withers within a few years, too," says a family sociologist.[4] A whopping one-quarter of the nation's children is growing up without fathers, resulting, says one scholar, in "the greatest social catastrophe facing our country."[5] Life without father is not only at the root of poverty and the crime and drug epidemics, say some experts, but also of low educational achievement by children and emotional and psychological devastation.

And such vanishing fathers are all too common: in one study on divorce, more than half the children who lived with their mothers had never even seen their fathers' new home; more than forty percent hadn't even seen their father in the previous year.[6] If men who want to be parents make such uncommitted fathers, what's a man who doesn't want to be a parent going to be like?

Paula knew a friend who had a child in spite of her husband's reluctance. "That kid is ten years old now and his father still resents him," she said. "It's so sad." Another woman juggles ten-hour days in real estate and two young daughters. When she asks her husband to stop watching TV and help out or play with the kids, he snarls, "You're the one who wanted them, so you do it."

So Paula didn't try to fight with Gregory about children. As the years went on, her assertiveness and independence grew stronger, while her commitment to the marriage grew weaker. At thirty-eight, she finally left Gregory for good. But she said that the "thought of having babies had been given up." She started dating, and when she found herself pregnant by a man she didn't love and never wanted to live with, she knew she had to have an abortion. She had just divorced and barely knew what she was going to do with her life. Although she doesn't regret the abortion, she regrets how the decision to be childless was made for her:

> My greatest anger and regret lies in not sitting down and really resolving the issue before Gregory and I got married. I wouldn't have let someone else make that kind of decision for me now. I

know you have to sacrifice a lot for kids, but it should have been my decision, my choice. I have regrets about that.

Today, Paula lives with a cat on a lake in a secluded converted barn with a purple kitchen and dozens of overgrown plants. She commutes forty minutes into the city to work as an administrative aide in a large library. Now forty-eight years old, Paula spends a lot of time alone spinning, weaving, knitting, and hiking with friends, both male and female. She said wistfully:

> I felt the time for children had gone by for me. The decision had been made; I don't think I had a lot to say about it, and I don't think I've ever really dealt with that. It never would have been okay to have a baby with Gregory. He would have resented it, and I would have ended up a single mom now which would have been very difficult financially and emotionally.
>
> With a different man, in a perfect situation, a perfect relationship, I'd have had a baby. It would have seemed the natural, really positive thing to do. It's not a real sadness in my life, but I do feel the loss. I haven't experienced something that would have been really important.
>
> But I also know on the one side, some kids are problems and instead of being a joy, they make their parents' lives very, very painful. You don't have control over what happens. That's one of the risks and it's a real scary thing. I don't have all that worry and strain. I don't have the pain of disappointment if the children don't turn out. Some of my friends are leading painful lives because of their children.
>
> On the other hand, as our parents die, they leave us, and without children, there isn't a sense of anybody after us. You know, nobody cares about me like my mom. If your mom doesn't love you, who does. That's something that I miss. I'll never have a child to say that about me. It's not a great sadness in my life, but I do feel the loss, and I'm concerned it may grow stronger as I get older.

Several women said they wished they could have been parents, but with only as much responsibility as a traditional father. Fathers "had it made" and it seemed the ideal way to be a parent. Janice, the forty-four-year-old attorney, who loves her career said:

> I would have loved to have been a parent if I could have put into it what the average man puts into being a father. But I just couldn't take on all the responsibility mothers usually do—you know, it's

always the mother, whether she's got a full-time career or not, who arranges for the sitters and day care, buys birthday presents for the kids and their friends' parties, plans costumes for Halloween, bakes cookies for school, and stuff like that.

With my husband, who only would have put into fatherhood the typical low-level amount of time and energy, having us as parents wouldn't have been enough for a child. On the flip side, I think my level of regret is about the same as a childless man my age—I would have loved to have been "a father," but I have many other ways to express myself and be creative and productive.

Like many women, Janice was forced to choose whether to have children or not without a fully committed partner. While researching *Hard Choices: How Women Decide About Work, Careers, and Motherhood*, sociologist Kathleen Gerson found that when men felt "cool to lukewarm" about parenting, "motherhood appeared almost as difficult and dangerous as if the partner were not present at all." In these cases, women feared that having a child would not only undermine their careers but also their relationships. That left the women with an uncomfortable feeling that they might end up with the "uninviting prospect of raising any child she bore largely alone."[7] Without a partner willing to share equally in parenting and all the additional chores associated with parenting, women feared that a would-be child would seriously damage their own emotional well-being.

So when a man doesn't want children, a woman has good cause to hesitate before taking the plunge. In such circumstances, as well as when women did not have mates, Gerson found that "choosing parenthood thus seemed a shortsighted and irrational act that promised to backfire eventually for these women. Childbearing was an immediate temptation they could resist."[8] Women in these situations typically chose childlessness "unenthusiastically," says Gerson, as the best of several bad alternatives.

In Dorothy's case, her husband wanted to be a parent but only of their own biological child. After ten years of marriage, it became clear to them that a pregnancy was not going to occur. They had a great marriage, and still do after forty-five years. Although Dorothy wanted a child terribly and would have eagerly adopted, her husband would not:

He just wouldn't. I think he was afraid. He just didn't want to. I hate confrontation and didn't push it.

Dorothy knew that she wouldn't be able to convince Jerry to want to adopt. Even if he later conceded, his adamant attitude against adoption was an indicator to her that it just shouldn't be. As time went on, Dorothy eventually adjusted to not having children, and by her late thirties, appreciated the freedom it entailed.

We lead a very wonderful life. We were able to do a lot of things our friends couldn't because they needed the money for the children. More than once, people would stop me and say, "You don't know how lucky you are that you don't have this problem or that problem." And we didn't. By my mid-thirties, I even asked the doctor for a diaphragm.

Not having children had allowed Dorothy and Jerry to retire in their early fifties and might even have saved Jerry's life. He had a heart attack a few years ago, and Dorothy suspects he might have had it a lot earlier and more severely had he been under more pressure. "You cannot have children and not have aggravation," she said.

Dorothy and Jerry are still exceptionally close. In spite of their strong marriage, though, Dorothy sometimes wishes she had pressured Jerry to talk more about adoption in earlier years. Both her parents and two best friends have died in the past decade, and the pinhole that the lack of children had punctured in her heart has grown larger recently.

I feel the lack more now. There's something missing and it's coming out much more at the present. Just the past few years I've been feeling this way.

Yet, Dorothy couldn't predict what might have happened if they had adopted a child. Would Jerry have come around eventually as a fully committed father? Would he always have resented the "imposition" of an adopted child? Would they have had a tough and tumultuous relationship that might have impaired Jerry's heart earlier and fatally? Dorothy couldn't answer these questions. She couldn't compare how much better or worse, more joyful or stressful, it would have been to have adopted a child against her husband's desires.

Seventy-five-year-old Lucille, on the other hand, was fortunate in finding a man who didn't want children. During her first marriage, she had a tubal pregnancy at age twenty-six. She was living with her husband and his overbearing mother in a three-room apartment at the time:

> It was very unpleasant and the pregnancy was a total surprise. If I had had a child at the time, it would have been a disaster. My husband was pretty much married to his mother and she didn't approve of me. After the tubal pregnancy, it got so bad that I moved out.

The doctors told her not to get pregnant again; the risks were too high. But that was okay; she was relieved to be out of the marriage free and clear and had a wonderful time during the second World War as a single woman.

> If I had had the child, I don't know what would have happened. I probably would have stayed married and it would have been disastrous. But as it turned out, I had a lovely time instead.

At thirty, she met Christopher and was "delighted" that he didn't want more children; he already had a son from a previous marriage and didn't want any more. Said Lucille: "It worked out beautifully for both of us." Lucille loved her career as an executive at the phone company; she kept getting promotions, was financially very well-off, traveled constantly, and loved her life.

> My life was in business; I wasn't involved with people and their children. That was the suburban thing and I was living a city life. My friends were from my job, and I never felt bad about not having children. I was too wrapped up in my career. I never felt deprived.

At fifty, she retired and started a new career in interior design. At seventy-five, she sells her paintings, helps manage the art gallery that she co-owns, is an avid golfer, and travels regularly.

> Having children would have been an experience I would have liked to experience. But under my circumstances, I have no regrets. If I had had children, it just wouldn't have worked. I haven't missed

not having children; in fact, not having them has enhanced my particular circumstances.

I think all through your life, you might always feel you missed something by not having the warmth and love that are supposed to go with having children. But if I had had children, it wouldn't have worked with my second marriage, and we've been very happy together. I didn't intend not to have children, but it's turned out very well for me. It just wouldn't have fit into my lifestyle.

Some women stall about having a baby because they are full of doubts, often with good cause, that their mates will share the parental load equally. Most men are not raised to be fully committed, nurturant parents; yet modern women often need a husband to share the load if they are to be career women as well as mothers. If only men would take on more of the parental responsibilities, the decision to have a child wouldn't be so conflicted for many women. Said demographer Martha Farnsworth Riche, national editor of *American Demographics*:

When I look at the data—whether it's time use, custody, or father's time with children—I see that men, on average, just aren't very interested in raising children. That continues to put an additional burden on mothers if they are going to have a career too. This is the missing piece: society pressures women to have careers and children, but they need men who are fully committed parents, too. If men would simply meet women halfway, having children wouldn't be such an issue.[9]

In Lisa's case, she *knew* that Adam would not meet her halfway. She always thought she wanted children, but she didn't think her husband, who was lukewarm about becoming a father, would have been a very good father. He was an only child born to older parents (his mother was thirty-four, his father almost fifty), was always a loner, had no experience with babies or young children, and never pictured himself with them. Although he wasn't emphatically *against* children, he wasn't particularly interested in them either, and wouldn't make a commitment to actively co-parent.

Had I been married to a different kind of man, someone who really wanted children and would make the commitment to be an active participant, I would have probably had children and been drawn into the whole family thing. I couldn't really see Adam giving up a lot of things for a child, though. It would be me doing whatever the kid needed, and I realized I didn't want that life.

In fact, we both agreed that our relationship might be in jeopardy if we had had children. We've learned a lot watching our friends parent, and we would have disagreed a lot on how to raise kids. I think it would have created a lot of anger and I'm glad we didn't have to face that.

Lisa, forty-six, and Adam agree that they're very compatible as marriage partners, but probably would not be as parents. Lisa says she's very happy; she loves her life with her husband and is content with the choice she made with her husband to remain child free. She has no regrets. They have no commitments—not even a pet, a plant, or a house. They rent their apartment and take advantage of their freedom.

Some women, however, find themselves childless yet burdened with many of the responsibilities of parenting. They are step-mothers.

Stepmothers: Women Both "With" and "Without" Children

Every day, some 1,300 divorced parents remarry, creating blended families and adding to the thirty-five million steppar-ents.[10] About 8.7 million children—one out of every five chil-dren—live in some 4.3 million stepfamilies in the U.S.[11] In fact, experts predict that by the early 1990s, more people will be part of a second marriage than a first marriage.

When women who do not have children marry men who do they become "instant parents." But their roles are constantly in flux: one moment they act as parents by disciplining, advising, or planning family events; the next moment they are "steps," inter-acting with children who are devoted to their absent and natural mothers; and yet at other times, they are "non-parents," retreating to allow their spouses to handle certain touchy matters.

Some women who have never had children look forward to suddenly being able to parent; others who aren't looking to parent find that the man they love comes as a package deal—"love me, love my kids." Making the transition from single woman to instant stepmother, however, is often a trying and difficult one. Writes Dr. Richard A. Gardner, a child psychiatrist and author:

> A women with no children of her own, when involved with a man with children whom she wishes to marry, may entertain unrealistic fantasies about how wonderful life will be with him and his children . . . After marriage, and the lessening of romantic euphoria . . . the bride may become oppressed with the new burden she has taken on. Other women ease into the role of motherhood and gradually become accustomed to its frustrations. Having it thrust upon her cannot but produce feelings of being trapped and overwhelmed.[12]

That's what happened to forty-nine-year-old Anna. "When I met Dan, I was almost forty and had never been married," she said, "I always thought I wanted to be a mother. In fact, part of what appealed to me about Dan was the fact that he had two kids. I figured I'd experience being a parent part time, but without all the hassles of having responsibility for them all the time." Dan and his ex-wife had joint custody; two weeks at each home and then the kids switched.

Although Anna fantasized about the new family and how warm and loving it would feel, she was totally unprepared for what happened. Her calm, ordered life was suddenly turned upside down by the hectic scheduling and the difficulties involved in trying to parent Heather, nine, and David, twelve. After working a long day as a market research analyst, she'd come home to all the daily hassles of having kids—taking them to the dentist, dance lessons, and softball, doing their laundry, helping with homework, coping with the noise and confusion (the twelve-year-old loved to blast his rock music; she wanted to ask him more frequently to turn it down but feared she'd sound too much like the "wicked stepmother"). And earning their love and respect was a very long-term process that never quite happened as fully as Anna had dreamed. She was always haunted by the specter of the wicked stepmother vs. the perfection of their natural mother.

Such instant stepmothers, especially those who have never parented, have the toughest adjustments to make, says Claire Berman, author of *Making It As A Stepparent*.[13] They're not used to the commotion that children can create, resent their privacy suddenly being invaded, and must grapple with jealousy and resentment as their new husbands devote enormous energy to children who sometimes resent their presence. Such a stepmother "is left feeling as though her nose is pressed against the window while the real party goes on inside without her," say Karen Savage and Patricia Adams in *The Good Stepmother: A Practical Guide*. All too often, childless stepmothers, who were eager to suddenly parent, find themselves as merely custodial stepmothers. They may have to share their precious weekends, holidays, and often vacations with children who may resent, alienate, and anger them. They are expected to shop, cook, and clean up after the children, play with them, advise them, and cater to their needs, yet they may not receive the unrequited love and affection that children often give to their own mothers.

"In most families the 'good' biological mother cannot be replaced in children's hearts and minds, and a stepmother's efforts at fulfilling this role breed resentment," write the authors of *Women and Stepfamilies*.[14] Even when stepchildren like their stepmother, they're often fearful that showing her affection would be disloyal to their natural mother. Yet stepmothers must give their time and energy to the children and may wince when much of their husband's income goes to the children and sometimes to the ex-wife. In fact, money is often a critical issue in stepfamilies, and it is cited as the second most popular cause for divorce in stepmarriages (problems with stepchildren are the number one cause).

When Christine married Gary in her late twenties, they agreed they'd have no children. She never wanted them since she knew she wasn't the "nurturing type," and Gary had already been through it. He had two kids, a ten-year-old son and a fifteen-year-old daughter, but they lived far away with their mother. After Christine and Gary were married for two years, it became clear that Gary's ex-wife's new husband was abusing the children. When Gary asked Christine if she'd be willing for him to pursue custody, Christine couldn't say no. It would have forced Gary to choose between his second wife and his blood children, no choice at all when he knew his children were being abused. But Christine felt like the rules of the game were changing in the middle and she couldn't help feel resentment. Christine soon became an instant parent to a twelve-year-old stepson and seventeen-year-old step-daughter who tested and challenged her from the beginning.

The first two years were "horrible." Emily (the stepdaughter) and Christine were rivals for Gary from the beginning; other times, the kids were nasty to Gary (their mother's doing, according to Christine). But Gary kept trying and putting out for them. Christine endured a thousand little insults and hurts over the years because she was the custodial stepmother, the "wicked" stepmother. But she grew to love the kids, and, at one point when she wanted to walk out on Gary, fear of what it would do to the kids stopped her.

Over the next three years, Emily had to have an abortion, Gary was fired, and Christine got an ulcer and had a tubal ligation.

> [But] sometimes [I'm] worried that I will regret that decision when I am old and alone and have no family, but my husband . . . reminds me that I *do* have children . . . [but] I wonder if these two kids, who are not bone of my bone or flesh of my flesh, will really care anything about me when I am old and alone.

Now, Christine is glad she didn't have children with Gary. "I so strongly disagree with the way he raises kids," she says. But she still adores him as a husband and glows in the warmth and stability of their marriage. The kids are honest and loving, and although there are constant ups and downs, Christine calls herself a very lucky woman.[15]

Unlike Christine, Cathy, forty-one, wanted very much to have children. She finds herself today with growing resentment toward her sixty-two-year-old husband for refusing to have a child with her. She had been married before, in her early twenties. She wanted children then but didn't conceive. After a long infertility workup, the doctors discovered that her husband had an extremely low sperm count.

But they told me not to tell him because it would hurt his ego. So here I was in the meantime, dying inside. I got so depressed, I couldn't function at all. I ended up hospitalized with a nervous breakdown. I finally broke down and told him. He was so immature at the time, he didn't even care.

It turned out to be better that we didn't have children, because we ended up divorcing a few years later when I was twenty-seven.

Cathy met her present husband two years later in the company where she was working as an executive secretary. He was older, wealthy, and a widower raising his daughter, then nineteen and only ten years younger than Cathy. They dated for three years before they married, and when they did, he insisted she quit working.

He didn't tell me until after we got married that he had had a vasectomy just before the wedding. But I still figured he'd change his mind, and I held on to hopes that he'd adopt or consider foster care later on. Although I was angry he hadn't told me, I just went along with it. What was I going to do?

For years, Cathy's relationship with her stepdaughter was difficult. Haunted by the over-idealized and dead but "perfect" mother, they found themselves in fierce competition over the most important man in their lives.

She had had her father all to herself for four years and didn't like me there at all. Here I was, a newlywed, and I couldn't even be alone with my husband. It was like I was competing with another woman rather than helping to take care of a child.

Cathy never felt close to her. Now that the stepdaughter is thirty-one, Cathy hopes that she'll marry and have children, although there are no prospects in sight at the moment. Said Cathy:

If she had a baby, it would help me. My need for a child would be taken care of. It would fulfill most of what I need. I keep hoping for that but nothing's happened so far.

So Cathy suppresses her resentment and now devotes her energies into volunteer work as an emergency medical technician. Carrying a beeper at all times, she runs off into the night whenever it goes off to staff the local ambulances. She's also out several nights a week in training classes, working her way up to become a full-fledged paid EMT.

> I love it. It feels good trying to save people's lives—it's my way of contributing to the world. And I know it sounds stupid, but I've sort of semi-adopted two eighteen-year-olds in the department. They call me "Ma" and come over to talk. I'm in heaven with them. I kid around with them; we're affectionate with each other. It's great.

Her husband resents her flying off whenever her beeper goes off in the middle of cocktails or when company is over, but she's emphatic about doing this for herself now.

> You're really limited when you're married to someone and they feel differently than you do. You just can't go ahead and do it any-way. Your life is governed by what they think.
> I'd really warn other women who want children and are thinking of marrying someone who doesn't. Those men probably won't change their minds. I think you eventually get used to not having children, but I don't think the feeling ever leaves.
> You get to a point where you really resent your husband for it, especially when you're angry. It's always there for me, and I have to stop myself sometimes from saying, "Well, if you had let me have children . . ." I could build a great resentment about it, but what good would that do?

But perhaps the saddest story came from Fran. Now fifty-one, Fran had married at twenty-four. Her husband was thirty-eight at the time, divorced, and father to four young children, ages two to ten. They lived in the same town as the children's mother and grandmother who were both bitter about the divorce. Fran felt she took the brunt of that anger and that it often infected the kids and their relationships with her, but she was hopeful it would end up okay. For twenty years, she mothered the kids on weekends and vacations when they'd come to their father's house.

> It seemed like a ready-made family and was as much as we could handle. I thought that, idealistically, it didn't matter if they weren't my own—they were ours. And I thought that was going to be okay. We talked about having our own children, but I was fine about it

never happening, although I think in the back of my mind I thought it would come about eventually.

It took a long time for Fran to get close to the kids, and she never felt she bridged the gap completely. She'd make headway with one or two of them, and then the next hour or day they'd be gone for the week, and Fran felt she had to start over again.

You think you'll get close, and you might be a confidante or friend one minute, but it was all temporary. In two hours they'd go back to their mother's and I'd just be their father's wife again.

There's a difference with children who aren't your own. You're never going to be first. There's a relationship you can have with your own kids—and a lot of natural parents don't even have it—but it can happen. With your own children, there's an acceptance that you'll love one another despite things you don't approve of or accept, that you'll still care about each other no matter what. But there's always a distance with steps. That acceptance doesn't happen. There's a missing link.

By the time Fran was thirty, she realized that her husband's children would not accept her completely as a second mother. Like other women in their twenties who marry men who already have children, Fran hadn't thought too much about having her own when she married. But by her early thirties, her priorities shifted, and she began to consider having her own baby. But like many other remarried fathers, her husband didn't want another child.

He didn't want to start another family and go through everything again. He got really upset—his vehemence surprised me. He'd walk away from those discussions with lots of fear that I might trick him by getting pregnant or something. I found out later that he harbored those feelings for years, that it wasn't resolved for him although it was resolved as far as I was concerned.

I'd spent a lot of time thinking about why I wanted a child, and I found they were selfish reasons, that I wanted someone I could rely on and care about and who cared about me as the years went by, and having that sense of being first.

But Fran and her husband couldn't communicate well on an intimate level, and the marriage began to unravel. For her own health and well-being, Fran was sterilized at thirty-five; her husband didn't even know. In her early forties, she went back to school to get out of the secretarial rut and came into contact with women friends who had been influenced by the women's movement. They empowered her to be more assertive. As the marriage deteriorated, as do two out of three remarriages with children,[16] she found the courage and independence to allow the relationship to completely fall apart.

After the separation, she tried to contact the children, then between the ages of twenty-two and thirty. In spite of her twenty years of caring for them and sharing Christmases, other holidays, and vacations together, they wanted nothing to do with her. Fran has had no contact with them since.

> It was a real shock to me. I realized that I had left my family hundreds of miles away to live with this man and his family. I had put all my time and energy into his extended family, making them my family, but I wasn't putting any time into people who cared about me. After the divorce, it was all gone.

Fran did make the transition, however, from clerical work to professional, and today loves her job as a staff trainer for a human services agency. Three years ago she started dating a man who had four children!

> I thought, "Oh, no, do I want to go through this again?" But these children are much older. They're very nice, and most of the relationship with them is long distance.

Fran decided to take the plunge, and she married him just six months ago. For awhile, the youngest daughter was spending a lot of time with them while attending a local college.

> There was always that distance. Anytime I did something against her wishes, she'd say something like, "well my mom wouldn't have done that—she would have let me have my way." That kind of implication.

But recently, that daughter has moved to another state to go to college closer to her mother. Fran thinks that having stepchildren this time will be okay, and that these will be long-distance and polite relationships that won't impact on the marriage much.

Fran's story, of course, is one of the worst-case scenarios. For Karen—the forty-five-year-old college professor from Chapter Six who never felt a maternal pang—being a "step" has been a casual, cool relationship. Her husband's sixteen-year-old daughter came to live with them last year after her mother died. Karen is pleasant to her, doesn't try to mother her, and Karen's husband is a fully committed father. Said Karen:

> I don't try to play a major parenting role with her. Her father's very involved in parenting and does a good job of it. I let her call the shots with me. I play the "I'll just be here" kind of role—more like an aunt-type person. She's under no obligation to have a real thing going with me like with a true stepparent. It's been a smooth transition.

When the children are older, the strains of stepparenting tend to diminish. Grown children are often grateful that their fathers have found someone who cares for them, especially if their fathers are widowed rather than divorced.

Mary, you might recall from the previous chapter, married for the first time at forty-five. Arthur was widowed with three grown children who were out on their own. Mary hardly held a baby until she was sixty, when one of her husband's daughters had a child. She approaches stepgrandmotherhood "cautiously," not trying to jump in with help and advice, but welcoming the get-togethers they have with grandchildren.

> As children have come into my life, it's been a pleasant experience, although not a close one. I am a stepgrandmother and don't try to be more, but they include me in things.

Of course, some stepfamilies make a smooth and fulfilling transition into a blended family. Rather than trying to mother stepchildren, successful stepmothers find other roles to play, such as mentor, friend, role model, guide, or aunt. Some experts say that stepfamilies that have a new, shared baby adjust better than those that don't.[17] That's not to say, of course, that women who don't have children can't become successful stepmothers. Many factors will influence how successful the stepfamily will be, such as how amicable the divorce was, how supportive and nurturant the father is, and how well the financial situation is worked out. But no one says it will be easy.

CHAPTER NINE

Infertility and Medical Interference

Unsuccessful treatment for infertility represents a profound tragedy for the couple who invested hope, time, and money and made lifestyle adjustments so that they might one day give birth to a baby. At some point, however, the couple and their physicians must acknowledge that further treatment is unlikely to be successful and that the couple should end their medical quest for fertility. . . .

Whatever life choices an infertile person makes, the remnants of infertility are rarely banished forever. . . . [it] is part of their lives forever.

—CONSTANCE SHAPIRO,
Infertility and Pregnancy Loss[1]

In 1972, Denise married in her early twenties and mapped out her master plan which was to first enjoy being a bride. "We thought it wise to build a couple before we were to build a family," she said. Although she went off the pill a year later, she continued to use contraception: "I wanted to make sure all the hormones were out of my system. I made sure we were doing everything wisely."

They began trying to conceive in the fall, planning on a spring baby; "that's how naive we were." Six years, two surgeries, and "cases of tear-soaked tissues" later, Denise and her husband were still childless. They are one of the 3.5 million American couples—one in every six—whose lives are shaken by infertility, a problem twenty-five percent more common now than in the 1960s. Late age attempts, sexually transmitted diseases, and the damaging effects of previous birth control methods are just some of the causes.

Everyone knows someone who's having trouble having a baby, even on TV and in the movies. Joyce Davenport, the diehard district attorney on "Hill Street Blues" was infertile (TV husband Captain Frank Furillo assured her that he married her for *her*, not her ability to conceive). Holly Hunter is so desperate for a baby in the kooky film comedy *Raising Arizona*, that her husband kidnaps a newborn quint. Glenn Close and James Woods pursue endless infertility tests until they turn to private adoption in the movie, *Immediate Family*. Ann Kelsey and Stuart Markowitz, the married lawyers on "L.A. Law" also turned to adoption only to have it fall through at the last minute. Luckily, Hollywood waved its fairy wand, and Ann miraculously conceived in spite of Stuart's dismal sperm count.

But we don't live in the magical world of Tinseltown, and even some people who do, like Ann-Margret (a stepmother who has always tried to have her own) and JoBeth Williams (who eventually adopted) and their mates, can't conceive or keep a pregnancy. Infertility can be a severe blow to couples in countless ways, sometimes precipitating a life crisis. Just the initial shock of a problem can rock a couple's foundation. Said Denise:

> We were very self-sufficient people, and we were taught that if we worked hard, we would get whatever we wanted—educations, good jobs, a home of our own, and babies in the nursery. No one ever warned me that you don't always get what you want, especially a pregnancy. This made me very desperate. Someone had changed the rules and hadn't told me.

Denise and her husband pursued medical help. Although about half the couples that receive medical intervention eventually conceive, Denise did not. They had "unexplained infertility," and after try after failed try, Denise began to feel helpless and hopeless.

Infertility treatments can take months, even years, and may cost thousands of dollars; in fact, each year, about $1 billion is spent in pregnancy pursuits. In the process, a couple's emotional well-being may be worn down. Some may feel that they are losing control over lives that had always been so well planned. Many suffer from emotional upheavals and are plagued by fears: fear that their spouse may desert them; fear that they'll never be a parent; fear that they'll be alone and lonely in old age. If the fears fester, escalating anxiety and tension may feed the fears even more. Sometimes, infertility victims may feel panicky, depressed, worthless, or vulnerable, or begin to doubt themselves and/or their relationships.

At first, Denise did everything she could to become pregnant. Like so many couples, she became an "infertility addict," obsessed with temperature charts, ovulation tests, postcoital exams, and fertility shots, as a way to exert some control. In a power struggle against nature, Denise became determined to win, to claim what she had always believed to be her birthright:

> I think I began wanting a pregnancy more because I couldn't have it than because I wanted a child. I had become so caught up in the obsession of the battle, in proving that I could have my own way, that I didn't focus on the child, the parenting, the lifetime commitment.

Gilda Radner, the late comedienne and wife of actor Gene Wilder, expressed a similar reaction:

> I found it very difficult to literally make the decision to have a baby. . . . but . . . Suddenly, when it's not going to be a natural event and it's put into your hands with experimental procedures and elective surgeries, the decision becomes an obsession. For me the issue became less whether I wanted a baby or not and more my inability to accept not being able to have one. [2]
>
> I couldn't take my fate: "You'll never have a baby." I began to beat my fists against a door that maybe I had locked on the other side." [3]

Radner was referring to an illegal abortion twenty years earlier and the nineteen years she pursued her education and career without a thought to pregnancy.

As Denise kept failing to get pregnant, she had to continually grapple with loss—loss of privacy, loss of control over her reproduction, over her daily life as medical procedures invaded her mind and body, and loss of her dreams. The supposedly most natural process in the world had became clinical, invasive, and impersonal. Every detail of her sex life and genitalia were examined and analyzed.

In time, Denise became depressed and angry, both common reactions for women toiling under the shadow of infertility. Women often become depressed because they have so little control and angry at their bodies for failing them, angry at fate for cheating them, angry at doctors who betrayed them with IUDs or other damaging birth control methods, angry at infertility specialists for their poking and prodding and their painful tests, angry at friends and family for pressuring them about pregnancy or for getting pregnant themselves, and angry at people who make stinging comments unthinkingly.

Yet partners typically react differently to the crisis of infertility and may grow angry at each other for not making each other feel better, for not understanding how they feel. Infertility wedges a barrier into what used to be intimate communication. Women, raised to value attachments and to show their feelings, typically are more devastated by infertility while feeling frustrated, angry, and hurt, by their husbands' lack of emotional support. One survey of infertile couples who had always expected they'd have children revealed that, while fifty-seven percent of the women considered their infertility the most serious crisis they'd ever faced, only twelve percent of the men did. Likewise, fifty-eight percent of the women, but only thirty-two percent of the men, felt they'd be missing a vital life experience if they didn't have children.[4]

As partners react to infertility on different planes, they may feel more and more distant or isolated from each other. At the same time, intimate, spontaneous sex—a joy in many marriages—may come to be monitored, planned, and forced.

Women who marry men who already have children may have the most difficult time dealing with infertility. Their men tend to be least committed to infertility workups since they've already had children. Many feel that if their wives want a baby, that's fine, but if there are problems, these men are the least apt to provide the kind of emotional support women need during this trying time. "These women are really the forgotten population, and it's growing all the time. These husbands just aren't as interested in medical treatment, and we see the wives in the clinic, day in and day out, month after month, all by themselves, without the emotional support women so badly need at this time," said Linda Hammer-Burns, Ph.D., a clinical psychologist at the University of Minnesota Medical School's Department of OB-GYN. These women are also much more limited in their options; men who already have children from a previous marriage are least likely to be willing to use donor sperm or to pursue adoption.

In Denise's case, her husband, Randall, did not have other children and was very supportive during their endless and expensive medical treatments. Yet the couple lived in emotional limbo for years. Every time a procedure failed and/or Denise got her period, they grieved again for the child they could not conceive. At the same time, they clung to a shred of hope that they still might succeed.[5]

But half of all infertile couples don't achieve a live birth, and, at some point, they must begin to mourn their dreamchild if they are to get through the infertility crisis. They must mourn because they've grown attached to their dreams of being pregnant, giving birth, and nursing and cradling their infant. They've imagined in their fantasies what the baby would look like, how she'd change their lives, how she'd bask in the glow of their love.

If couples are to get beyond the sorrow of infertility, they must mourn the loss of those dreams, the loss of whatever part of their self-identities are wrapped up in those dreams, and the loss of a destiny they had always assumed they'd pursue.

But that grieving process for a child that never was or will be can be a struggle in lonely isolation. Infertility is truly an "invisible disability"; its losses are largely unrecognized by others.[6] There's no real person missing, no shared memories, no cultural or public recognition of the loss, no funeral. Other people don't know about their emotional pain unless they choose to share it. But the pain can hurt and paralyze its victims until it is reckoned with.

The Transition

If a couple can't produce a baby, they must first recognize their infertility as a loss that requires them to move through the stages of mourning and later to either adopt or choose child-free living. If they deny their pain and loss and refuse to acknowledge and talk about it, these feelings can fester and infect the marriage. That's what happened to Deanna, a forty-three-year-old California photographer. Not being able to get pregnant was so painful to her that she tried ignoring the possibility there was a problem and she never pursued medical intervention. But her marriage couldn't take the strain and stresses of chronic infertility.

> I expected to have children anytime, and my husband had high hopes each month, putting a great deal of stress upon me every month counting the days. He left me after eight years, when I was twenty-nine, basically due to my childlessness. It was a very difficult time for me, and it took me twelve to fourteen years to recover emotionally.

Other couples seek medical help until they're either successful or decide they must stop trying. Couples can't rein in control over their emotions and private lives until they cease their quest for a baby, says infertility expert Constance Shapiro, author of *Infertility and Pregnancy Loss*, and a Cornell University professor of human service studies. Only after acknowledging their loss can couples move through the mourning process, accept their loss, and eventually redefine their identities and self-concepts, their expectations, hopes, and plans, and forge ahead. Some will pursue adoption, but others will not, and may need to mourn the loss of a child even more deeply.

Sometimes, it's a seemingly easy transition to acceptance, especially among women for whom there was little choice. Older women, for example, who grew up in an era when fertility problems weren't discussed openly were offered few options by their physicians. Many older women interviewed for this book spoke of accepting their childlessness without an emotional crisis. Some gathered strength through their belief that God had purposes for them other than being parents.

Ruth, eighty-five, the widow of a college professor, lives alone in a retirement apartment. She married at twenty-six but never got pregnant, and the doctor didn't know why. She spends her days now in a wheelchair, helped by a nursing aide during the day. Said Ruth:

> It was never a crisis for us. We were both brought up in godly families and were taught that you're born, you die, and in between you accept. That's how I've lived all my live. I learned to accept. You just can't cry all the time. I just took things as they came.

Florence, a fifty-three-year-old bookkeeper, still married after thirty-four years, never got pregnant and never saw a doctor about it, assuming he couldn't help anyway. She just let it be. "I love children, and I was envious at one time of people who had them," she said. "But by the time I was thirty, the feeling passed and I got over feeling that I wanted them."

Other couples facing infertility, however, may need to forge out new meanings for their lives as well as for their marriages. Not being able to have children may undermine the function or fulfillment of their marriage, perhaps even their purpose on earth. Couples who come out of the infertility crisis most successfully are those with the greatest ability to reframe their marriage goals and identity. Other factors that help are strong marriages, high self-esteem, financial security, and strong careers that provide a sense of identity and self-worth.[7]

Women, in particular, must shift their identities and goals for the future from being a mother to being a nonmother. This transformation to nonparenthood, in fact, can be as profound as that to parenthood, say sociologists and experts on involuntary childlessness, Anne and Ralph Matthews. "Nonparenthood is likely to have as significant an impact on family and personal identities as parenthood itself."[8]

To ultimately reckon with infertility, couples may need to mourn their loss just as survivors mourn the death of a loved one. If they deny their experience as a significant loss or minimize its importance, they could get stuck psychologically. Communication and the expression of emotions are very important at this time—common emotions include shock, denial, anger, guilt, yearning, helplessness, and hopelessness. Although psychic pain may persist for months, perhaps years, involving spells of weeping and despair, recognizing the pain is part of the mourning process, which is the natural, healthy way to deal with loss. And through that process comes acceptance, and only through that acceptance will hope and energy return.

Loss is part of everyday life and grieving is a learned skill that allows us to accept our losses and pave the path to regaining control over our lives and toward self-growth. Psychoanalyst Judith Viorst, author of *Necessary Losses*, describes how everyone must cope with losing and "letting go":

> Throughout our life we grow by giving up . . . our deepest attachments . . . certain cherished parts of ourselves. We must confront, in the dreams we dream, as well in our intimate relationships, all that we never will have and never will be. Passionate investment leaves us vulnerable to loss. And sometimes, no matter how clever we are, we just lose.[9]

Deanna remembers how her feelings first shifted from desperate hope to desperate sorrow, and then eventually to acceptance. Although her infertility will always be a tender spot, the new importance that her work took on in her life became the silver lining of her childlessness. It is not a direct compensation for not having a child, but it is a positive way to channel her energies and enrich her life with new meaning and purpose.

> My work has made a great difference in feeling useful and busy in a positive way. My work now consumes ALL my time to the point that I need a housekeeper. My husband has to drag me out of my home office to go out for recreation. I have such a deeper meaning and purpose to my life now that children would be in the way. I am enjoying my "childless" life now in being free to pursue worthy causes and lifelong dreams and ambitions.

Thirty-eight-year-old Terri, mentioned in the introduction to this book, never had any career aspirations and thrust her energies into raising and training horses, designing and building a luxury home, and working out all the details involved in subdividing forty acres she and her husband purchased ten years ago. How was the transition for her?

> Having a family was really important to me and I never questioned that it would never be. But after six years of going to doctors, doing all the tests and retests, having four operations in one year, and then finally being told I couldn't have children, a great sense of relief washed over me. I was so glad to be finally told something definite.
>
> I spent the day crying and then locked myself into a room with a typewriter and spilled my guts out from Friday to Sunday night typing and typing. When I came out on Sunday, I felt renewed.

Some women acquired a sense of peace by viewing their infertility as their fate. Although many were not religious, they knew that to continue struggling against their infertility would be a struggle against themselves. Margaret, sixty-six, had fibroid tumors throughout her thirties and a hysterectomy at thirty-nine.

> After that final surgery, I just said to myself, that's the way the cards are dealt. This is it. It's all over with. I think it's a lot harder when you're anticipating whether you're pregnant or not all the time. But once you know, okay, this is it, I remember thinking. I just have to pick up and get on with my life.

One woman referred to the serenity prayer as a source of strength: "God grant me the serenity to accept the things I cannot change, and the courage to change the things I can, and the wisdom to know the difference."

As the women relinquished the belief that they must be a parent and came to accept that they could be creative without being procreative, and productive without being reproductive, they were able to get on with their lives.

One important step at this point is to strengthen the marital bond; if women are not going to have their emotional needs met by having children, they must be able to get it from their husbands, said Dr. Linda Hammer-Burns. "If the relationship isn't very emotionally satisfying for the woman, a woman is much more apt to leave the marriage after an infertility experience. The infertility becomes a watershed—it doesn't have so much to do with childlessness as with the need to get emotional needs met. I've heard women say that their husbands are okay if there are children, but if there aren't, the situation isn't tolerable."

In fact, a small study by Hammer-Burns found that half of the couples who remained childless after infertility broke up, primarily because the women did not find the marriages emotionally rewarding enough if there were to be no children. "After leaving the marriage, these women felt much more at peace with themselves," said Dr. Hammer-Burns. Couples that do stay together, however, become very close. They've weathered a life crisis together and forged out new goals in their relationship. Women interviewed for this book as well as for Diana Burgwyn's book, *Marriage Without Children*, found couples with a history of infertility feeling very close to their husbands and satisfied with the relationship.

Why Some Don't Adopt

Getting on with their lives may mean either adopting, drifting into a childless lifestyle, or actively choosing to live child free. To adopt successfully, experts stress that infertile couples must first successfully mourn the loss of their biological dreamchild as discussed above. Adoption should not be a direct *substitution* for a biological child, but a separate decision to embrace a nonbiological child with total heart and spirit.

Of the infertile women who didn't get pregnant in 1988, only seventeen percent turned to adoption, and less than half of those most expected to adopt did—the married, white, infertile, childless women between thirty and forty-four years of age, according to a surprising study released by the National Center for Health Statistics in 1990.[10] Although previous estimates stated that some two million couples and one million singles seek to adopt as few as 20,000 babies through agencies every year, the study said that only 200,000 women actually sought to adopt in 1988. Nevertheless, many couples are daunted by the two-to-five-year-long waiting lists for healthy white infants and can't afford the $8,500 average sum to adopt, much less the $10,000 to $30,000 or more it takes to adopt privately. Others don't have the emotional stamina to wait through a strange woman's pregnancy knowing that about twenty percent of private adoption contracts fall through. Or they don't have the emotional strength to get through home studies which seem invasive, judgmental, and interfering. Said Denise:

> We kept saying we ought to get on an adoption list, but we didn't, not because we were against adoption, but it was a way to stay sane, to not be violated again. The adoption agency would have asked a lot of questions like the doctors did and would have probed into everything about us.
>
> We were so raw and fragile from the infertility experience that we didn't feel strong enough to go through that scrutinizing. So it was more self-preservation than a decision not to adopt.

Other couples fear, sometimes justifiably, that they may be rejected for adoption. Couples with health or financial problems, for example, or who are too old or too handicapped, may not be accepted. Just fifteen years ago, for example, partners of different religions were turned down. Barbara, now forty-eight, was one of them: she and her husband couldn't adopt because she was Catholic and he Presbyterian. Married at twenty-seven, she never used birth control, and got pregnant two years later.

> I just assumed everything would be normal. After we'd been married two years, I didn't realize I was pregnant until I had this horrible miscarriage at five months, bleeding and bleeding on a hike.

Later diagnosed with endometriosis, Barbara spent the next six years trying to get pregnant, but she kept bleeding profusely at unexpected moments instead.

> I'd be downtown and I'd suddenly just start gushing blood. I'd call my husband, desperate for him to bring me a coat. I never knew when it was going to happen.

After nearly a dozen D&C's, Barbara was given medication that suppressed the bleeding. But she never got pregnant, and she and her husband couldn't adopt.

Other couples don't adopt because one partner doesn't want

to, sometimes out of fear: fear that they won't bond adequately with an adopted child; fear that the child had inadequate prenatal care or has unknown genetic problems; fear that the biological mother may come to reclaim the child; fear that the child will grow up only to pine for and search out his/her biological mother.

Some women feel that society devalues adoption and may reject it because of that. When a group of seventy-one infertile women, ages twenty-five to forty-five, were asked about societal beliefs, they reported that love in adoption is second rate because it lacks the biological bond, that the kids are second rate because their genetic past is a mystery, and that adoptive parenting isn't "real" parenting.[11] Women who feel this way are still infertile, according to the authors of *Let's Talk About Adoption*,[12] rather than *no longer* infertile. If they did adopt at that stage, they'd see their new child as a constant reminder that they were denied a biological child. To be successful, adoption must become a first choice rather than the second best. Only when infertility is transformed into an opportunity, an affirmation, can the option of adoption be most successful.[13]

Other women aren't attracted to parenting a child who doesn't carry their own genes and biology. They need to experience pregnancy and childbirth and don't feel comfortable parenting a non-biological child. Ellen, the therapist first mentioned in Chapter Three, remarried at forty-two, had tubal surgery, and then went through *in vitro* fertilization only to shift into psychological nonparenthood at the age of forty-five. She spoke of why she didn't consider adoption:

> In some ways, I already feel like an adoptive parent with my clients. I'm really curious what it would have been like to be pregnant, give birth, and see what our genes would have produced. But I didn't want to be a parent enough that I wanted to go through the process of adoption.

Terri put infertility behind her a decade ago after four operations. She never pursued adoption because having her own children was very important to her. When newborns were offered to her on two separate occasions during the past decade through relatives who were doctors, Terri hesitated.

The first baby call came while we were still going through our infertility workups and we couldn't think about it seriously then. But the second baby call came just four years ago and really threw me. My mother would say, of course, you adopt, but her desires weren't mine. She wanted me to adopt what came along, but I wanted to be pregnant.

Terri had to examine within herself what was important to her and what her needs were in wanting a child. She did not accept either infant, and most of the time she's relieved that she didn't.

Some women don't adopt because of the fear that the adoption will turn out bad and they're afraid to risk it. They'd observed adoptions that had heartbreaking results. Ruth, the eighty-five-year-old widow of a college professor who never knew why she never got pregnant, felt this way: "We had talked about adopting but had seen so many families on campus that had adopted and things just didn't turn out well."

Others are daunted by the dismal statistics of potential emotional trauma up ahead: Although one to two percent of children in this country are adopted, they comprise five percent of the outpatients at mental health facilities, ten percent of patients in inpatient facilities, and six to nine percent of the learning or emotionally disabled in schools.[14] Many adoptees go through emotionally troubled times at some time trying to come to grips with why their natural mothers gave them away.

And finally, some couples just drift into never adopting, much the way that fertile couples sometimes drift into nonparenthood. Perhaps they couldn't admit a final defeat to infertility or perhaps their drive to parent wasn't strong enough to motivate them to pursue all that is involved in seeking to adopt. Sylvia, seventy-seven, now married for fifty-four years, was told two years after she married that her high blood pressure could be fatal if she ever attempted a pregnancy.

We just accepted it and went on with our lives, which were always extremely active and busy. Once we were told not to consider getting pregnant, that was it, the decision was made, and I never thought much about it after that. Period.

I guess we talked about the possibility of adoption, but we were just too involved ourselves in our careers and the community. The jobs took a great deal of our time and the years went by.

Sylvia eventually worked her way up from a clerk to a top-level executive at Sears. Her career became the focus of her life and she rarely gave a thought to children after that. "I've no regret, not even twinges about it," she said. But Sylvia was lucky. She found a path to living without children without a lot of soul-searching and coming to grips with what she wanted in life. Most experts on infertility insist that in order to become free from the tyranny of infertility, one must consciously mourn the loss and then redefine their goals.

Child-Free Living

Experiencing feelings of anger, fear, rage, desolation, and hope-lessness are part of the healthy process of mourning, say experts on death, grief, and infertility. It is through that process of ac-knowledging sad and bad feelings that you can achieve a sense of peace in accepting the loss and turn these feelings around into a positive life change.

To go beyond acceptance into a positive affirmation of child-free living, rather than childless living, Jean and Michael Carter, authors of *Sweet Grapes: How To Stop Being Infertile and Start Living Again*, speak of making a declarative choice to be child free.

That does not mean resigning yourself to a life without chil-dren, say the Carters, themselves former infertility victims who transformed that tragedy in their lives into a positive life change. Rather than focusing on what you don't have and drifting into lifelong childlessness, the Carters turn it around, "believing that for every loss there is the potential for gain.[15] What child free means to us is finding the gain that comes with the loss of fertility, seeing within the negative the possibility for something posi-tive."[16] They suggest that by making a conscious, deliberate deci-sion to live child free, you can regain control over your life and free yourself from the shadow of infertility. By focusing on what you can have and achieve, this view of childlessness provides opportunities for other growth experiences and new goals.

Choosing to be child free after infertility is not giving up hope, the Carters stress; it is finding hope of a good life again, only this time without children. Actively choosing child-free living allows you to gain by investing renewed energies into chosen directions such as work, hobbies, family, friends, community service, church, art, romance, sports, etc. This active life choice allows you to take advantage of the benefits of not having children, without deprecating the value of having children.

The value of making this life choice is not so much whether it's the "right" choice—for there is no "right" or "wrong" answer in lifestyle decisions—but in the fact that a choice is consciously made. The correct choice is the one that's honest, most comfortable, and mutual in a relationship. Only by *choosing* your path can you can regain control. People who drift into a childless life do not take the opportunities to seize their own destiny and invest renewed energies into new gains and goals; rather, they aimlessly float to wherever the tides of fate carry them.

The transformation from childlessness after infertility into child-free living is not necessarily a shifting of priorities, the Carters stress. Rather, it is a way to fulfill the goals you had for parenting in other positive, constructive ways. People typically want children as part of a desire to change their lives and to nurture and love. Couples choosing child-free living may do this in a myriad of ways.

After six years on the infertility merry-go-round, Denise, for example, realized she was not going to get pregnant. She and Randall then re-examined their motives for wanting children.

> We're competent loving people and we thought we could do a really good job parenting. But over the years we've seen hundreds of really smart competent people have really tough times parenting.

Everyone Denise knew at the time was becoming a parent. "I wanted to be accepted," she said. "I didn't know how to be a 'nonmother.' What would I do with the rest of my life?"

During her years of infertility, Denise and her husband bought a puppy, became active in their church, became leaders of the church's youth group, and purchased their first "handyman special." Denise had started to change her life in creative, meaningful ways, was nurturing a puppy she adored, and was helping and guiding teenagers at church as well as rebuilding a home. These activities helped her to turn her energies away from infertility and toward others while giving herself an opportunity to nurture and nourish. As she and her husband began to build the house of their dreams, nail by nail, they also began to build a support group in their city for infertile couples.

At the time, we didn't know what child free was. There was no such a thing at the time. The only people who didn't have kids were Aunt Sally and Uncle Harry, who were in their seventies, and you never knew why they didn't have children. No one talked about it.

During their infertility, Denise and Randall watched as more of their friends became parents and had a really tough time parenting. Said Denise: "Our lives in comparison seem so sweet and calm." She didn't downgrade the importance of motherhood but rather began to upgrade the value of her own life. As time went on, Denise started to embrace some of her friends' children with warmth and love. Her volunteer work with the youth group grew more important to her. Her support group began to grow, and each successful pregnancy or adoption was a personal joy and success.

We slid into child-free living without realizing it. You think that child free means not having kids in your life. Part of that free is to feel free to bring children back into your life, a freedom where you no longer feel a loss of not having children, but you feel a gain of being able to bring children back into your relationship without feeling sad anymore. It's a change of attitude.

Denise's statement reflects her transition to acceptance and allows for growth and the ability to forge creative adaptations out of sorrow, pain, and loss. Denise has also realized that she doesn't have to work and achieve through her career because she doesn't have children. Instead, she devotes her time to working on their lake house, on her garden, and on cooking all her meals from scratch.

> My home is my career. It's not that we don't want kids—that's too negative. We have lived without children for years, and other than the pain of the infertility, we have lived them very happily.

Denise observes her neighbors who have jobs and try to be supermoms too—juggling jobs but still driving their kids to Little League and gymnastics, doing the shopping, making dinner, keeping the house clean and neat, and feeding the dog.

> One of my friends told me that her life was so out of control. I see some of these mothers trying to prove they're supermothers; it's a compulsion. I feel now so much more in control and with an inner calm and peace, partly because we've been through a life crisis. I don't get upset about things anymore. I take things as they come and try to let it roll off.

Denise has made the transition from being childless to being child free. The Carters stress the difference:

> One of the features that distinguishes the acceptance of childlessness from the choice to live child free is the amount of work that goes into achieving each. Acceptance comes quite naturally if you don't deny the loss; it's mainly a matter of time and endurance. The transformation to child free, however, requires a conscious effort—the work that goes into making decisions.[17]

That means talking and talking and talking about feelings of ambivalence, choice, goals, loss, hope, despair, and dreams with your partner rather than assuming they know how you feel. For the Carters, what came out of all the talking was that, although their option for a biological child had closed, they still had choices and opportunities from which to choose:

> The most important thing was that we realized that we *did* have a choice. We could be child*less*, defining our lives by what we lack, or we could be child *free*, affirming the potential gain that comes of living without children. We chose the latter. . . . Instead of being unsuccessful parents-to-be, we were very successful nonparents. Failure was no longer the major theme of our lives . . . Neither one

of us had realized how much of our lives had been consumed by infertility until we chose to live child free.[18]

Yet the Carters warn that the child-free choice is the "closet choice." Other infertile couples find it threatening, parents are disappointed, and friends don't understand why adoption isn't chosen. Typically, couples find little support and must find solace in their own resolution, hoping that others will be as glad for them in their affirmation as they are for other infertile couples who eventually get pregnant and adopt.

As the transition becomes complete, women speak of the relief and peace that washes over them, as well as the feeling that they have become masters of their own destiny again, transforming the energies they invested into trying to get pregnant to other outlets. From changing their view of childlessness from a tragedy to accepting it as an opportunity for new experiences, they make room for other possibilities. Says Judith Viorst:

> Losing is the price we pay for living. It is also the source of much of our growth and gain. Making our way from birth to death, we also have to make our way through the pain of giving up and giving up and giving up some portion of what we cherish. . . . And in giving up our impossible expectations, we become a lovingly connected self, renouncing ideal visions of perfect . . . life. . . .
>
> And in confronting the many losses that are brought by time and death, we become a mourning and adapting self, finding at every stage—until we draw our final breath—opportunities for creative transformations. . . .
>
> And we cannot become separate people, responsible people, connected people, reflective people without some losing and leaving and letting go.[19]

The Legacy of Infertility

Although very little research has looked at the lifelong effects of infertility and involuntary childlessness, experts report that once the decision to be child free becomes definite, relief usually follows, coupled with renewed energy. As the uncertainty and pain gradually recede into the past, the pursuit of new goals and purposes is possible. As couples make positive changes in their lives to take advantage of the benefits of child-free living, in time, the thought of a pregnancy may seem too disruptive and birth control helps to avoid that dissonance. Some women start using birth control or have their tubes tied as a "declaration of independence" from infertility, as Jean Carter put it, and to seize control over their lives, getting off the cycle of hope and despair each month.

As women move into their forties, the issue of having children tends to fade as their friends' children grow up and leave home. "Trust that your childlessness will be less of an issue when your friends and their children are older," says Merle Bombardieri, clinical director of Resolve's national office in Boston (a national, non-profit organization that offers counseling, referral, and support to people with infertility problems), and author of *The Baby Decision* and the fact sheet, "Child-Free Decision-Making."[20]

Margaret now says with hindsight that if she were going through her infertility again, she would now consider adoption more seriously, though she doesn't know if she would actually have adopted or not. Nevertheless, she said that her infertility did stop haunting her:

> Has it gotten easier over the years? Well, it certainly hasn't gotten harder, that's for sure. There's no doubt that most of my friends have their families scattered all over. They do not live close by, and their grandchildren are not constantly in their lives.
>
> Of course, I've missed out on the pleasures of grandchildren, but then again, some of my friends have children but won't have grandchildren. There are no guarantees. Also, I know that there were some years that I didn't have all the strains my friends had. I think I've always had a much broader life with more freedom than my friends did.
>
> Although I think it's better to have children, it's certainly not the end of the world without them. It really isn't. You can lead a full life. It's all in your attitude.

Couples who shift to child-free living shouldn't feel they have to justify their decision to others, Bombardieri stresses, or that they need now to demand excellence or brilliance from themselves just because they don't have children (although devotion to a career is often one's greatest satisfaction). Women who become child free after infertility must learn to enjoy and nurture themselves and develop holiday traditions and a family system based on friendships, neighbors, and other relatives. Child-free women can forge a path to inner peace and feel gratified that they are passing on something of themselves to the next generation by working with children, or by putting their nurturant energies into artistic or intellectual pursuits, gardens, religion, or meditation.

Although infertile women who decide not to adopt fear that they will be continually haunted by the searing pain they've endured during infertility, Bombardieri and the Carters stress that once a couple has grieved, the piercing pain subsides into a periodic pang. Say the Carters:

> Only part of your current pain is from actual lack of a child. Some of it is part of a grief process you're in the midst of. Another part is the maddening uncertainty of whether or not you will ever get to be a parent. If you decide to remain child free, you can stop trying and stop wondering. You'll emerge from the heavy tent of grief, ready to start a new life.[21]

> Deciding to live child free is not a magic potion that takes the painful loss of fertility and makes it disappear. We still have, and probably always will have, sad moments when we remember our dreams of children or have experiences we would like to have shared with a child. Choosing to accentuate the gain doesn't mean completely losing the loss.[22]

Rather, expect a relative peace that comes from reconciling yourself to the understanding that there will be conflicting feelings in our lives. Child free doesn't mean permanent liberation from feelings of loss, the Carters stress. Rather, it means acknowledging the potential for gain that comes from the loss. "It means becoming big enough to embrace both the loss and gain."[23]

Although infertility is part of one's life forever, says Shapiro in *Infertility and Pregnancy Loss*, women interviewed for this book and for Diana Burgwyn's *Marriage Without Children* seem well adjusted to not having children as they move into their forties and older. Some researchers have suggested, in fact, that the emotional distress of being infertile and remaining childless fades in midlife. Childlessness may become an issue again in old age, but not as an identity crisis or an emotional issue, but rather as a factor in forming support networks.[24] (See Chapter Fifteen on growing older.)

Perhaps infertile women without children seem so well adjusted because of the human need to justify to oneself that one's decision was the right one—a process called cognitive dissonance. Occasional ambivalence, twinges of regret, or sadness about whether child-free living was the right choice may occur regardless of dissonance and is also normal, just as adoptive and biological parents may sometimes wonder whether becoming a parent was the right road to take. Men and women who couldn't have children and didn't adopt may also from time to time have concerns about their generativity—not passing on something of themselves to the next generation—or about never becoming a "full adult," but always remaining only a child to their parents. Others may be concerned about being at the end of a genetic line, or feeling "old" without the vitality of children to keep them young.[25] (See Chapter Fifteen for more on these feelings.)

For a woman with a history of infertility, certain times may feel particularly painful. Menopause may be one—infertility at this time becomes a finality, suggests Shapiro, (although some research suggests that older women can continue having babies after menopause with donated eggs). Fears about going into older age without children may surface again as other losses occur at the same time: declines in health and stamina; death of parents; unmet career goals; and friends retiring, moving away, even dying.

But humans have a remarkable ability to adapt to their circumstances. And since there are many benefits to living without children (see Chapter Thirteen), those who can focus on the rewards and use their additional time and resources to enrich their lives and pursue new opportunities, will forge ahead with renewed vigor and learn to appreciate and adapt to their lives without children.

CHAPTER TEN

Women Who Love Women

Are lesbians immune to a culture of compulsory motherhood? Of course not. We were girls before we were aware
lesbians, and we were raised by families that expected us
to become mothers. We read the same books and saw the
same movies as our heterosexual sisters. And today we
live in the same world, one which purports to value motherhood above anything else a woman can do.
                                —NANCY D. POLIKOFF,
                                    Politics of the Heart[1]

Just like straight women, some lesbians are baby oriented, some
aren't, and a lot fall in the middle. In years past, the vast majority
of lesbians who were mothers were wives first who bore children
in heterosexual relationships that they later left. Many lost custody of their children because of their homosexuality. Today,
more and more lesbian mothers who come out retain custody
though it's still not a sure thing. And more lesbians than ever are
having children in lesbian relationships, although some must lie
to social workers to adopt and to artificial insemination centers to
receive donated sperm.

Yet, lesbians who don't have children still outnumber those
who do: only about fifteen to thirty percent of lesbians have children, and most of these children were born in heterosexual marriages that later broke up.[2] Historically, for many socially and
politically active lesbians, the issues of feminism, lesbianism, and
independence from men were tied up with issues of motherhood.
Traditionally, motherhood meant subjugating one's needs self-
lessly to serve others. Motherhood was too binding, too restric-
tive. It was antithetical to liberation. Worse yet, it represented a

146

caving in to the patriarchal pronatalist value system the lesbian movement tried so hard to reject. To become a mother, after all, meant having to allow the needs of others to take precedence over your own needs. But as the lesbian movement gained strength and numbers, having children then became a civil rights issue for lesbians. Lesbians began to assert more actively their right to have children, too.

But before lesbians consider motherhood, they first must grapple with their identity as women who are different because they love women instead of men. Although some lesbians believe they were born with a propensity for loving women instead of men and recognize it from a very early age, most don't see their homosexual desires until early adulthood. Fifty-year-old Ilene, the caterer who lives in Oregon, didn't realize she was gay until she was in her early thirties. Growing up in a traditional upper-middle-class Roman Catholic family, Ilene assumed—just as most girls growing up in the 1940s assumed—that she'd have a traditional family. "I had the idea that I'd have children all along," she said. "I'd go out with boys and think about children's names that would go with their names."

After college, Ilene worked as a secretary and still hadn't met "the" man. Although her long-range plans were to settle down, she always took advantage of her child-free status. She'd work for a year or two, then take the next year off; work another year, then take six months off. In her early thirties, however, she was promoted out of the secretarial pool and her career skyrocketed. It was the 1970s, and more and more homosexuals were coming out.

> I didn't know what was wrong with me. All of these years I wondered why I didn't meet the right man and settle down and have a family. And then suddenly one day, the light bulb finally went on. It finally popped in me and I thought, "Oh! Women! That's what it's all about." As soon as I realized that, I immediately met someone who I started seeing and soon loved, and then I really wanted a family.

Ilene is part of the ten percent of the population believed to be homosexual. She came out at the time when few lesbians were starting families. Although now there seems to be a "lesbian baby boomlet" occurring, Ilene and her partner thought about having a baby at the very beginning of this trend, when lesbians were just starting to realize that they, too, could have children.

At the beginning of the decision-making process about whether to have children, the issues for lesbians are very much like that of straight women. In Cherie Pies's book, *Considering Parenthood: A Workbook for Lesbians* (San Francisco: Spinsters/Aunt Lute, 1985), the chapter on "Choosing Not To Parent" covers the same topics as other decision-making books on parenting. It includes the pros and cons of becoming a parent, coping with having children on a daily basis, and the importance of forming alternative family networks and relationships with children if motherhood is rejected.

But Ilene and her partner, as lesbians, had other issues to consider, too. Which woman would be the biological mother? What would happen if they split up in the future—what would be the legal status of the nonbiological parent? What rights would *her* parents, as grandparents, have in that case? Through what method should they have a child? Adoption? Artificial insemination through a center or a male friend? Sexual relations with a man? Should he be informed of their intention, or remain ignorant of his potential biological child? If they try to adopt, should they lie and have one partner pose as a single parent rather than as a lesbian couple since many states forbid lesbians from becoming foster and adoptive parents? Which woman should pose as the potential adoptive mother, and which as the friendly, helpful roommate? What would it be like for the child, growing up with two mothers and no father? Who should they tell about their lesbian relationship—their doctor, their parents, their child, their child's teachers and friends, their neighbors, their caseworker if they opted for adoption?

Ilene was ambivalent about having a child, but her partner definitely wanted one, so the decision about who'd be "the" mother was easy. Said Ilene: "It must not have been all that important to me because I knew I didn't want the primary responsibility. I would be the aunt; my partner would be the mother."

They looked into artificial insemination, but it was too expensive—$300 for a month for two inseminations. They considered asking an acquaintance to donate his sperm but were unsure about who to ask. They were looking into adoption, when the relationship began to fall apart. When Ilene was offered a great job on the West Coast, she decided to take it and leave the relationship. After that, Ilene didn't think much about children. She was busy traveling several weeks a month in her new job; she spent a year in Sydney, Australia, then a few years back in California, and then a year in London. At forty-four, she had a hysterectomy. She was surprised at herself for the lack of emotion it brought forth:

> I was told that it was very natural to grieve when you lose the ability to have children. I was surprised by the lack of feelings I had about it. I'm not sure it was ever something that was very important to me. I never felt a biological clock urgency.
>
> Having children would have perhaps allowed me to have those family gatherings which is what I miss as far as not having children. But I also know I'm imagining a romanticized version of the Sunday dinners which I remember from my childhood.

A year after her hysterectomy, Ilene got involved with another woman, a physician who could easily support them. They decided to leave the rat race and moved up north. There are no children in her life, and although she occasionally thinks, "Oh wouldn't it be lovely to have a child," she realizes that the reality of raising children was never important to her and rarely enters her mind. Ilene found it easy to let go of any presumptions she held about having children, probably because she never found herself very baby-oriented to begin with. Yet, she admits that if all the elements that go with having children had been in place, she probably would have had children anyway. "I guess if things had been different—had I met a man I loved early on—I might have had children," she said.

Laura, forty-five, also recognized her lesbianism slowly and also said that had she found herself in a loving, long-term relationship with a man, she'd probably have had children. But her life just didn't go that way, even though she tried hard at it for years. On the other hand, she didn't view it as a serious loss, either, maybe because she was brought up to value careers instead. As a child, she always received the implicit message that motherhood was not very appealing. Her mother never took much of the responsibility for child care, choosing instead to work full time at the family-owned dance school.

> My childhood was not a particularly happy one for me or my two older sisters. My father was something of a tyrant—to call my father a misogynist would be kind. There were always live-in housekeepers doing the cooking and child care. I think that communicated a powerful message about the dubious joys of domesticity and child-rearing.
> To my father, women were dumb broads, but his daughters were expected to be smart. I had to prove that I was smart, so I decided to be a professor.

With the message that raising children was dreary work but the masculine world of careers was much more important, Laura went from Vassar on to graduate school for a Ph.D. It was the 1960s, and Laura became a feminist, though not a lesbian.

> I was interested in men and went to bed with men. I wanted a capital "R" relationship, but nothing wonderful ever materialized. At the same time, I always had women friends, but I never thought of them as competitors for men. I always thought I was straight, but I can look back now and say, oh yeah, I guess I was in love with my sophomore roommate, but didn't realize it at the time.

In graduate school, the women's movement hit campus with a wallop:

> The issue of lesbianism always came up and I dealt with it in my head at an incredibly theoretical level and was mostly very afraid of it. That was really the first time that I knowingly met and hung out with lesbians.

Although Laura assumes that other people assumed she might have been a lesbian in graduate school, it wasn't until her mid-thirties that she had her first lesbian relationship. Her partner had two children; Laura helped parent them for several years and grew attached to them. But her partner was "a nut" and the relationship was "an absolute disaster." The woman became physically abusive and Laura finally realized she had to disentangle herself from the relationship, but she feared the woman would pursue her. So she left town without a word, without a goodbye, and never communicated with the family again.

> I've had some taste of the parenting experience and I'm glad for it, although I'm so sorry for the outcome, for leaving the children so abruptly and never being able to be in contact with them for fear their mother might find me. I still have a very sad, lasting feeling of guilt.

But helping to parent the two children made Laura realize she had been right about parenting: "It's an awesome sort of responsibility with many difficulties and ways to go wrong. I think kids are fascinating and really love seeing my two friends' little kids, but I can also appreciate the other side."

But Laura hasn't been involved with anyone for awhile. Although Laura now is only interested in women, she believes that her lesbianism is largely the result of fate and circumstance, largely the way that some straight women view their childlessness:

> I had some flexibility in the decision about my sexuality and the fact that we're living in an era of AIDS helped tip the balance. Some people see themselves as strongly lesbian and nothing can derail them from that. For others like me, there are some accidents of personal history from which certain feelings and options are made available. Who knows, if one of those fellows I was interested in earlier had wanted to get married, maybe I would have walked off into the sunset, but that never happened, and I became less interested as time went on.
>
> As far as children, they were only thought of in the context of a relationship with somebody who wanted them. It wasn't going to happen unless a set of conditions happened, which never did.

Laura estimates that about one-third of her lesbian friends have children (which is consistent with official estimates), and just like straight mothers, some are so involved with their youngsters she finds she has less and less in common with them these days. One friend, for example, had a child three years ago and continues to focus most of her interests and energies on raising the child. Although Laura adores him, she tires quickly of her friend's limited interests and resents that the mother won't do anything without him. Just like straight women without children, Laura finds herself drifting away from her friend; she devotes her primary energies to her career as a city planner and to her circle of friends. She has a special relationship with her niece (who she'll take traveling this summer as a graduation present) and her friend's three-year-old, as well as a coworker's three-year-old, but has few lingering doubts about not having children.

> Regrets? I guess I'm ninety-eight percent glad and no more than two percent sad that I don't have children. I get to see what kids are like without having to have them myself.
> You just can't have it all. You can't both know what it's like to have children yet live a life of freedom by not having children.

Before the 1960s and 1970s when many lesbians felt safe enough to come out, women with gay tendencies either totally suppressed their desires or were closet lesbians. In looking back, who knows how many of the old "Boston marriages" were lesbian relationships or not. Homosexuality was so taboo, many women hardly acknowledged to themselves their homosexual desires. Several older women I interviewed for this book lived with other women for years. Of course, they could have been platonic relationships which provided an important sense of family and intimate companionship, but they also may have been lesbian relationships. I didn't ask outright because I knew from other researchers who had interviewed older, never-married women, that to do so could ruin my rapport with them.

Eighty-seven-year-old Lillian, for example, as described in Chapter Two, was divorced during the Great Depression. She paired up with a girlfriend to survive this grim period, and they never separated after that, until Mary, her best friend, died of cancer in 1975. Whether the relationship was sexual or not doesn't really matter. Mary was Lillian's best friend, roommate, partner, and confidante. She fulfilled Lillian's emotional needs and sense of belonging for the forty-three years they lived together. The network of friends they developed are still Lillian's friends and main source of support. Since she never remarried, children were never thought about again.

> I never missed not having children. In fact, I never even thought about it. And I can't say there have been drawbacks either. I made certain decisions and never looked back. And I'd make the same decisions again today.
>
> It's probably a blessing for the children never born to me that I didn't have them. Although at one point in my marriage, I thought I couldn't wait to have children, the feeling passed and I've never had that maternal kind of feeling since. I love kids, but I think I was born without a maternal drive.
>
> Mary was definitely my best friend, always. After we were established, I never thought about remarrying.

Marsha, now sixty-six, also threw "the baby out with the bath water." Once she discarded the notion of marriage, she abandoned any thought of having children. Just to recognize her sexual orientation violated every norm she grew up with. Being a lesbian in her times was mutually exclusive to having children, unless they had been conceived in an earlier marriage. Although Marsha didn't recognize her lesbianism until after college, she remembers always being different in that she rejected the patriarchal system at an early age and was always "rebellious against the traditional role of women." The traditional role was marriage and children; the two always went together, and Marsha rejected them as a package. Instead, she wanted to go to business school, but Wharton wasn't accepting women in those days, so she majored in economics instead, where women were treated like "numskulls." Although she had crushes on girls from time to time, she didn't consider lesbianism until after two traumatic experiences:

> I dated a lot of men in college, but one night I had too much to drink and I was raped—what people call date rape these days. I was so worried about being pregnant that I told my mother, who took me to the doctor. I wasn't pregnant, but my mother was so upset with me.
>
> After college, the same thing happened again. I had too much to

drink, and my date took advantage of me. Again, I was so scared to death I was pregnant that I even tried to do a self-induced abortion. I eventually got my period, but those experiences really scared me, and although I've continued to have relationships with men on and off throughout my life, I've always felt far more connected with women.

Once Marsha realized that she had no interest in becoming married after a brief engagement in her twenties, she never thought about children again. She earned a Ph.D. and taught college for years coupled with a lifelong commitment to social causes, including civil rights, the peace movement, women's rights, socialism, and local politics. Her attitude was very much like never-married women who didn't want to be permanently attached to a man who might try to control them, and she relinquished any thought of children with the rejection of marriage.

> Unless you were in love and wanted to get married, having children just didn't appeal to you in those days. I just didn't see myself as a mother and wife; instead I was very career oriented. I wanted to live my life my way and not be tied to some man, having to do housework and all that. It just didn't appeal to me.

Music and her love affairs were always Marsha's passions. Over the years, she's had long-term relationships with two men (one was married, the other was bisexual; neither was interested in marriage) and seven women, including one that had terminal cancer at forty, whom Marsha nursed until she died.

After a hysterectomy at fifty, cancer in her early sixties, and anti-estrogen hormone therapy, Marsha has no sexual drive left, yet she is now approaching the twelfth year of living with a woman she loves deeply. "She's much younger than I am, but I know this is a very important relationship to her, too," said Marsha. "We'll be together until I die."

Although estranged from her family for her politics and nontraditional lifestyle—only one brother knows she's gay—Marsha feels complete and has no fears of growing older. Her network of attachments through her lover, her teaching, her social activism, her local community of retirees, her cats, her singing, and her dancing provide her with plenty of emotional sustenance. She has also sort of "adopted" six older women, all widows (some with children), all straight and in their eighties, and all alone. "They're not well and they need somebody," Marsha said. "I like them; they're interesting women, and I feel for them. Perhaps our relationships are in place of having our own families." As far as having children, well, it was a moot point with Marsha:

> Having children just never crossed my mind. It's just never been part of my life. I knew I didn't want them early on, and in the lesbian communities in which I've lived at different times of my life, most lesbians didn't have them, at least not in my generation.

Although still a "closet" lesbian, with most of her straight friends not knowing she's gay, Marsha has always lived a very politically active and nontraditional life—and children have never been a part of it.

Rachel Guido DeVries is also a lesbian with no desire to be a mother. Divorced at twenty-nine, Rachel came out as a lesbian and plunged herself into writing that same year, leaving her career of pediatric nursing behind. At forty-three, she's a novelist, poet, sculptor, and teacher of feminist and creative writing. Living with the same partner for eleven years and in the same community for almost twenty years, Rachel feels loved and loving, secure in a tight social network with other lesbians, many of them mothers.

> I never felt the emotional desire to physically bear or have a child, and I view not having children as a joyous choice. I feel privileged to have that choice, to be able to come and go as I want.
>
> What concerns me, though, is the class distinction in how choices are made. I'm concerned about blue-collar women, who are less aware of choices, who are afraid to come out as lesbians, and are unaware of their choice not to mother.

In her poetry and sculpture, Rachel ponders the meanings of the "notmother." They are "freedom dreamers" who express nurturance and love in nontraditional ways. Rachel rejoices in their ability to love and to soar freely. But at the same time, although she feels no sadness or regret about being a "notmother," she feels a physical pang of loss:

Physically, there's a sensation, a nostalgia about my body's loss in a physical sense. I'm very aware of my body not fulfilling its physical potential—there's nothing sad in it, but it's like a homesickness my body feels. It's like still wanting to smoke cigarettes after quitting for five years—there's a physical sensation that I want to smoke, but it's not related to emotions at all.

Much has been written in the gay literature about being a gay parent. Yet, very little has been written about not becoming a parent, a "notmother," as Rachel calls it, although the majority of lesbians are *not* mothers. One problem that has surfaced, however, is that some lesbians without children resent how new mothers become so self-absorbed that they turn their energies inward and abandon the exhausting political and social work of trying to loosen the rigid social and political fabric of society. Although lesbians who don't become mothers don't begrudge those who do, some believe that motherhood is a sort of copout for some gays, used as a way to seem more normal again. Thirteen years ago, Irena, a fifty-year-old political activist and writer, wrote an essay about not having children; she still stands by her words.

A normal woman wants children; I am a normal woman; I want children. This kind of short-circuiting of real feelings is quite common with many women, women who cling to fantasies created by others. These fantasies, many women think, will keep them in the mainstream, will prevent them from appearing different or conspicuous.[3]

When lesbians become mothers, something happens: their primary identity shifts from being a lesbian first to being a mother first, said Harriet Alpert, a psychotherapist who specializes in lesbian issues and is the editor of *We Are Everywhere*, an anthology on lesbian mothers. Lesbians who become mothers often admit, though begrudgingly, that they find themselves having more in common with heterosexual mothers than with lesbians without children. Said Alpert: "This is very disturbing for some lesbian mothers, especially for women who feel their lesbianism is really part of their core beings."[4] At the same time, it distances the lesbians who don't have children from those who do.

As some lesbians have become disillusioned with the idealized vision of a cohesive lesbian community that would provide a sense of alternative family, motherhood has become more appealing. "We are all worn down by the personal traumas we experienced with lovers and friends that shattered our naive beliefs in building one large lesbian community. Once I was no longer energized by the feeling of being different, I began to seek ways of fitting in," says Nancy Polikoff, an adoptive lesbian mother, in *Politics of the Heart*, another anthology on lesbian parenting.[5]

These kinds of pressures also tore Irena for years. She wanted to fit in, and part of her longed to have a baby. She, too, was bitterly disappointed in how the lesbian community failed to provide a secure, permanent home:

> The collective experiments ended in frustration, bitter anger, a hard silence that severed what everyone had hoped would be permanent ties.
>
> Expectations were so high, we wanted these groups to fulfill so many divergent needs, they were destined to disappoint. For me and for many other women it was a sobering kind of experience, to say the least.[6]

Emotionally, it was hard for Irena to sort out her feelings about children. She was haunted by fears that without children she'd lose all intimate connections. In her worst vision, she envisioned her life as empty as that of a bag lady's—isolated, alone, and forgotten. And just like straight women, she felt an enormous pressure to deliver a grandchild to her mother. Irena was born in Poland during the Holocaust; she and her mother emigrated to the U.S. when Irena was eight—the only members of their family to survive World War II. Irena was an only child and pressured like other child survivors and children of survivors to carry on the family line. Irena also wondered as more and more lesbians would turn to motherhood, what sense of family would be left for women like her, a lesbian without children?

These issues pulled at her throughout her thirties. At forty-nine, Irena lives without a partner and leads a hectic professional life as the executive director of the New Jewish Agenda, has just published a book of essays, and teaches writing on the college level. Though occasionally she still questions her decision to remain childless, she takes pride in having resisted the enormous pressures she felt to have children, in dealing with her fears, and remaining true to an instinct she knew was leading her away from a traditional family. But as we'll see in the next chapter, for women who wanted babies, lesbian or straight, letting go is not easy. Lesbians without children are in a double bind: they are pressured to live in a straight society and must defy the norm to come out as a lesbian; then in the lesbian community, they're pressured now, just like other women, to become mothers. Said Sandra Pollack, editor of *Politics of the Heart*:

> The whole society is more conservative and family oriented. Lesbians are seeing they too can have children and there's a lot of support in the community to do so. It's becoming a more acceptable pattern for lesbians. The whole tone of society, in the gay community as well, is back to motherhood.[7]

Yet, lesbians who choose motherhood are obligated to defend the rights of lesbians who choose not to mother, says Polikoff, "especially to support those women who make feminism their full-time work. No one else will say that their choices are as valuable as ours. No one else will say that it's strong, positive, and self-affirming not to have children, that it's more than just 'all right.' What's more, our decisions to have children will be used to reinforce the isolation of lesbians without children from mainstream society."[8]

How well the lesbian community grapples with these issues of mothering vs. nonmothering remains to be seen.

CHAPTER ELEVEN

When Not Having Children is a Loss

When I find myself in times of trouble, Mother Mary
comes to me,
Speaking words of wisdom: Let it be.
—JOHN LENNON AND PAUL McCARTNEY

I will always have an inner grief about not having children, and this grief will not just waft away. Part of me will
never be reconciled to not being a mother. . . . [Yet] now
a lot of the grief is in the past and I feel I can leave this
issue and move on in my life. In a lot of ways, it is a great
relief. I was expending a lot of emotional energy . . . and
now I can redirect that energy.
—VIRGINIA, 41[1]

For women who choose not to have children, the state of being
childless is a voluntary condition that usually produces little, if
any, dismay or dissonance. Children were not desired and not
missed. Although child-free women may occasionally wonder
what it would have been like to have children, many say that it
was hardly, if ever, an emotionally-laden issue for them. If they
had wanted children, they would have had them. They chose not
to have them, and they live accordingly.

Yet, many women without children are not "child free": they
didn't choose it; they didn't consciously mean for it to turn out
that way. They find themselves childless for whatever reason—no
right relationship at the right time, an unwilling partner, an unre-
solvable infertility problem, and so on. For many of these women,
not having children represents a loss, whether mild or severe.

159

This chapter will talk about the emotional issues associated with that sense of loss, and how women face what that loss means to them. As with any loss in life, the better able a woman is to confront the emotional pain she feels, the better able she will be to move on. She may pass through a transitional stage of dealing with the sense of loss, and then leaving it behind, "letting it be," and getting on with life. This chapter will address those coping strategies of facing and dealing with loss that allow women to grow from the experience and spring from it into a life full of advantages and freedoms. It will also explore how women without children feel about social pressure, stigmas, stereotypes, and some people's perceptions of them as selfish.

No Doubts, No Regrets

The voluntarily child free, the "early articulators" who never foresaw children in their future (see Chapter Six), seem to carry little, if any, sense of loss or sadness about never having them. For example, Karen, the remarried and child-free college professor, recalled always thinking that remaining child free was the right thing for her and has only viewed it in an affirmative, positive context:

> I never assumed I would be a mother. As far as memory serves me, I don't ever remember a time that I had any interest in it. I never saw it in my future or expected it. My husband and I used to talk about it regularly to make sure it wasn't a neglected issue, but I was pretty firm. I've never felt ambivalent about it.

Karen has had no doubts, no regrets. Her feelings about children have never wavered. Forty-year-old Jackie, an only child who has been married for nineteen years, feels the same way. She had a tubal ligation five years ago.

> I just never wanted children. I was never smitten by the maternal bug. I like individual children, but the idea of having children was never appealing to me, and that feeling has always been there. I'm reinforced every time I go grocery shopping and see moms with screaming toddlers and their constant demands. It would drive me crazy.

Candice, forty-three, an Afro-American and an only child, is now a financial officer for a law firm. She has felt no interest in children ever since she was a child. She had a tubal ligation at the age of twenty-three, and she has never been ambivalent about not having children or experienced any shred of regret. Said Candice:

> "Though I have vacillated about wanting to be married, I have at no time ever wanted a child—not ever for one second. And I still feel that way."

Ah, but these women are still relatively young. What about older women? Very little research exists about older childless and child-free women except in the gerontology literature (See Chapter Fifteen). What's out there however—including the women interviewed for this book, other books on child-free living,[2] and the few papers in the literature—shows no evidence of growing regret, especially among these "early articulators." If they still feel resolute about no children as they pass through that biological clock time zone, then they seem to remain resolute throughout their lives.

Recall Lynn, fifty four years old who realized by twenty-two that she never wanted children and has always been grateful that she miscarried her one pregnancy during her brief marriage. "The idea of having children is not a pleasant one to me and I can't think of any negatives for not having them," she said. "There was total relief when I realized I wasn't going to have to go with that pregnancy." Although she is an only child with very few family connections, deeply misses her long-time lover who passed away several years ago, and feels very isolated in the city where she lives now, she still never imagines or wishes she had children.

Betsy, fifty-seven, married and retired already for ten years, feels the same as she did as a teenager: children would have interfered too much with her life. Said Betsy, "Regrets? None that I can think of—oh, yes, there's one thing I dislike—I can't get a family discount on my Florida fishing license! Seriously, I feel we've made the right decision. No children—no regrets!"

Neither Dolores at sixty-five, a "postponer" (who at first didn't think they could afford children) nor Helen Brooks (the Texan horse lover) at sixty-six, an "early articulator," has wavered in their views either. Dolores couldn't think of any regrets or down sides to not having children: "I'm very comfortable with my choice. I've no sadness or regrets, ever. Oh, maybe once in a while a little glimmer, but nothing I'd dwell on or say I missed, never." Helen said that "there haven't been any hard parts" about not having children, "just a lot of good parts about it."

Sylvia, seventy-two, said she was so clear about not having children that it wasn't even a decision for her. She's been married to the same man for forty-three years, and when she told him before they married how she felt, he went along with it. She's spent the years studying music, painting, and maintaining a home.

> I just didn't want children; I had no desire for them. All my friends had children, but for me it wasn't even a decision, just part of my life. I never felt the need for it; it wasn't even an emotional thing. I don't even think about it. My feelings have never changed.

And even at one hundred years of age with never a sister, brother, niece, nephew, or even any cousins she could think of, Marjory Stoneman Douglas (see Chapter One) feels the same today as she did seventy-five years ago when she was twenty-five: "I never wanted children. And I don't want children now."

One woman, a full-time psychology professor at an Ivy League University and the mother of three sons under five, asked me at a picnic when we were discussing this book: "Don't you think psychological defenses are protecting these women's hidden feelings? Have they all dared to look deep into the wells of their hearts? If they'd made a mistake, would they be able to admit it? Wouldn't cognitive dissonance have played its defensive role in masking these women's true feelings?"

But why must we question women who express no ambivalence about children? Are there not just as many mothers racked by self-doubt who might have been better off, for their own and their children's sake, had they not had their children?

Other women without children, however, find themselves childless by twists of fate and by default in a shadow of ambivalence.

Chances are that at some time these women reflected upon children and motherhood as an emotional issue related to issues of attachment and loss. And one of the early phases in reckoning with the irrevocability of never having children may be panic.

The Panic: That Relentless Ticking Clock

Who knows if hormones have anything to do with it, or if the monumentally pervasive social and cultural pressure to have children is so ingrained in virtually every part of our social fabric that a woman who has not acted upon her biological ability to have children may feel compelled to do so when she's up against the clock.

In either case, many women panic when they foresee their biological clock somberly sounding MIDNIGHT. For some, the panic lasts for as little as a day, and grips them as early as in their early twenties. For others, time's urgent tick isn't heard until the early forties or drags on for years through the muddy waters of ambivalence, causing bouts of agitation and anguish.

As a woman imagines her biological "alarm" about to go off, signaling "Time's up!," she may feel fear, anxiety, and/or panic about time and her life passing out of control. Forty-one-year-old Tammy, for example, has no children because she never made the definite decision to have them. Although she thinks she's okay with that non-decision—childlessness by default—she's been growing more anxious as her biological time to have children quickly runs out:

> Coming closer as I am to a definite cutoff, an absolute limit that tells me I no longer have the option to have children, I no longer can choose to have children, I feel a scary kind of pressure. Am I making a mistake? Will I come to regret this more and more over the years. I'm having more and greater internal conflicts about the decision or *lack* of decision as I get closer to the point of no return.

Although Joan, the former child actress/model, now a forty-year-old pediatric nurse, never felt a sense of panic, she remembers feeling a sense of urgency to have a child:

The only time I recall wanting a child was when I was twenty-three- to twenty-four-years old. I was single, a feminist for whom no man was worthy (or even adequate), and I developed a five-year plan. I gave myself five years to save money, get pregnant by a male with good genes, move to Vermont, and live alone with my child, a shotgun, and a St. Bernard dog.

But then Joan met her husband-to-be. She dumped her five-year plan and got married. They put off children while they tested the waters of marriage, which proved to be sweet but, as time passed, the list of reasons not to have children seemed to grow. At the same time, the urgency for a child passed, never to return.

Many women muse that their biological clock panic seemed to have more to do with missing the *experience* of pregnancy, childbirth, and breastfeeding than the experience of parenting.

Gwen, the thirty-seven-year-old, never-married editor and writer, remembers:

> When I was about thirty-three years old, my biological clock went off for about six weeks and I actually had second thoughts because I thought maybe I was missing something. The only things that really interested me though were pregnancy and childbirth, which I think are fascinating biological phenomena and must be exciting to experience. I haven't had any problems with this since then.

Laura, the forty-five-year-old lesbian city planner, also thinks her major regret about not having children is missing out on childbirth:

> I clearly think that being pregnant and giving birth, when they don't go wrong, and in spite of all their commoness around the world, are still extraordinary life experiences and ones that I have not had and will never have.

As Pamela, the sixty-one-year-old ever single dancer, looks back, she remembers a sense of panic at forty that was brought on by a brief pregnancy. It wasn't until she realized she was pregnant, that she decided she wanted a child badly.

It was a momentary crisis. I got pregnant, it was a slipup, and I realized that this was the last moment and I'd be sorry if I didn't follow through. So I decided to have the baby. But then I had a miscarriage! But by this time, I really wanted the pregnancy. I frantically thought about men whom I could ask to father a child. Later, I realized of course, the man wouldn't be anyone I'd marry, and anybody I'd ask to be a father wouldn't be so irresponsible that he could ignore he had a child in the world.

So then I looked into adoption, and was told it was easier to adopt internationally, although preference was given to couples. Anyway, the more I thought about it, the more I realized that this was a horrendous undertaking I was contemplating, to be the sole bread earner and sole emotional support, especially for a child who might have difficulty adjusting to this culture. Finally I gave it up. At some point, I realized you can't do everything.

But some women struggle in panic, up against the wall, as the clock's final bell looks imminent: will they or won't they have a child.

Paula, the divorced librarian whose husband of eighteen years never wanted children, said her friends in their thirties still drive her "nuts" with their insistent need to hash over and over again their confusion about children:

My women friends get crazy sometime in their mid-thirties. Something switches on; they get so driven. I don't know where this comes from. We spend hours with it; we hike up a mountain and down a mountain; and a few women will drop back and the whole topic of conversation is, "Do I have a baby or don't I." It becomes an obsession; they get very pressured. There's something else going on besides what rationally makes you choose to have children or not.

When the pressure of time gets them, I see women say, "This is it or not at all," and that's as far as they get in the thought process. You have to get past that and evaluate your life and relationship. There's a lot more beyond just wanting a baby—there's, do you have what it takes to create a strong healthy child?

I really think that sometime in your early forties the decision's made and you get your common sense back again. If you get through that, you come out the other side and you begin to stabilize, look around, and see things more clearly.

In the meantime, however, women may experience a range of disquieting emotions.

Feelings of Loss and Fear

When women consider children but end up not having them for whatever reason, they must reckon with that loss at some point and grieve for it in some degree. Women who made a very conscientious decision not to have children seem to feel this the least. And it's commonly recognized that women with infertility problems experience a severe loss. Yet, women who always thought they'd have children but whose life paths have turned away from maternity because of twists of fate and circumstance have also sustained a real loss—the loss of a dream or image they had held most of their lives, for the baby they'll never see, for never knowing what might have been. With that loss vanishes a whole way of life, for a mother's daily life for almost twenty years is radically different in many ways than that of a woman without children. Mourning is how we face loss, and however it hurts, with feelings ranging from isolation, loneliness, helplessness, and sadness to perhaps even despair, facing the loss is the only route to accepting it. Acceptance is the hallmark of the end of grief and mourning.

Forty-three-year-old Diane remembers experiencing anxiety and then depression when she first started to come to terms with her permanent state of childlessness. She went through the mourning process before she could put the image of having children behind her:

> I was really grateful I didn't have a child in my first marriage which ended in my late twenties and was a real disaster. By my late thirties and several relationships later, I was really depressed that I'd never have a child. I had a really good cry and was really unhappy for awhile. It was a mourning period and I had to readjust my priorities.

After Ellen remarried at forty-two and went through two ectopic pregnancies and an *in vitro* fertilization, she let herself grieve:

The whole infertility process was very traumatic. A lot of grief came up. It was too much pain in too short a period of time and it had become too much of a focus in my life. The process kept bringing up feelings of inadequacy, pain, and grief. I had to face it and allow myself to go through all the feelings of grief.

Gail is the financial consultant who was sterilized at thirty-five because of pressure from her doctor and a husband who wasn't committed to children. Although she remembers a brief depression after the surgery, she was quickly distracted by the demands of a head-spinning promotion.

My attitude was somewhat cavalier at the time—I was coming into a point in my life where I was making decisions and feeling very good about making decisions, and I guess it was a little bit of a trip for me. And I made the decision to be sterilized in this context. But you don't realize with something like this that you are making a very big decision.

Gail tended to minimize the importance of her decision to herself and didn't fully confront and process her sense of loss when she was sterilized. Her defenses kicked in to help her cope by protecting her from dealing with issues of loss and fear and thereby allowing her to reassert a sense of control and mastery over her life. But since she didn't reckon with her pain at thirty-five, it's been resurfacing lately at age forty-three.

I can't say I wake up every day and think about not having children, but I'm feeling the residuals of my decision. I sometimes feel a sense of loss more than before. I don't say, "Oh, gosh, I really wish I could be at the school play," but there are moments when I think what would it have been like. But I keep myself so incredibly busy that I don't spend a lot of time internalizing on the emotional scale, and maybe that's going to hit me with a wallop some time in my life.

I am not in an enormous grief over this; it's a part of my landscape. It's not something that causes a great deal of pain, although if there were a lot of loss or failure in my life, it probably could and that may happen down the road.

I think there's potential to create some baggage for you later on when you aren't well prepared psychologically and emotionally or well resolved at the time.

Gail got choked up and tears welled up in her eyes. "I think for me, regret will come stronger later and I'll have to deal with it."

Since Gail didn't deal with her true feelings earlier, they continue to haunt her. Often, to prevent ourselves from feeling out of control or overwhelmed, we all use what psychologists call defense mechanisms to cushion ourselves from anxiety or fear to get through a hard time. In moderation, these are natural and healthy ways to deal with emotional pain, but if we continue to use these defenses to keep the uncomfortable feelings indefinitely at a distance without ever acknowledging in our heart of hearts that we sense the pain of a loss and that it hurts, the feelings are bound to resurface at some time in the future when we least expect it. By preventing ourselves from dealing with our pain, we can't begin to heal emotionally and move toward acceptance.

Like Gail, most of us were never taught how to deal with loss. To come to grips with whatever losses we sustain, we must bring unconscious feelings to the surface, making them conscious feelings. When psychological energy is tied up in holding the emotional pain at a distance, it can never be internalized. And it is only through internalization that we allow the loss to become part of us, not apart from us, and this is the essence of the mourning process.[3] Women who care about not having children and don't emotionally deal with the loss, may find themselves, as Gail did, having to deal with it later.

Often, tangled up in feelings of loss and panic are fears: fears about what the losses mean for our lives, about lost connections with the next generation, about growing old alone without a caring child to look out for us, and fears of insecurity.

Irena, the only child, never-married lesbian said she has always feared that, without a child, she'd lose the connections vital for a sense of *guaranteed* and *permanent* security.

> I fear that I will not build up the proper immunity to resist the erosion [of losing connections and relations]; I am afraid I, too [like a homeless shopping bag lady], will end up alone, disconnected, relating to no one, having no one to care for, being in turn forgotten, unwanted, and insignificant, my life a waste. In the grip of this terror, I can only anticipate a lonely, painful old age, an uncomforted death.[4]

In her late 30s, when Irena became most depressed about how fragile and transient friendships can be and how inconsistent lovers may be, she wrote:

> It was the myth of a child, a blood relation, and what it could bring me, which seemed to me the only guarantee against loneliness and isolation, the only way of maintaining a connection to the rest of society. And certainly one of the difficulties for me, as a woman who now knows that she will never bear children, is to let go of that myth without sinking into total despair.

Irena reminded herself, of course, "that children are not a medicine or a vaccine which stamps out loneliness or isolation, but rather that they are people, subject to the same weaknesses as friends and lovers." She knows she was raised with the myth of the idealized family, one in which warm, loving blood bonds, thicker than water, flow gently between parent and child, but its power still dominates her fantasy life. Yet she also knows that although true affection bonds certain children and their parents, many families are estranged, ties are irrevocably severed, no comfort or love is exchanged. But the fear that she will be without the "permanent" and "guaranteed" child relationship still creeps into her thoughts at her weakest moments.

One of the most haunting fears is fearing regret itself. Many women expressed their contentedness with their current lives—lives being well lived in their thirties, forties, and fifties. But they were scared about how they'd feel later on. Many said that the only thing that really bothered them about not having children was the fear that they'd regret it later on. They wondered whether they were making a big mistake.

And whether they feared regret or not, many feared old age without children: "My only regret about being childless concerns aging and being alone," said one woman who expressed how many felt.

Yet, studies show that, "Overall, there is little evidence that important psychological rewards are derived from the later stages of parenthood," concluded two sociologists who examined six U.S. national surveys that looked at happiness and satisfaction in people over fifty. Having children contributed to neither happiness nor overall satisfaction in later life.[5] And the effects of being childless in later life are described as "benign" by gerontology researchers. (See Chapter Fifteen for more on the effects of childlessness in later life.)

The Pain and Anger Imposed by Would-Be Grandparents

One of the most difficult aspects for women who do not have children is coping with the pain and disappointment this "nonevent" may cause their mothers who were eager to be grandmothers and feel cheated by their childless daughters. If siblings have children, the pressure lets up, although some women said that when the grandchildren are from sons, the grandmothers still pressure them because having grandchildren through daughters is different. Said Janice:

> My mother doesn't approve of the way my sister-in-law brings up her children, and she's really disappointed that I never had kids. She's said that a daughter's children would be more like her own, but a son's children belong to his wife. She feels like a meddling mother-in-law now with her daughter-in-law and her grandchildren, whereas she thinks if I had children, it would be much more gratifying for her.

Most difficult for a daughter, however, is when her mother has no other grandchildren prospects. Gwen, for example, feels "okay" about not having children, considering that she had "no positive reasons to have children." But her mother's loss continues to sadden her.

> One of the most painful things about my choice is that it has greatly disappointed my mother and probably my father, too. My mom really wants to be a grandmother and started to hint around at this a lot. I think she has finally accepted that I won't be having children and neither will my sister, so she'll never be a grandma.

Irena was under even more pressure. As the only child in her family to survive World War II, she was brought up by her mother with the unstated assumption that she would contribute to regenerating the family. And she always fantasized that she would have a child, for to do so, as we saw in Chapter Ten, would insulate her from losing intimate connections. But Irena came to realize that her fantasy was largely a legacy from her own dissatisfied relationship with her mother. By becoming a perfect mother, she could "annihilate the impatient critical voice within myself, the voice that has kept me insecure and dissatisfied."

> Thus, my desire to become the perfect mother, to act out that fantasy, has in reality nothing to do with having a child, but rather with my desire to experience something I wish I had experienced. It is not a child I wish to mother, it is myself.

> According to the myth of motherhood . . . if I do not have a child I will never experience that caring, that uncritical peace, that completely understanding sensibility. Only the role of mother will allow me that. This is clearly the wrong reason for having a child—one which can be ultimately disastrous.

And so Irena followed a different path. But it has, nevertheless, been excruciating for her to deny her mother the grandchildren she always assumed she'd have. "The 'you're-the-last-of-the-line' argument always makes the woman who chooses not to have children appear perverse, stubborn, ungiving, selfish." Irena has had to withstand that kind of pressure and trust that her instinct to follow a different route was the right way for her to go. Yet, she hears the excitement and envy in her mother's voice informing her of new babies. "I have often resented the fact that nothing that I could achieve could elicit that tone of voice, that kind of lasting, enduring satisfaction . . . underneath it, I know, lies a silent, unstated criticism of me."[6]

Children always try to gain their parents' approval as a way to earn their love. Fear of disapproval sometimes triggers feelings of emotional abandonment, even when we're grown children. It's not that our past rules our present, but rather, that it inhabits our present. As we separate from our parents, it's often still difficult to be able to accept their disapproval. Denise, for example, feels empowered by having successfully shifted her focus from six years of agonizing over infertility to accepting and enjoying her child-free status. She's proud of her transformation and how she's organized a support network for other couples who have trouble conceiving. But her mother and mother-in-law have never understood, and Denise feels their pain as well as her own pain for never being able to bridge a communication gap between them.

Both our mothers are in their sixties and whenever we tried to talk infertility to them, they couldn't talk about it. Robert's mom would tell everyone, "It was Denise's problem; she couldn't give Randall a child." We just tried to roll with it.

I don't think they've ever realized the depth of our anguish or the height of our peace since we finally made it through. Randall's mom just died, and with he being an only child, it was really sad. We'd try to talk about important things, but she just couldn't before she died.

Our moms suffered a great loss, too. They've had to just sit there while everybody else brings out their grandmother brag books, and all they've got are pictures of our German shepherd. If they've been able to achieve a sense of resolution, we don't know.

But mothers can also anger their daughters like no one else, pushing all the wrong buttons. Mothers may feel they've a right to interrogate their children about why they don't have children. Jean Veevers in *Childless by Choice* reported that parents "cannot be put off with appeals to privacy or with superficial answers . . . in many if not most cases, parents feel that one of the rewards due to them for their years of child care and support is the right to grandchildren."[7] They *expect* grandchildren and grow more restless as their peers become grandparents. When daughters don't procreate, they may be not only curious and resentful that they're not getting their due, but ask their daughters where *they* had gone wrong.

Thirty-eight-year-old Natalie, a professional environmentalist who never felt maternal and has no desire for children, feels that her decision is her own and hers only. Although all her friends either have or want children, she's never felt pressured to have her own children. But her mother, who already has two grandchildren through Natalie's sister, is "relentless."

We came from a very warm, loving family. If there was any real negative, it was that my sister and I were always the center of attention and concern. But now, she's very unaccepting of my choice.

She says, "Was I such a bad mother?" She takes it very personally. I've learned to laugh at it, but sometimes I get really angry. She can be so inappropriate. A very good friend of mine who was pregnant called my mother once looking for me, and my mother started spilling her guts out: "What about Natalie? Do you think she'll ever have a baby? I'm just so distraught that she's not going to have children."

Why can't she recognize that I'm an adult, able to make my own decisions, and I've made this one for my life. I'm happy with it and she just can't respect that.

Several women described tension in their relationship with their mothers, who interpreted their daughters' rejection of motherhood as "spitting in their face," and as rejecting them and their way of life. Fifty-year-old Ilene, mentioned earlier in this book, recalls that her large extended family was very family oriented. Her mother had been a nurse until she married at thirty-two and was glad to give up her career to raise her two children, one girl and one boy. But Ilene didn't grow up to be the perfect daughter her mother had imagined:

As the only girl, I was spoiled. But I remember as a young child, I wanted to be married and live exactly the kind of life my parents were leading. But later, I didn't marry. I didn't have children. I rejected my mother's lifestyle, but in my rejecting her role model, she interpreted it as my rejecting her, and our relationship has been strained ever since. She's eighty-two, and we're a little better at our relationship now, but we still can't talk about a lot of these things.

Whereas Gwen feels sad that her mother will never be a grandmother, she's also angry at her for hinting at it from time to time:

She'd die if I ever became a single mother, but the fact that I don't have a mate, which I would very much like to have, makes her persistence even more painful to me. What if I had wanted children? How did she think her hints and pressure would have made me feel if I wanted something I couldn't have? I'm disappointed enough that I haven't found a life partner.

Lisa, the forty-six-year-old weaver first mentioned in Chapter Four, had a tubal ligation at thirty-five. When I asked her if there had been conflicts with her parents, she said:

It was awful with my mother. Two years ago, she said, "Don't you regret not having children?" I said, "Mother, I'm forty-four years old, you want me now to start regretting things I can't change." My parents aren't as close to my brother's kids as they'd like, and they wish the grandchildren had been mine because I'm closer to them. But it's gotten me angry. I remained firm: "Hey, if you want a grandchild, adopt one. I'm not having a child for you. You're not going to bring it up." It was very difficult—my mother just couldn't imagine why I didn't want kids. My grandmother called me the most selfish person she ever met.

The Transition

Just as women with infertility problems must undergo a transition to reorient their assumptions and goals, many other childless women who didn't make the conscious decision *not* to have children need to do the same. Sometimes, the transition will occur in the foreshadow of menopause. Grief may resurface as the ability to have children passes; anger may well up at the body that betrayed them; the thought of imminent menopause may bring up feelings of being out of control. Sometimes, the transition is hard to recognize:

"It may first appear as a vague sense of unease. Or it may take the early form of a slight depression, for no known reason. There may be a sense of foreboding, shifting, change," describes Nancy Peterson, author of the book about never-married women, *Our Lives for Ourselves*.[8] The midlife transition may begin with feelings of disquiet and upheaval, which may result in a woman questioning her lifestyle, choices, goals, and fantasies. Reassessment and renewal are the rewards for successfully following through:

The transition is like a shaking-out process, a seventh-inning stretch in the middle of life, a time to make some adjustments, take a longer view. It would be interesting if we could know the effects of biology and hormones on all this, because the midlife transition is sometimes caught up with a final concern about childlessness and may directly precede menopause . . . or it at least foreshadows the beginning of the premenopausal period for most.[9]

At some point, a woman will need to stop dwelling on what she has no control over anymore, i.e., having children, to focus on what she can control. Some women may form new commitments to their careers and/or extended families; some take advantage of their financial security to abandon a strenuous worklife; still others may take the opportunity to focus their energies on nurturing themselves and devoting more time and energies than ever before to their physical and mental well-being and spiritual growth. Recall Diane who went into a depression upon coming to terms with her childlessness in her late thirties:

> I was really upset about never having children and then I just said, "Okay, I'll never have children," and I readjusted my priorities. I began to really appreciate my free time. I started taking classes at night, going to a health club, visiting museums.
>
> Now, I have a much different outlook. I don't feel needy that I have to search out a man to get married and have a child. Unconsciously, it was a tremendous burden. Now, I let relationships into my life not because I want to get married and have children but because there's a nice friendship and a sense of sexual excitement. It's much nicer now, more relaxed; men don't feel under pressure from me to make the relationship work.

Ellen, herself a therapist, went into therapy to help guide her through what she knew were important issues related to grief, aging, and loss.

> It's only been in the past few years that I've felt whole enough and ready enough to give to a child. The sadness is that it was too late. I went through a time processing a lot of feelings of loss: loss of mother, of not being able to be creative biologically, of learning how to be creative and generative without having a child. I have had to accept myself as the product of all my decisions: this is what happened, and now I have to make a concerted effort to have a rich life, which I have. Part of that work is really focusing on our relationship because we felt we were out of sync. It'll never be a complete process, but that work has really helped a lot.

Some women felt helped by "permission givers," important people in their lives who communicated that it was "okay" not to have kids. Diane was at first taken aback at her mother's attitude:

My mother said, "What do you need children for?" She's been married to my father now for forty-six years. It's not a great relationship but they're still married. She said that having a child is just a lot of aggravation. You know, she told me that at twelve! I thought, "How selfish of her—the one joy in life, and to tell me not to have children."

But now, years later, it's helped tremendously. Sometimes I say wistfully, "Wouldn't it be nice to have a child," and she still says, "What do you need it for? It's such a tremendous responsibility and financial burden."

The "permission givers" for Andrea Brown, the thirty-six-year-old DES daughter and literary agent whose husband definitely won't have children (see Chapter One), were the older women in Florida she spoke to who said not to worry about not having children.

My stepmother, who's been married to my father fourteen years now, has two sons and she has said to me many times that she envies my decision. She's seventy now, and she says she wouldn't do it over again. My aunt, too, says she wouldn't do it again. They all feel they had no choice. That helped make it easier for me.

For many women, childless aunts or influential professors who served as positive role models gave the message that it was "okay" to not have children. These women were leading lives of positive autonomy, unburdened as mothers were, fulfilling other worthwhile goals in the outside world. Some women recalled as young girls that they admired such a woman who lived so differently than their mothers, who showed them there was another way.

Acceptance and Relief

Once women are well into their forties, the sense of urgency about children begins to fade and women begin to feel relieved to put the issue behind them. People stop asking about it. Peer pressure finally lets up. Parents stop mentioning it anymore. Friends' children leave home, and women without children begin to feel more in step with women their age who are mothers. The issue of children fades, becoming an issue of youth. Women come to accept their lives as they are. Women who actively chose not to have children still felt relieved and glad that they hadn't had them. Other women put the issue in the perspective of their entire life. Said seventy-five-year-old Lucille, who was told never to get pregnant again after a near-fatal tubal pregnancy at the age of twenty-six:

> I've probably missed a great experience in life, but I don't know, not having gone through it. No, I don't regret it for my lifestyle, for either of my marriages; the first marriage was a disaster, and in the second, my husband already had a son; it wouldn't have worked out. I think I would have liked to have had children, for the experience of it, but I don't feel deprived. You can't miss it if you don't have it.

Iris, the seventy-seven-year-old widow who married too late for children (see Chapter Seven), taught school for years and continues to be active in the peace and civil rights movements. For her, children have become a "non-issue."

> I just don't think about children. I've never felt any regret, never. In my heart of hearts, I'm sure I missed something, carrying a child, watching it grow, but it hasn't been a drawback—I've seen it all with nieces and nephews. Life would have been different with certain pleasures, even ecstasies maybe, but it doesn't distress me. I've had other things. It just doesn't engage my interest to think about it. I know I've missed things but, on the other hand, a woman with children has been denied what she thought she'd like to do and has missed what I've had.

Others said glimmers of regret surfaced from time to time, but they were only occasional and easily put in the context of their entire lives. Irena still sometimes wishes she had had a child early. But she's also proud of herself for listening to her own heart and mind.

> Often, of course, I wish I had done it, done it in those uncon-scious years when so many women I knew were doing it. . . . Still, there are moments when I can actually assert a certain amount of pride in the way I have chosen to lead my life, when I can feel extremely good about the fact that I did not succumb and did not

keep myself in line. I am pleased that I withstood the pressures, that I kept my independence, that I did not give in to the myths [of perfect families] which surrounded me. . . . I experience momentary delight in the fact that I escaped and did what I wanted to do (even when that was somewhat unclear), that I did not give in to the temptation to please my mother, did not give in to the pleas of my father's ghost to keep him alive, did not conform with the rest of my friends, but instead kept myself apart and independent in some essential way. In moments like these, I can easily take responsibility for my life and say it is the life that I have chosen.

None of this is ever very simple. There are pleasures that one gives up when one decides not to have children. But as I keep telling myself: you can't have everything. The act of choosing inevitably brings loss. It is a difficult lesson to understand and accept. I keep trying to relearn it.[10]

Charlotte, seventy-one, twice divorced and a victim of unexplained infertility during her second marriage, lives alone, one hand paralyzed, in a trailer park of retirees.

I've always been very disappointed that I didn't have children, but I don't concentrate on it much. No good in making myself miserable. I feel I failed in some way with my two marriages, but there's no point in making your life unhappy over it. It's a misspent life if you spend it terribly unhappy over things you can't change. It's past; it's gone. You can't undo it. A good sound outlook is the greatest asset you can have—it helps you through life.

Seventy-four-year-old widow Grace Downs, who married too late for children, still lives in the four-bedroom house she shared with her husband. Said Grace: "Oh, sometimes I think about it, but I don't dwell on it. I have enough to do. I belong to myself; I don't have to consider anyone else."

When older women were asked to respond to the fears younger women had about growing old without children, they answered with the grace of age—of having lost husbands, parents, sisters, and dreams, of accepting their losses, letting them be, and getting on with life. Said ninety-two-year-old Carol, who lives with her husband in a low-income, senior citizens housing project:

I had regrets about not having children for a short time in my late thirties, but just a short time. It was just something I accepted. I'm not sad about it; it's just part of life. It hasn't been an issue. Young women shouldn't be scared about it—you have to accept life's decisions as they come. You can't foresee everything.

If you're lonely in your old age, it's your own fault, not your circumstances. If you're not friendly and take part in things, you'll be lonely. Of course, if you have children, sometimes they take care of you and sometimes they don't.

Religious women, such as eighty-five-year-old Ruth (see Chapter Nine), found solace in their faith and God's will. Clara, eighty-four, the widowed schoolteacher with unexplained infertility, lives nearby more than twenty-five nieces and nephews; she has humbly accepted her childlessness. The disappointment and sadness from early on gradually and gently turned into acceptance:

> I've had a fruitful life, a busy life, a happy life, and I don't know if I'd want to change it. I wish I had had children, but as long as I didn't, I accepted it. It's like you wanted to go to the movies yesterday and you didn't go. You might have a regret, but you pass it off—that's the way it was. It hasn't interfered with my life. I can't say it's been rewarding not having them, but on the other hand, I haven't suffered either way. I would have liked to have them, but I just accepted life as it came, as God's will.

One woman may never be a mother; another will never have a sister or know her father. Perhaps another will miss never being the concert musician she had dreamed of becoming or the compassionate healer. There is a certain grace that comes in accepting what one has no control over. Some psychiatrists say that it is perhaps our losses, even more than our gains, that define our life experiences. Says psychoanalyst Judith Viorst:

> In the course of our life we leave and are left and let go of much that we love. Losing is the price we pay for living . . . [but] we should understand how these losses are linked to our gains. . . . In confronting the many losses that are brought by time and death, we become a mourning and adapting self, finding at every stage—until we draw our final breath—opportunities for creative transformations.[11]

On Social Pressure, Stigmas, Stereotypes, and Selfishness

Once a woman reckons with her own feelings about not having a child, she's got to deal with everyone else's feelings about her not having children, starting with pressure to have them.

In 1955, a mere one percent of women expected to remain childless, for whatever reasons.[12] In 1980, 9.4 women out of ten favored marriage, yet four out of five (eighty-two percent) said that they didn't think children were an essential ingredient for a full and happy marriage.[13] By 1988, ten percent said they didn't expect to have any kids; another fifteen percent weren't sure.[14] And a 1990 Virginia Slims Opinion Poll showed that six percent fewer women than the year before believed a marriage, kids, and career combo was ideal; rather, more were willing to forego the children.[15]

These trends show that it has, no doubt, become easier and more acceptable these days to remain child free. Cultural pressure has let up. But there's a long way to go, women in their forties said. Pro-choice liberals talk about respecting a woman's right to make her own decisions about her reproduction, yet few seem to respect the child-free choice. Said fifty-year-old Hope, an "early articulator":

> There's a lot of support for someone who's had an abortion, and there's a lot of support for people who've postponed babies and have infertility problems, but people are always surprised when I say we've chosen to be childless. They think it's a little strange, weird—there's no cultural support. It's interesting where the line for societal support is drawn.

We've already seen how mothers can put the squeeze on daughters to have children, but friends can too. Friends who have become mothers may, indeed, sincerely wish to convey the joy of parenting to their childless friends, but they also may long for another pregnant friend to revalidate their own choice to parent. In fact, Planned Parenthood has a saying that friends can get you pregnant faster than husbands.

New mothers, coping with the difficulties of new parenthood, may feel their choice threatened and challenged by carefree friends unburdened by children. "I may also feel envious of some aspects of their lives," researcher and mother Carole Wilk admitted when she studied career women and their childbearing choices, "and at the same time guilty because of this envy."[16] Some women interviewed for this book thought their friends envious or jealous while others merely resented the intrusion of their friends' pressure on a private, personal decision. Said forty-four-year-old Nancy Lucas Hampton:

> I wish people would accept my choice. I think couples with children are envious of those without, especially if they've had grave difficulty raising a child. I suspect they want me to have children so I can commiserate with them.

The majority of women commented that they'd had to learn how to respond to the casual, conversation-opener, "Do you have children?" or "How many children do you have?" Some had a pat answer like, "No, we married too late," or "No, we weren't able to." Hope, intentionally childless, still thinks that such questions create an awkward situation:

> I feel like I have to explain my decision, but I don't. I also feel the need to apologize, that maybe I made a mistake, although I really don't feel that way.

Louise, forty-two, married and child free, got so fed up with questions from relatives that she lied to a cousin, saying that she couldn't have children.

> I thought surely that would stop her in her tracks. It did, though only for the time being. The next day she phoned and very excitedly informed me about a girl she knew who went to a doctor that can work miracles. Would I like his phone number. Naturally, I was flabbergasted to have gotten caught in a lie, and have never lied about it again.

For Terri, such a casual question would anger and hurt her when her feelings about her infertility were still raw. These days, she's still a little uncomfortable when people ask and tries to avoid pity from others. One of the joys of getting well into one's forties, in fact, is that people stop asking.

Regardless of one's age, however, stereotypes persist, the women interviewed said. The gentler ones are the maiden aunt schoolteacher . . . the woman who adopts all the neighborhood children, like stray cats . . . the battle-axe career woman. . . . The harsher ones are . . . barren . . . frustrated . . . dried up . . . ballbusters . . . odd . . . coldhearted "child haters" . . . "People think we eat children for breakfast."

But the most pervasive and persistent cultural criticism that women without children heard was selfishness, with all its negative connotations. The freedom to do as they pleased without having to consider others may indeed sound selfish, women said, and perhaps may even be, but the reasons parents give for having children sounded more selfish to them.

Although prospective mothers are rarely asked to justify why they're going to have a baby, they cite all kinds of reasons: to cement a marriage; have someone to love and return love; to be needed; prove their true womanhood; become a "grownup"; please parents or a husband; pass on the family name; provide a link to the future; and be cared for in old age.[17]

Others view kids as vital for a meaningful marriage, a sort of insurance policy for emotional well-being and prestige, provided the children do well.[18] Some children are begotten, not so much for their own sake, but for the rewards they'll bestow on their parents—satisfaction, status, respect, love, elder care, surrogate success, etc. And many aren't conceived for any particular reason at all, but by "assumption." For example, one-third of college students don't even consider whether they'll have children or not—they just assume they will—while five percent assume they won't.[19]

In other words, children are conceived today largely to gratify the parents. One study of married couples concluded that children were wanted as "love objects," for their emotional rewards and connections, their function of bonding together a marriage and family. They're considered necessary for a cohesive family and to buffer the parents against loneliness and an impersonal world.[20] We also have children because we yearn for a change, and having a baby seems such a positive one.

There's nothing wrong with some of these reasons except that many are themselves, totally erroneous. As we've seen, having a child can be threatening to parents' emotional well-being while requiring years of endless responsibility and hard work.

True, children can be the route to indescribable love and a deep, unexplained passion, unlike any other love. Yet that profound love may exact a high price. Motherhood is a package deal, and tied up with the pride and joy are also the endless hours of caretaking chores, sacrifices of the mind and body, and the full spectrum of gut-wrenching emotions—from the despairing to the sublime—not to mention extraordinary amounts of time and money.

One common reason baby boomers have children is part of their personal quest for self-fulfillment. In their self-conscious, deliberate way, boomer women want children so as not to miss out on this important role in life, to have a "real" family life, and to enrich their own lives with their children's love and affection. One demographer suggests that children are to baby boomers perhaps "the priciest of baubles."[21]

So, are today's motives to have children narcissistic, selfish, and self-serving? (Ironically, these same adjectives are often used to describe women who decide not to have children.) Family sociologist Jessie Bernard, herself a mother of three, says:

> It has been pointed out that the reasons for wanting children are equally, if not more, narcissistic and may be equally, if not more, selfish than the reasons for not wanting them. Those who want children as a guarantee of immortality; to keep the family name; to take care of them in their later years; to achieve for them; "just for the experience"; for "self-fulfillment"; and for any of the myriad other reasons often given for wanting children are no less narcissistic or selfish than those women who choose non-motherhood.[22]

In fact, it's just the opposite, said many of the women interviewed for this book, including thirty-eight-year-old Nina Silver, a divorced, child-free musician and writer in Manhattan:

> It's the ultimate in arrogance to have kids to become immortal, to fulfill your needs for old age, loneliness, generativity, or immortality—to bring a child into the world to fulfill those needs is the ultimate in narcissism.

Natalie agreed: " 'Who's going to take care of you when you're old?' my mother keeps asking. I say, 'That's a pretty shitty reason for having a kid. I would never do that to anybody.' "

Said Joan:

> To have children to avoid loneliness in old age is selfish. Inappropriate. It means CONDITIONAL love—to give so you can receive later. That is not a good reason to have children. It is faulty in reasoning. No contract was signed. Guilt can be waved as a flag in a child's face, but a child can choose to reject feeling guilty.

Lisa treasures her freedom to take off every weekend and summer with her husband and resents her grandmother calling her the most selfish person she ever met:

> "How could you not have children because you want to travel and all," she said. I know a lot of people who have children so the children will take care of them when they're old. I find that just as selfish. Selfish is just not a word I see in terms of having or not having children.

Susan, a forty-one-year-old divorced and remarried technical writer specializing in software manuals, said that selfishness is what allows her to be her own person to the fullest:

> The best part of not having children is the freedom to be selfish about how I spend my time. I can pick up and go when and where I want and don't have to worry about having screwed up someone else's life.

Indeed, weren't some women who suspected they might not have been great parents being less selfish by not experimenting on a vulnerable child? And besides, women living on their own without the responsibilities of raising children weren't harming anyone; they were living their own lives quietly, and, in fact, often reaching out professionally or as volunteers to help others.

Ilene had this to say about selfishness: "You know, I think I'm a little selfish, but I don't know if I started out like that or ended up like that."

Besides being called selfish, some women recalled freak reactions they'd gotten about not having children. Said one child-free married woman living in Utah:

I used to feel defensive since I live in a state controlled by a religion that thinks having babies is a surefire way to get to heaven, so have as many as possible whether you're good at raising them or not. I even had a lady come right out and tell me that I was selfish, and if I didn't have children all I was was a legal prostitute.

Said an ever-single fifty-five-year-old woman in North Dakota: "One man from my hometown said, 'If you don't get married and have a family, you are nothing.' "

Some women think they symbolize a threat to certain people whose daily lives are largely mandated by their roles as parents. One woman felt denigrated, "just because I didn't want to 'give life' to another person, but wanted to live a life of my own without the responsibility of someone who would dictate my actions for two decades or more." Many women were leading autonomous lives, not hurting anyone and not neglecting anyone. They were just independent, and it wasn't really fair, some women felt, for that to be called selfish.

Middle America also tends to distort these women's lives. They live out their *own* fates, yes, unhampered by children, but do they deserve Phil Donahue's treatment of the voluntarily child free? In 1990, he presented a show called "People Who Hate Children." When women and couples explained their conscientious, well-thought-out reasons why they shouldn't have children, the audience booed and hooted them. The transcript of the program identified each voluntarily child-free guest as "(name), Dislikes Children." That such coverage on child-free living could be so sensationalized in 1990 perpetuates negative stereotypes about women without children.

A few women in their early forties, on the cusp of the baby-boom generation, felt stung by a motherhood backlash that devalued their choice. Deanna, forty-three, whose infertility broke up her first marriage and casts a spector of sadness over her second marriage, said: "Other people definitely devalue me because I'm not a mother. One lady yelled at me for not giving my poor husband children! Some people feel sorry for me; others think I'm terrible. We don't associate with families now."

Some women who chose not to have children for their own

sake and for the sake of the unborn children, are saddened that the open-mindedness of the late sixties has been closing up.

> Ironically, nonmothers are in the situation many housewives said they were in during the late 1960s and into the 1970s. Then feminism was so vital and had so much impact that women who stayed at home said they felt devalued. Left out. Now it is I who do.

Thus wrote Paula Weideger in a 1988 *Ms.* magazine article about womb worship and how society seems to be reproaching women who aren't mothers, whereas in the 1970s, women who didn't pursue careers and choices other than motherhood were reproached. Weideger senses a new hierarchy of values now where smug mothers "perch at the top and nonmoms huddle down below," just like the male-dominated hierarchy that this generation of women has been trying to break up.[23] Nancy Hampton, who was divorced during her prime childbearing years, said: "I sense a feeling of superiority on the part of those with children, as if they had accomplished a feat I was incapable of."

For psychoanalyst Roberta Joseph, making the deliberate choice to forego children was to preserve the less dramatic but by far more peaceful status quo: "Because of who I am, I must forgo certain experiences to assure that I have what I need most." But defending that nonconformity in the baby-bouncing 1990s is again harder to justify and sustain, Joseph says. "The current baby boom that I am declining to join in part reflects a backlash from the more confident and expansive seventies, when women seemed finally to be disencumbering themselves of sex-role stereotypes."[24]

That pro-baby backlash was so strong for some women that discussing child-free living with people who were parents or prospective parents became a taboo topic. It was seen as too risky a topic to tackle because of the fear that they might be attacked by people who were staunch pro-baby and couldn't understand someone who wasn't. They felt that others didn't respect their decision and so they weren't really comfortable talking about it with people who were going to argue with them. As a result, many kept their feelings about not wanting to have children to themselves.

Lissa is a forty-five-year-old librarian in California. She knew by her twenties that she wasn't interested in having children, but she felt her position was always vulnerable to attack:

> I feel I always have to defend myself for my decision not to have children, something parents never have to do. Other than my aunt, who validated my choice when I was in college and then only in secret, no one was on my side. I generally hide my feelings, not wanting to look like a freak.

Lissa is grateful, however, for finding a group of women who had similar feelings and with whom she could talk about not having children.

Interestingly, older women without children tended to express very little concern or awareness of stigmas, stereotypes, or of being devalued. We can only guess whether this was a function of their age and distance from being concerned about children—an issue of early middle age that seems to fade with the years—or of their growing up way before the self-expressive 1960s and 1970s. Yet, most of them admitted to never really talking about their not having children. No one ever asked them about it, and they never brought it up.

In fact, in looking for women to interview for this book, I found many older people reluctant to ask childless friends or relatives if they were willing to be interviewed. Not having children was a topic that had never been discussed. One of my mother's best friends, for example, is a woman I have known since first grade who would gladly help me in any pursuit I chose to undertake. Yet, she could not bring herself to ask her oldest and dearest friend of 50 years, a woman without children, if she were willing to have me call or write her. In another instance, a sixty-five-year-old man couldn't face asking his sister, a very successful banker, if I could call her.

For these people, childlessness was an unspoken taboo topic, never to be discussed. Perhaps one reason they didn't want to bring it up is because not having children has been frowned upon by society and may still be devalued by and large. One small study which assessed college students' perceptions of parents vs.

nonparents, for example, suggests that people are still judged by their fertility status: parents were perceived as having more positive qualities, and the more children they had, the higher their positive attributes rating.[25]

In any case, women will continue to not have children, and how well they fare will depend on how they put their emotional issues to rest and form a web of important social relationships that matter to them. The next chapter explains how women without children form their social relationships and family networks and find ways to care and be cared for by others.

CHAPTER TWELVE

Nurturing and Networking

> Love, commitment, continuity—these create deep and
> indelible bondings. Whatever the structure they exist in,
> they are the material of which kinship is made.
> —KAREN LINDSEY,
> *Friends As Family*[1]

The last chapter reviewed how women who had wanted children
go through a period in their lives in which they reckon emotionally with the issues associated with not having children. This
chapter will begin to talk about how women without children go
on to live vibrant, rich, satisfying lives. It will focus particularly
on how those lives are full of family and friends and people who
care. Of course, women don't need children to be embedded in
a web of important social relationships. And although children
aren't necessary for emotional well-being and a loving life of being
fully human, friendships and kinship networks are—whether they
are comprised of blood family or alternative family members.
Such relationships are the necessary connections that are key to
a fulfilling old age, not children and grandchildren per se, as we'll
see in Chapter Fifteen.

These social connections may be fluid attachments that ebb
and flow over the years, and they may be few. In fact, just one
confidante is overwhelmingly powerful in promoting emotional
well-being.

Whereas many women feel a strong need to nurture, some
women without children think there may be something wrong

with them for lacking a "maternal instinct." Society would have us believe that "we will only feel at peace, sure of ourselves, when we have fulfilled the glorified 'instinct'. . . . [that] you are not a full woman until you are a mother," writes Nancy Friday in *My Mother, My Self,* herself married and child free.[2] Yet, many researchers don't believe that women are born with the innate need to bear and raise children. The truth is that some humans—male and female—like to take care of children and/or other creatures that need them, but " 'Some human beings do not like it at all,' " Dr. Leah Cahan Schaeffer, author of *Women and Sex,* told Friday. " 'It is not some great biological imperative, which if frustrated will ruin or impoverish a woman's life.' "[3]

Yet, many societal forces encourage us to have children and promote the idea that they are vitally important for achieving satisfaction and fulfillment in life. Although such pronatalism may make women without children feel uncomfortable, "different," or "lacking" in some way because they violate the norm, understanding pronatalism's important role may help. Society pressures and supports people to have children to encourage them to undertake the very difficult and underpaid but essential job, necessary to perpetuate the society. Perhaps if there *were* an overwhelmingly strong maternal instinct (how come no one ever talks about the paternal instinct?), such strong cultural pressure wouldn't be necessary. But for the sake of the human race and society, we need people who want to parent and so society encourages all to become parents.

Psychoanalyst Erik Erikson says that humans must sometime in midlife achieve the stage of development called "generativity" to become a balanced person. Only by passing on a part of themselves to the next generation will a person become a mature, healthy adult. Although having children is an obvious route, generativity can also successfully be achieved by helping to make the world a better place, be it through volunteer work, important political or social causes, or even through creative works. One route to achieving inner peace, in fact, may be by immersing ourselves in causes greater than ourselves.

Needing to Be Needed

Most of the women interviewed for this book, including those who never felt maternal longings, expressed a need to pass something on of themselves. Many women fulfilled this need by teaching, nursing, or by helping or guiding husbands, other people's children, friends, or animals. By doing this, women felt needed and helpful. In addition, an important fringe benefit of helping others was the forging of vital social connections.

For years, unmarried and other women without children have been teachers and nurses. These career paths were not only two of the few professions open to women, but they also served to fulfill the need to nurture and to pass on something of themselves that improved the world. At seventy-seven, Iris continues to be active in a women's peace movement, doing her part to improve the world. She married too late to have children but she never missed them—she saw kids every day during her high-school teaching career.

> I'm very fond of children and have a reputation for being very good with little ones, but I've never felt a strong maternal instinct. Between my students and nieces and nephews, I've always had outlets for any nurturant tendencies I've felt, but I never wished that I could be a mother, too. Yes, children are wonderful, but I've always been very glad to give them back to their mothers.
>
> No, dear, I'm not concerned at all about generativity and immortality. I don't think it's important. What's important is that while we live here on Earth, we do what we think is good, and I feel I have and continue to do that.

The roles of college professor, mentor, and advisor on campus make Judy Long—the feminist sociologist who never felt maternal—feel totally fulfilled.

> I won't be passing on a large estate to anyone, but I'm very much concerned with the next generation. I feel like I've made an enormous contribution in my lifetime, especially related to equality for women. I do it every day.

Joan, the forty-year-old pediatric nurse, who is married and child free, put it this way:

We are both very nurturing people. We nurture one another and our pets, and as a pediatric nurse, I am available for my patients, guiding their parents to good parenting skills.

Almost every week, *someone* comments how amazing it is that I can work with sick children—children who have cancer, who have been abused, who are psychotic. They say they could never do that and how strong I must be. I am not stronger than the average person. I am just not distracted by children of my own. I am free to focus on the health and welfare of the child at hand. This is a blessing.

For many women like Joan, work provides the essential outlet for them to give of themselves. Rachel Guido DeVries, who left her career as a pediatric nurse to become a full-time writer, went through a transformation at the age of twenty-nine when her husband said he was ready to start a family.

I just knew at that instant that it wasn't what I wanted. At the same time, I began to take my writing very seriously and realized that I didn't have the energy to sustain my life as a writer and be a mother. I just didn't have the desire to bear and raise a child.

That same year, Rachel came out as a lesbian, divorced her husband, and left nursing. She was published soon thereafter and, as we saw in Chapter Ten, is now a novelist, poet, and sculptor. She also teaches creative writing to students from grade-school to university level.

All my entire life, from my earliest memory, people have said to me that I'd be a great mother, that I should have children, or now that I'm forty-three, that I should have had children because I'm so nurturant, so giving, so energetic.

People have this monomaniacal notion of nurturance. Yeah, I have these qualities and have had them my entire life. And all of the work that I do is a form of nurturing. Writing is an expression of it, teaching is an expression of it, and nursing was, too.

I think the ideal reason why women have children is to give their child what they understand about the world and to offer it. Clearly, that's what I do every day. Here's what I understand, here's what I know of the world—here, you take it; do with it what you want. If it's useful, good; if not, dump it.

There's a whole range of nurturance outside of maternity and I don't think enough people recognize it.

Some women, because they did not have children, were available to nieces and nephews who needed them at critical times. Many also recalled themselves having been strongly influenced by a childless aunt who made them feel special. In turn, some became surrogate aunts/mothers.

Fran, fifty-four, for example, the financial consultant who was always too independent to marry, raised her teenage niece and nephew for ten years because her sister had such a tough time with them. Fran said that although she is not a mother, she has certainly parented, and that "having them, I would say, has satisfied 99 percent of any maternal longings I might have had."

Sixty-nine-year-old Hilda also helped raise a niece and nephew for nine years when her sister-in-law abandoned her four- and six-year-olds. Today, Hilda calls them, "my kids," and her niece expects her to be there when she has her baby next year. Said Hilda: "They consider me their mother. They take me out on Mother's Day, call me several times a week, and so on."

Other women, though they didn't raise a child in their homes, mentioned a special niece or nephew with whom they had unique relationships. Linda, thirty-nine, a "postponer" who never will have her own children, regularly talks to her twenty-year-old nephew on the phone:

> He's always been in trouble in school and like me, he's always been a little too mouthy for his own good. I feel very attached to him. He's come to live with us for weeks during the summer and I often talk to him. When things aren't going well with him, he'll tell me, and sometimes, just hearing my voice, he gets so choked up he can't talk.
>
> My younger brother—he's six years younger—is like my kid, too. He was always my baby, in a way. He just had a baby, and we're going to talk to him about being the child's guardians.

Linda has a commuter marriage with her husband, spending weekdays in a city three hours from home. Linda talked about her best friend, who lives there with three stepchildren: "I always spend at least one night a week with her family, helping her out. I take the kids roller skating, help her fourteen-year-old with his homework, tutoring him, helping him prepare for finals. I feel a part of her family." Linda has another friend with five teenagers; she and her husband make a point to connect regularly with the ones they feel especially close to.

Eighty-two-year-old Edith, who had an abortion during the depression, always adored and was adored in return by her cousins' children. Her beloved cousin is dead now, but Edith has regular contact with the kids: "These children—now in their forties—have always given me warmth like I've never seen. One of them wanted to help me move a few years ago, but I wouldn't hear of it. But they'd be available for me if I ever needed them. I know they would."

Betty, seventy-two, married and voluntarily child free, who never, ever, had an urge for her own children, feels very connected to her sister's children:

> I've always been very close to the children in our family. My sister died ten years ago and her children are grown, but my nieces live nearby. I talk to them every day, and see them at least once a week. I won't have to turn to them when I get old—in fact, they'd turn to me.

Other women take a broader approach to expanding their social networks and connections with younger people, feeling satisfied with more casual and occasional contact. Seventy-four-year-old Grace Downs, for example, lives down a country road from her brother and sister-in-law. Grace and her husband had no children, but they'd house one or two out-of-state college hockey students in their farmhouse for a year. Grace continued the tradition after her husband died nineteen years ago. This upcoming year, though, Grace was planning something different: her favorite niece was going to move in because she'd been accepted to a college nearby. Grace had offered to not only help pay tuition but to share her home. She looked forward to how the relationship might develop.

Some women, however, like Marjory Stoneman Douglas, the

environmental writer and crusader from the first chapter, has no nieces or nephews. Ms. Douglas, in fact, doesn't have any relatives left. She said she doesn't miss having them either. When she reached her eighties, however, she needed some help and enjoyed the developing friendship with a forty-year-old neighbor who helped her read her mail, get to the doctors, etc. She struck up a sort of deal with him: in exchange for being her "surrogate" caregiver in her aging years, he would become an heir.

Some women chose not to have children because they didn't want the responsibility and caregiving that goes into raising children. And they didn't want others to think that they needed a dose of kids every so often. When Lisa, the forty-six-year-old weaver who originally thought at twenty-six that she had to have a baby to quit working, answered a question about whether she had developed any special relationships with younger persons, she replied:

> I almost resent the question. It's assumed because we don't have children, we want to be involved with other people's children. People feel that we should be exposed to their children because we are missing that aspect in our lives. Well, if I wanted it, I would have had one.
> One friend to me, "Wouldn't you like to watch my son play baseball?" No, I wouldn't—people assume that you need children, that you should get involved with children or youth groups if you don't have any. That's more acceptable to them than someone who doesn't want much to do with children.

Lisa had, in fact, several special relationships with friends' children—one was a young woman going to college nearby who was far from home, and the others were two orphaned teenagers of one of Lisa's best friends who had died of cancer several years ago. But she still resented friends assuming that she yearned for contact with youngsters.

Nina Silver, the thirty-eight-year-old divorced, child-free musician and writer on the verge of remarrying, took perhaps the broadest view on family and friends. After a childhood of sexual abuse by her father, and both parents denying the abuse years later when she confronted them, Nina has turned away from her nuclear family with the exception of one half-brother. She has redefined the meaning of family for herself:

> My family is humanity. My nurturing is in my daily compassion-
> ate dealings with people and in my performing musical and nonmu-
> sical writings in which I strive for intimacy, vulnerability, and the
> sharing of new ideas and spiritual openness for social change.

Nina planned to put much of her nurturant energies into her new husband, a path that several women took. Others said their aging parents needed them and sapped most of their caregiving energies. Other women found less traditional routes to nurturing and guiding. Denise, for example, who gradually adopted a child-free lifestyle after years of infertility, started an infertility support group ten years ago. Today, she considers it her extended family and career:

> When we speak publicly on child-free living, we always suggest
> that people nurture something. A lot of the nurturing my husband
> and I do is throughout support groups and hotlines. Many have had
> or adopted children, and I enjoy them and feel sort of responsible
> for them in some ways. I've come to learn that a person can be a
> mother as a nurturer without having her own children.

Denise emphasizes that most people should recognize their need to nurture or nourish whether it be through other people's children or parents, pets, plants, friends, or senior citizens. "If you're living child free and you don't have nurturant relationships in your life, you're missing a lot," she said.

Many women, however, felt fulfilled by putting all their social and nurturant energies into adult-centered lifestyles that didn't call for children. Their network of friends, often formed through neighborhoods and community contacts, had grown into their extended family networks. Sylvia, for example, has lived in the same neighborhood ever since her childhood, and she has no plans of ever leaving it: "I've known these people forty and fifty years; we're a close-knit group."

A few women turned to their church, not only for solace, but as the route to enlarging their kinship networks. Florence, fifty-three, childless due to unexplained infertility, got involved with her church fifteen years ago. After working full time as a bookkeeper every day, Florence goes out almost every night to a church activity, including Bible study, meetings, and Bingo. Kids are at most of the meetings, and she usually ends up holding one of her favorites. Two days a week she visits elderly women in nursing homes. Said Florence: "Our church is a very close-knit group. It doesn't matter what age you are, we're there for each other and these people will be there for me, should I ever need it."

A variation of churches for the nineties, in fact, may be self-help groups. More than twelve million Americans help themselves by belonging to one of the half-million groups across the country. They focus on problems ranging from drugs and drinking to gambling, overeating, and surviving incest, cancer, surgical menopause, and mastectomies. These groups not only bring people together on a regular basis and give them a place to belong, but they also give them a place to express their emotions, fears, and weaknesses, to provide an opportunity for them to nurture and help others, and to forge ties, a common identification, and goals with others.[4] Several of the women I interviewed used such groups to not only help them with their problems and/or addictions, but also to provide a regular source of support and social contact. Janice, forty-four, belongs to an overeaters self-help group; Julie, fifty-five, belongs to Emotions Anonymous; and Rosemary, seventy-two, has been a member of Alcoholics Anonymous for more than forty years.

Other women felt very fulfilled by community volunteer work. Gwen, thirty-seven and never married, had just signed up at two hospitals to "cuddle" abandoned babies; thirty-eight-year-old Lehn, married and child free, is a Brownie leader for a troop of six- to nine-year-old girls; Susan, forty-one, shows movies on social issues to teenagers in a juvenile detention center and leads discussions with them; Hilda, sixty-nine, continues to write million-dollar grants and work daily for early intervention programs to prevent teen pregnancies; Sylvia volunteers full time planning jumbo fundraising events for the Red Cross and her community cultural center; and Marjory Stoneman Douglas at one hundred continues to lecture widely and write articles about saving the Florida Everglades.

Helping others provides an important source of inner strength and social contact, according to researchers at the Institute for the Advancement of Health in New York. People who help others are not only less socially isolated but have been found to gain important health benefits, too: "It now appears that the brain cannot do its job of protecting the body without contact with other people. It draws vital nourishment from our friends, lovers, relatives, lodge brothers and sisters, even perhaps our co-workers and the members of our weekly bowling team," write psychologist Robert Ornstein and physician David Sobel in *The Healing Brain* (Simon and Schuster).

Other women are still searching for their way of bestowing a part of themselves to the world. One woman is thinking about sponsoring a poor child in a developing country; another a foster child. "I suppose some lucky people know what they want to give from the beginning, others search for a long time, and still others never find it," says Cheryl Merser, author of *Grown-Ups: A Generation in Search of Adulthood*. "But there's a need for all sorts of gifts, and there'll be time to find one; it's not as if we're shopping for a world that already has everything."[5]

Other women felt they were still in the decision-making process of how to expand their networks: one woman who had had no contact with her brothers for twenty years was now making a concerted effort to see them and their children more often. Another in her early forties, just six months after a tubal ligation, was now seriously considering the adoption of an older child. She had no regrets about her sterilization, for she felt she was too old to go chasing after a toddler, but she and her new husband had a strong desire to expand their family.

Interestingly, adoption holds a special symbolic meaning for child-free women, Jean Veevers found in her landmark study of child-free couples, *Childless by Choice*. Many couples she studied mentioned that they always thought they might adopt sometime in the future, a theme that cropped up from time to time in the interviews for this book. Cathy, forty-one, first mentioned in

Chapter Eight, still clung to the hope that her second husband, sixty-two, may someday be willing to take in a foster child; Jill Layton, forty and stricken with multiple sclerosis, said that one of her greatest regrets is that she never had the guts to adopt an older child. Ilene, fifty, said that she and her lesbian partner talk about foster care often:

> It's a recurring theme for me. Being a mother was something I chose not to do, but when I read about abuse in foster care, I get a little tug, "Why don't you help out?" I don't know if we will or not, but we discuss, say no, then discuss it again. Right now, our builder, who has adopted a couple of foster children, told us his church is looking for foster homes. I don't know if we'll do it or not.

Although few ever actually adopt or take on foster children after years of voluntarily child-free living, Veevers felt that such thinking allowed the child free to feel that the door was always open so that their child-free decision and lifestyle would not seem irrevocable.[6]

Whereas many women over forty said that the doors to having children were shut for them, Judy Long believed that she could always change her mind:

> I have no regrets about not having children. It's absolutely been the best decision for me, and besides, it's always reversible. If I wanted to reorganize my life, I could certainly take in a child at any time and raise him or her.

Pets

Another very important source of nurturing and emotional satisfaction for many women was pets. Veevers found that voluntarily child-free couples had pets at about the same rate as other couples—about two-thirds had pets, but that only a small minority, however, considered their pets "surrogate children."[7]

About three-quarters of the women interviewed for this book had pets; of that group, two out of three adored their animals, considering them important substitutes for children.

A few turned to horses as the objects of their love. Terri discovered her passion for horses after years of infertility.

I've never had real career aspirations. Instead, I've put those energies into nurturing animals. There's nothing more fulfilling to me
than my horses. I bred my mare, raised the baby, whose birth I
missed by ten minutes. They totally fulfill me. I spend every day
with the baby who's three now. There's an intimacy there that I
can't get anywhere else, and it absolutely fulfills me.

In fact, more and more Americans—with or without children—consider their pets true members of their extended family.
"More than two out of three Americans think of their pets as family
members; some twenty percent in surveys say they are as important
as a child," Dr. James Wilson 3d of the University of Pennsylvania
School of Veterinary Medicine told the *New York Times*.[8] And a
growing body of research backs him up. Pets can play a critical role
in the emotional and physical well-being of their human owners,
according to a 1988 National Institutes of Health report. Animal
companions not only provide an important source of social stimu-
lation and reliable companionship (in some cases more reliable
than family members), but they also fulfill an emotional and social
void in many Americans' lives, according to the NIH report.[9] And
other research has suggested that pet owners are not only happier
and healthier but need medical care less often.[10]

Terri has a puppy, too. Dogs, in fact, seem to be the best
pet "stress buffer," research suggests, because they are so responsive and relationships with them tend to be the closest.[11]
Gail, the forty-three-year-old consultant who had her tubes tied
at age thirty-four, freely admits that her two kennels of Golden
Retrievers—one in the garage and one in the house—are "un-
questionably a substitute for children."

I raise them, show them, adore them. Around the time of the
sterilization, I raised a litter and kept several dogs from it. In looking
back, I think I kept all these dogs from that period of time as an
unconscious substitution.

Louise, a forty-two-year-old Manhattan executive secretary,
married and voluntarily child free, said:

I'm a devout animal lover, most especially dogs. I have a five-
year-old yellow Labrador who means the world to me and I suppose
he is somewhat of a "substitute child." However, he only requires

being played with, walked, fed, and loved. He doesn't require the one-hundred-percent emotional involvement that a human child does, for the rest of the parent's life.

Judy Long denied that her Siberian husky or Siamese cat were surrogate children ("They're members of the family!"), and she repeatedly interrupted our interview to coo to one of them and make sure they were comfortable. Barbara, the forty-eight-year-old businesswoman who suffered from years of endometriosis before she put her infertility behind her, said her pets run her life:

They're spoiled rotten. When the decorator came to redo this couch for $7,000, I told her, don't even bring me a fabric they can't come in on. One dog chewed a Chinese rug. Oh well! They rule me. This dog goes everywhere with me. When we go away—which we do often—they never go to kennels. I hire housesitters and I'm so picky you wouldn't believe it. The cat upstairs, she's nineteen years old and has never been in a kennel. The dog sleeps in the four-poster guest bed!

Only two women said that if they weren't willing to have the responsibility of a child, they certainly weren't interested in the responsibility of a pet. Said Lisa:

No way, we don't want pets. We don't garden; we won't even buy a house. All those things that require time or nurturing would be a tug on our freedom. We just don't want the responsibility. My husband says he'll never own anything he has to feed or paint.

Yet, Lisa still considered herself a nurturant person—with her husband, her women friends, and a few of her friends' children.

Friends

And finally, many women, especially single women, said that their friends were their most important kinship link. Many younger women (in their thirties and forties), however, felt they'd drifted away from friends who had become mothers and tended to form new friendships with other women without children. Their friends with children were just too distracted to put the energy and attention into the friendship. "My social circles have most definitely changed as a result of my not having children," said Candice, the forty-three-year-old divorced financial officer for a law firm.

> In most cases, friends having children has terminated the friendship. The person is just not available the way he or she was before and very often their conversation changes from the interests we had in common to babytending—a subject in which I have no interest. Usually after I delivered the shower gift, said itchy-kitchy-coo once, and admired a set of snapshots, we saw no more of each other.

Younger women were split about whether they felt a particular kinship with other women without children vs. just finding less and less in common with friends who were mothers. Women with infertility problems often found it too painful to spend a lot of time with families with young children. Voluntarily child-free women, on the other hand, found it too annoying. Said Linda, thirty-nine, who postponed children indefinitely:

> My husband and I just find ourselves gravitating to people who don't have children or whose children are grown. We had good friends with two kids, but they wouldn't ever leave them with a babysitter, not even to go to good restaurants. It got to be such a pain in the neck, we stopped seeing them.

Natalie, age thirty-eight and voluntarily child free, sounded wistful when she spoke of her old friends:

> When my friends have kids, their lives change. One by one, I see them get really tied down, and it definitely changes our relationship. There just aren't a lot of things you can do with them. You end up going to their house, but they're really distracted. You stop going to the movies together; you stop going away together on weekends.

Younger career women found their friendship network often developed through co-workers. Whether the women had families didn't matter because the work environment never included them. Gail has always entertained a lot on the job: "I interact with so many women in nonfamilial situations and have so many friendships that way that people's children are secondary to what I know about them."

Janice, the forty-four-year-old attorney said:

> Several of the other lawyers I work with are women with children and I'm good friends with some of them. But I hardly ever see their children. When we spend time together as couples, we usually meet for dinner in a restaurant or go to the theater or movies. They sometimes talk about their children, but they know that's not a common thread between us and don't focus on it much. We have a lot of work issues to talk about instead.
>
> On the other hand, I've drifted away from some of my old friends who have become mothers. We used to share all our problems together, and now all their problems are related to their having children, and we just feel too different now.

By the time women are in their fifties, however, having or not having children seems to matter less and less. The children are grown and either living away from home or living very independent lives if they are at home (as are almost one-quarter of America's twenty-one- to twenty-four-year-olds!). Women without children feel more valued again by mothers at this stage, especially if they're friends at work. The middle-aged mothers are more focused on re-establishing careers, a domain that women without children had successfully traversed. They were also interested again in a social life that didn't involve children. What was most important at this stage in life was whether friends were married or not. Without much exception, single women tended to socialize with other single friends, widowed or divorced, and couples stuck with couples.

Never-married women and long-time single women particularly valued their friendships, counting on them for long-term intimacy and involvement, commitment, and reciprocity.[12] Some were starting to plan to grow old with such friends. Diane, a divorced forty-three-year-old middle-level executive, said that her closest friends were single and childless, too. "My girlfriends and I have all decided we'll be a support group for each other." They talk about how they'll retire together and not have to worry about being alone. Lesbians, too, were particularly confident of their friendship circles and had definite plans to settle in one of the lesbian retirement communities that were starting to form.

None of the older women interviewed cared anymore whether their friends had children or not. Companionship at this point was more a function of whether other women were widowed yet or not. Many of these older women, however, had come from large families and relied on siblings and their spouses and children for intimate relationships. Today's younger woman without children is more apt to be from a smaller family and won't have as large a kinship network as the older women interviewed. It is too early to tell whether or not they will form intimate connections with friends and successful alternative network systems.

CHAPTER THIRTEEN

Wealth, Health, and Time to Enjoy Them

He is free who lives as he chooses.
—EPICTETUS

No man is free who is not master of himself.
—FRANCIS BACON

Women without children undeniably have two valuable resources that women with children very often complain about not having: money and time. This chapter will explore how women without children may have what is comparable to winning up to a million-dollar lottery and having three months more a year in leisure time to enjoy it. It will also explore some of the health differences found between women who have never had children vs. women who have.

On Money and Careers

Money, of course, contributes to both the freedom and control women without children feel they have over their lives. Although only a few women considered the cost of children as a primary deterrent for not having them, most women acknowledged that they fully appreciated the extra money they knew they had, though few could imagine just how much that was. In fact, women without children have the equivalent of winning a lottery valued at $250,000 to $1 million (depending upon their lifestyles and incomes).

Cost of Raising Children

The U.S. Department of Agriculture estimates that a *no-frills* kid, i.e., one receiving just the basics, costs the *average* consumer more than $100,000 to raise to age eighteen, and another $100,000 for college. The nonprofit organization, Zero Population Growth (ZPG) reports that a no-frills child costs $150,000 plus $160,000 for a private college, or $77,000 for an in-state public college.[1] All piano and swimming lessons, computer toys, sports equipment and uniforms, halloween costumes, camps, birthday parties and presents etc. are extra.

For upwardly mobile baby boomers, however, who earn more than $50,000 (a reasonable income for an average two-career couple), the cost climbs to one-quarter of a million dollars without college: $264,249 to be exact, according to *Money* magazine, for food, clothing, and shelter for twenty-one years. With two kids, the savings are minimal: each child will cost $209,500 instead.

When *Money* (July 1990) calculated some of the extras many baby boomers spend on their children, the price tag doubled and even tripled (and included a six percent average annual inflation). Crib-to-college costs for parents easily hit $600,000 and more (see sidebar).

Costly "Extras" Many Boomer Parents Spend on Their Kids

• Preschool child care/nursery school: With fifty-seven percent of families earning dual incomes and another quarter of households headed by single parents, many young children need day care. Four years of group care costs an average of $24,000; four years of in-home care, $63,000.

• Piano lessons, five years: $5,000.

• Private education: $143,000, grades K–12.

• A four-year Ivy League college education: $300,000 (includes a seven percent annual inflation rate, and would require an $8,000 annual investment earning nine percent annually for a 1990 baby;

if the investments were to begin when the child enters first grade, the annual investment needed would be $15,400 a year!).[2]

To calculate the cost of children at different income levels, economists estimate that one child costs up to thirty percent of a family's annual income. In other words, a child-free couple needs to only earn sixty percent of what a two-child family needs to maintain the same standard of living. Having a child, therefore, may not only mean giving up a lifestyle, but a standard of living as well.[3]

But that's not all. If a parent, usually the mother, quits her job to stay home with her child, her lost income—the "lost opportunity cost"—needs to be factored in. Highly educated women can estimate that cost to be about three times the direct costs to raise a child. For a middle-class family to raise a no-frills child costing $125,000 (the average between the U.S. Department of Agriculture and ZPG's estimates), the lost opportunity for mom to stay home is therefore estimated at $375,000,[4] a luxury fewer and fewer families can afford.

The Indirect Costs of Raising Children

The cost of having children to a woman's career, however, cannot be so easily calculated. If a woman takes five years off for childrearing, what are her chances of climbing her career ladder as quickly as the woman who takes no time off? Does having children cost women top jobs? Does it shift women from the steep career ladder to the flatter "Mommy Track?" According to a 1980 Urban Institute report on the impact of children on family well-being, research confirms that "there is a loss of wages as a result of dropping out of the labor market, and the longer the time out, the larger the loss."[5] Women without children are disproportionately at the top: *Ms.* magazine reported in 1989, for example, that sixty percent of the top female executives don't have children.[6] Of those under forty, sixty-five percent don't have children (compared with only ten percent of male executives).[7] And a Harvard economist predicts that as career women increasingly think of themselves as executives who might happen to have children—rather than as mothers who have careers—up to thirty percent of women managers will not have children.[8]

In general, couples without children earn fifteen percent more than couples with children.[9] For couples between twenty-five and thirty-four years of age, the difference jumps to twenty-four percent, according to *American Demographics*.[10] And for women managers of comparable educational status, those with children earn about twenty percent less.[11] If you consider the difference over time, say, for a mother earning $30,000, her childless counterpart would earn some $4,500 to $6,000 (fifteen to twenty percent) more each year—that's $81,000 to $108,000 over the next eighteen years, not counting inflation!

Add all these various factors together, and you can see how a woman without a child may enjoy a million dollars more to spend than the mother next door.

On Time and Travel

Not only does the married woman without children have thousands of dollars more to spend, but she also has another three months (twelve-hour, five-day work weeks) in leisure time a year; an unmarried woman without children has almost four more months of leisure to spend as she pleases.

A woman without children does an average of four hours less housework a week than a woman with children. That adds up to a total of 208 hours a year, or seventeen more vacation days (twelve-hour days) in saved housework each year.[12] (Other estimates of time spent on housework, though older, are even higher—515 hours [forty-three days] of housework a year for one-child families, 719 hours [sixty more twelve-hour days] more housework a year in two-child families).[13] In making a comparison between married with unmarried women, the average married woman does 7.5 hours more housework a week (that's 390 hours or thirty-two days a year) than her unmarried counterpart.[14]

When a woman has children, time is not only swallowed by more housework, but also by child care. Women with children, employed and non-employed, spend another average ten to eleven hours per week taking care of children. That's another 520 hours a year or forty-three days worth of child care activities.[15]

If the children are preschoolers, the differences are even greater. Mothers of preschoolers spend four more hours a week in child care and 7.5 hours a week in housework than women without children. That's 11.5 hours a week, or the equivalent of fifty more days a year for the childless counterpart to enjoy avoiding housework and child-care responsibilities.[16]

And the women's movement hasn't helped much, according to a recent work by sociologist Arlie Hochschild. Ten years ago, career mothers thought they were having it all, but the truth is, they were (and still are) doing it all; well, at least almost all. Husbands do about twenty percent of the cooking, cleaning, and laundry, compared with eight percent in 1965.[17] That's a great improvement, but there's still a long way to go.

Women are stuck in a "stalled revolution," Hochschild says after studying how fifty two-career couples coped with housework and child care. Whereas these wives thought they had fairly equal relationships when their wedding bells rang, Hochschild found that working women do a "double shift," that there was a giant gap between how much housework and child care today's modern mothers thought they'd do after children, and how very much more they actually did. After women got home every night, they'd do another equally arduous shift of work. She calculated that working women end up doing fifteen hours more housework and child care each week than their husbands—in a year, that's *a month more of twenty-four-hour days*, and in a dozen years, it's an extra *year* of twenty-four-hour days.[18]

What do women without children do with all the extra money and time? Many of the women interviewed have traveled far and often. Others have built "dream houses" they helped design and build. Although many women without children have strong career commitments, many women interviewed for this book used their extra money and time to leave nine-to-five jobs, either setting up their own freelance endeavors or not working at all for months at a time. This finding is consistent with a study comparing child-free vs. parental couples. It found that over time, child-free women who had stated in their mid-twenties that careers were a primary motivation for not having children had, indeed, shifted their priorities away from careers by their mid-thirties.[19]

Another study of fifty-seven child-free couples and fifty-five parental couples (average age thirty) in Canada tried to find out whether child-free couples actually took advantage of their freedom and spontaneity. It found that four out of five of the child-free women were so committed to pursuing their career goals (compared with only half the mothers), that they were not in fact "jet-setters" globe-trotting around the world. The study also reported no significant differences between the two groups in travel, recreational activities, and formal group participation. The child-free were, however, less organized and lived according to fewer plans than the parents. "Their reluctance to plan is consistent with their emphasis on being spontaneous and avoiding routine."[20] Over time, however, the researchers concluded that the child-free couples fell into their own routines to which they stuck to fairly regularly. As one woman interviewed for this book said, "We live a quiet, well-ordered life, and I like it that way."

In many ways, having children determines a way of life that not only includes more housework and child-care, but is comprised of, to a large extent, many child-centered activities that fill the day, from school sports and plays to lessons, homework, and driving the children to and fro. Life without children is much more undetermined and left open. How it's filled is up to the women involved.

On Health

Most medical research has focused on men in the past. And since women without children are an "invisible minority" to a great extent, even less research has focused on the health effects of not having children. One link that's been known for some time, however, is that *not* having any pregnancies is a risk factor for breast cancer. Women who have never given birth have two to three times the risk of getting breast cancer than women who had children before the age of thirty. The risk of breast cancer in women without children is about the same as for women who delay their first child until after age thirty, according to the National Cancer Institute.[21]

Evidently, there is no increased risk for breast cancer among women with infertility problems. Curiously, the risk increases for women, ages twenty-five to forty-five, who rarely have intercourse or who have partners with infertile semen.[22] Other risk factors are also important, however, including high social status, early onset of menstruation, late menopause, family history of breast cancer, obesity, and a high-fat diet.

Women without children may also be at higher risk for ovarian and/or endometrial (uterine) cancer. "With ovarian cancer, the thinking is that women whose ovaries are stimulated by repeated ovulations are at higher risk compared with women who've had ovulatory cycles interrupted by pregnancies," says Linda Carson, M.D., director of the Division of Gynecological Oncology at the University of Minnesota's School of Medicine.

With endometrial cancer, women who frequently don't ovulate appear to be at higher risk; women without children may be disproportionately represented among these patients since being anovulatory (not ovulating) is one cause of infertility.

It must be kept in mind, however, that not only are these epidemiological risks, not specific risks for a particular woman, but that other risk factors seem very important. In breast cancer, factors such as age, early menarche, late menopause, family history of breast cancer, late age of first childbirth, obesity, high-fat diet, and perhaps oral contraceptives and alcohol consumption also play important roles. For endometrial cancer, age, diabetes, high-blood pressure, early menarche, obesity, long-term intake of estrogen, early onset of menstruation, and liver diseases are also important risk factors.[23]

Women without children may be at higher risk for these diseases because of the longer exposure to the toxic effects of unopposed estrogen—during pregnancy, estrogen seems to somehow be neutralized or transformed to a less toxic state or even into a protective state. Women who never have pregnancies, therefore, are exposed to estrogen's toxic effect indefinitely, without any breaks from ovulating and stimulating the endometrium.

Older women without children (over age fifty), may also be at higher risk for sudden cardiac death (ischemia), a painless and undetected condition that affects tens of thousands of Americans each year. This tentative conclusion was drawn from a small case-controlled study of fifty-one female heart-attack patients over fifty and a control group that lived in the same region. Women without children were disproportionately represented among the victims: twelve, or almost one in four, of the victims had never given birth.[24]

The Framingham Heart Study suggested that married and divorced women were at higher risk for coronary heart disease than women who had never married. And that risk climbed with the number of children. Interestingly, female clerical workers were found to be at higher risk than professional women, but only if they had children.[25]

Some preliminary evidence also suggests that never having children may be a risk factor in having less bone mass, a precipitating factor for osteoporosis. Women with children seem to have more bone density, perhaps because of calcium deposition during pregnancy, higher hormone levels during pregnancy, and/or because mothers have had more weight-bearing exercise carrying the pregnancy and young children around, says Dr. Mona Shangold of the Hahneman School of Medicine in Philadelphia.[26] But again, other risk factors are important, including early menopause, low body weight, low calcium intake, lack of exercise, alcohol use, and smoking.[27]

However, women without children may be at *lower* risk for stress incontinence, uterovaginal prolapse, lower back osteoarthritis, benign breast disease, and obesity (which is a risk factor in many diseases, including high-blood pressure, diabetes, heart disease, and cancer).

Women who do not go through pregnancy and vaginal childbirths are less likely to have their muscles on the pelvic floor damaged or stretched. When these muscles are injured or weakened, urine leakage during coughs, laughter, and exercise can occur, a very common problem among middle-aged women. Weakened pelvic muscles can also cause the uterus to fall into the vagina or flop backwards, and such prolapse can prompt a hysterectomy.

"There's definitely a marked difference in the rate of uterovaginal prolapse among women who've had or not had children," observes Wulf Utian, M.D., professor and chairman of obstetrics and gynecology at Case Western Reserve's medical school. "Though other risk factors such as chronic cough, obesity, smoking, hormone deprivation, and congenital factors also act on weakening up the tissues, the major promoting factor is childbirth."[28]

Dr. Utian says that he's also observed much more lower back osteoarthritis in women who've borne and raised children. Pregnancy and childbirth strains and can damage the spinal column; mothers also spend several years lifting children, carrying more groceries, etc—all activities that can strain the lower back.

Researchers suspect that the more pregnancies a woman has, the more weight she gains and the harder it is to take it off. One reason may be that the fewer children a woman has, the more likely she is to exercise, work in the labor force, and achieve a higher socioeconomic status. All these factors have been linked to reduced weight problems.[29]

Furthermore, divorced women may tend to be thinner. Although thinner people may marry more often (they're considered to be more attractive), marriage and parenthood tend to put pounds on, with its obligatory meals. Divorce, on the other hand, is so stressful that it may disrupt one's eating patterns and reduce the amount of social support to sit down for meals. One hypothesis is that married women without children are therefore probably thinner than mothers, whereas divorced women without children may be thinner yet.[30]

On overall health, the child free seem to have the upper edge, though studies conflict. One study that analyzed the health and well-being of 2,480 married urban couples concluded that "parenthood detracts from the physical and psychological health of husbands and wives, particularly among younger couples." Childless couples ranked highest on health and well-being (factors such as physical disabilities, impairments, chronic illness, and other physical problems), "empty nesters" next, and active parents the lowest, according to a University of Arizona sociologist.[31] In the older segment of the sample, however, childless women were found to report poorer health, presumably because many were involuntarily childless due to physical problems, compared with younger couples in which a greater proportion are voluntarily childless.

Another analysis looked at a sample of 338 elderly persons, comparing parents with nonparents. Adults who never had children were not only better off financially, but also "in terms of health, the childless both are in better health and are more satisfied with their health than parents," concluded the sociologist in the Canadian study.[32]

However, when the effects of children on well-being were analyzed in 5,000 households annually throughout the 1970s, researchers from the Urban Institute in Washington, D.C., found no evidence that motherhood was connected with physical disabilities. The only link they did uncover was that women who already had physical problems were less likely to have children.[33]

Although no differences have been observed in age at which menopause occurs, symptoms of menopause, or differences in dosage of hormone replacement necessary after menopause, Dr. Utian said that some evidence suggests women without children have fewer complaints during the change of life, as do women with higher incomes, higher educational levels, and women who have never married.

Researchers have found marital status linked to overall health and longevity, yet no one evidently has looked into fertility and longevity. What has been uncovered is that divorced and separated men and women have the worst health, widowed people the second worst, and then single people; married persons tend to be the healthiest and to live the longest.[34] And these relationships hold true even when individuals live with someone other than a spouse.[35] But the National Center for Health Statistics has not looked into women's fertility status and longevity. Although one may guess that women without children may have overall less physical and emotional stress during their lives, especially professional women who do not find it difficult to support their single-headed household, whether this impacts on health and lifespan has not been studied. "These are really good questions, but I don't think anyone knows the answers," says Dr. Utian. "There's so little investigation into the health status of women in any group, much less into women without vs. women with children. If we could identify differences between the two groups, we might be able to prevent or counsel women to prevent additional risk factors but, at this point, nobody knows the answers to these questions."

So women without children have a lot more time and a lot more money than other women, and a mix of health risks and benefits. These are some of the more tangible advantages and risks to not having children. But many of the costs and benefits are intangible. Next is a summary of the intangible pros and cons of what it's like not to have children.

CHAPTER FOURTEEN

The Ups and Downs of Child-Free Living

> You gain some things by having children and you lose
> some things when you have children. There are costs and
> benefits either way. There's no free lunch. You make
> choices and you live through the consequences of them.
> You can't have it both ways.
>
> —LAURA, 45

Just as parenting is a mixed bag, so is life without children. Whatever a woman's balance is between the rewards and the drawbacks
of childlessness, however, will largely determine her sense of liberation vs. deprivation in living without motherhood.

This chapter will not only talk about the emotional and psychological costs and benefits to not having children, but also about
feelings regarding control vs. risk in women's lives. It will also
explore happiness and marital satisfaction differences among
women with and without children and address some times in
women's lives that were described as particularly difficult by some
because they didn't have children.

Relishing the Rewards

Whether women were resolute in never wanting children or sor-
rowful because they wanted but couldn't have children, almost
every woman interviewed for this book came to appreciate the
rewards of child-free living. The rewards were many:

• Exhilarating freedom and independence, and the ability to be spontaneous: "Freedom to live my life as I want without the demands and pulls that children make"; "The ability to control my own life"; "I can use all my time as I want"; "Freedom to pursue my career without having to worry about how it's affecting a child."

• Avoiding the stresses and responsibilities of being a parent, such as fighting with the kids; problems with drugs, alcohol, discipline, health, school, peer pressure, pregnancy, etc.; worry over children getting physically and/or emotionally hurt; "Freedom from worry about having screwed up someone else's life."

• Avoiding the day-to-day drudgery of cleaning, laundry, cooking, shopping, child care, and other incessant demands of children.

• Avoiding the pain and disappointment of having children who don't meet your expectations.

• Freedom from financial worry; enjoying more money.

• Enjoying an exceptionally intimate relationship with your mate, spending more time with your mate, avoiding the hassles with your mate about childrearing.

• Freedom to indulge a lifestyle without having to work too hard or make too much money.

• Not having to disrupt an already fulfilled and busy life.

• Ability to pursue careers, education, and other creative outlets; ability to continue in a learning, self-growth role rather than a teaching role.

As Deanna expressed it:

No messes, no school hassles, no friends running through the house, no worries for their health and lives, no added expenses, doing whatever we please when we please, sleeping late, staying up late, going where we want when we want, no drug problems, no teen pregnancies, no financial burdens with young marriages or babysitting their kids. Not watching them die either!

More than one woman referred to the following letter to Ann Landers; although cutting and sarcastic, it still struck a chord with several women:

There's nothing sadder than the childless couple. It breaks your heart to see them stretched out, relaxing around swimming pools . . . suntanned and miserable on the decks of boats, trotting off to Europe like fools with money to spend, time to enjoy themselves and nothing to worry about.

Childless couples become so selfish and wrapped up in their own concerns that you feel sorry for them. They don't fight over the kid's discipline. They miss all the fun of doing without for the child's sake. It's a pathetic sight.

Everyone should have children. No one should be allowed to escape the wonderful experiences that come with each stage of development. The happy memories of those early years: saturated mattresses; waiting for sitters who don't show up; midnight asthma attacks; rushing to the emergency room to get the kid's head stitched up.

Then comes the payoff, when the child grows from a little acorn into a real nut. What can equal the warm smile of a small lad with the sun glittering on $2,500 worth of braces—ruined by peanut brittle. Or the ear-splitting shrieking of twenty hysterical savages running amok at a birthday party?

How empty is the home without challenging problems that make for a well-rounded life and an early breakdown. The nightly reports from your wife are like strategically placed blows to the temple. And when the report cards come, you have to face the truth—your senior son is a moron.

Children are worth every moment of anxiety. You know it the first time you take your son hunting. He didn't mean to shoot you in the leg. Remember how he cried? He was so disappointed that you weren't a deer.

See what the years have done to the childless couple. He looks boyish, unlined and rested. She is slim, well-groomed, and youthful. It isn't natural. If they had kids they would look like the rest of us—depressed, worn out, and haggard. In other words, normal.[1]

The Sobering Drawbacks

But not having children also has a handful of serious drawbacks, some women said. These include:

• Never knowing the experience of pregnancy, childbirth, nursing, and raising a child.

- Missing the sharing, growing, day-to-day exchanges involved in raising a child; missing out on the joy and love they can bring.
- Having no one to pass on values, talents, family heirlooms and memories, or the family lineage.
- Having no grandchildren.
- Fearing that regret will grow in the future.
- Fear that old age will be lonely with no child to lean on.
- Depriving parents of becoming grandparents.
- Losing friends who become preoccupied with parenting.
- Coping with social disapproval; feeling left out of a family-centered society.
- Occasional feelings of sadness and loneliness.

Deanna again summed it up well. Still living in the gloomy shadow of infertility, the drawbacks sting her sharply:

> Not giving my husband a child, not loving or caring for them, not playing with and enjoying them, not having them on holidays, not having grandchildren, tolerating other mothers "baby/child" talk, missing out on all the love and joy they seem to bring.

Of course, many child-free women do not view these factors as losses or deprivation but as freedoms. For them, not having children was and remains the most natural and obvious thing to do. Not one of the almost two-dozen women who knew firmly in their twenties and thirties that they didn't want children felt any differently as they grew older. Perhaps, as the irrevocable nature of the decision became permanent, cognitive dissonance and rationalizations eased over any wrinkles of doubt that might have surfaced. But perhaps too, since these women made their decisions so conscientiously and deliberately, the decisions were the right ones for them. Chances are that the more choice a woman exerted in determining her childless/child-free status, the less she'll have lingering, agonizing doubts. "People are usually more committed and willing to defend a choice that is consciously and rationally made," says psychologist Jeffry Larson of Brigham Young University, who has studied the literature on voluntary childlessness.[2]

On Control and Risk

Regardless of whether a woman has chosen to not have children or whether she ever misses having a child or not, almost every woman interviewed for this book relished her freedom and the control over her life that not having children allowed her.

One of the scariest things about becoming a parent, after all, is the lack of control, for raising a child is unpredictable in a myriad of ways. People who need to feel "in control" may find the daily task of raising children very difficult. Those who insist on retaining control may exact a heavy toll on their children, while those who sense they're losing control may feel scared and unstable, and in extreme cases, anxious and depressed.

"This loss of control over self and future was the most frequently cited motive for wishing to avoid parenthood," found one researcher who studied forty-four child-free marriages. "Parents were described as 'losing control'; children as taking over and pulling the strings, jolting the parents into immediate, gratificatory action."[3]

Women who don't have children avoid many risks—the risk of having an emotionally or physically handicapped child, of disrupting their marriage, career, and/or lifestyle, of having to cope with drinking, drugs, premarital pregnancies, and devastating diseases. Women without children are also spared thousands of little worries and many major ones too—from junk food, TV trash, neighborhood bullies, team tryouts, and fights over pants that are too tight to problems with grades, accidents, health, and behavior. As the world seems to grow out of control—and beyond the control of parents—battered by crime, drugs, and diseases, and threatened by pollution, overpopulation, soil erosion, species extinction, overdevelopment, deforestation, even global war, and so on, the risks of bringing a child into such a world may feel overwhelming. Also, women without children don't have to worry or cope with the strain of trying do it all, becoming harried, hurried, and hassled in the process.

Having a child, after all, takes a giant leap of faith and in many ways is a higher risk today for women than it used to be. More mothers than ever have to work outside the home, juggling the demands of marriage, kids, and a career. Raising kids is harder in our drug-torn, violence-prone, nuclear-armed, media-blitzed society. Women are also more likely to divorce than in years past, and when they do, are at much greater risk of becoming poorer and forced to struggle with raising children solo.

Said Hope, a voluntarily child-free fourth-grade teacher:

> Raising kids is scary. I don't know how people make the decision to have kids; they must have a built-in self-confidence. I think it's a heck of a responsibility to be responsible for someone's basic personality, how happy they are with themselves, their self-esteem. I feel very relieved I don't have to worry about those stresses.

Some women didn't have children because it was the least risky alternative, often the path of least resistance. Some didn't marry because they weren't sure about the potential of the marriage; some didn't risk getting pregnant with a particular husband or at a particular time because the risk seemed too great; others feared how a baby might unsettle an already fulfilling marriage and lifestyle. Still others who considered adoption later backed off, again, avoiding such an unknown.

Yet, not having children has its own risks, as Kate Harper pointed out in her 1980 book, *The Child-Free Alternative*—the risks of being different than most people, of being misunderstood or devalued by others, of discovering later that missing this human experience might turn out to be more important than you thought. "You take the risks that any pioneer faces: getting lost, or finding once you get to where you are going, that it has not been worth the journey."[4] On the other hand, as we've seen, some mothers say the same thing.

Nevertheless, by avoiding motherhood, women without children can retain a strong sense of control over their lives and can take, instead, professional and recreational risks, or "scale down" to a simpler lifestyle. Linda, for example, upgraded her job every few years, moving hundreds of miles at a time and maintaining a commuter marriage on three different occasions. Lynn went to Denmark on vacation after her divorce and decided not to come back for twelve years. Janet, always single, just quit her job as a college administrator after working full time for twenty years and isn't too concerned about when she'll find another. At fifty, Ilene decided to "drop out" after years of working at a career that required a lot of travel. She's moved to the Oregon coast with her lover and now works part time as a caterer and in a bookstore.

Many mothers, of course, also make many changes and there's no way to actually compare the two groups. The point is that, although women without children may feel out of control when they're up against the clock, once they accept their child-free status and take advantage of it, they are bound to feel more in control. They can be masters of their own fate and fortune with typically much more money, time, and other resources on hand, compared to mothers.

On Happiness and Marital Satisfaction

But how do women fare in regard to happiness? satisfaction? With children, marital satisfaction forms a U-shape when mapped out—it's high at the beginning, dips down the entire time a couple raises children, and then edges back up when the kids leave home. Regardless of whether the kids were "good" or not, adopted or biological, "when the last kid leaves home, the marriage improves," says University of Nebraska sociologist Lynn White, who conducted an eight-year study funded by the National Institute on Aging.[5]

In general, couples without children, including the voluntarily child-free, "undecideds," and "postponers," are happier with their marriages than mothers. In general, the fewer financial hassles and the more the partners share chores, the happier the wives are. Mothers lose on both counts—they're under more financial pressure, and they've got more chores but less time and help to do them. Child-free wives, however, have fewer financial concerns and more equal marriages in terms of sex roles. As might be expected, researchers have found that wives in child-free marriages are happier.[6]

In sum, one reseacher put it this way:

Data on the health and well-being of couples . . . suggest[s]that parenthood detracts form the health and morale of husbands and wives, particularly among younger couples. This phenomenon is probably social rather than biological, since former parents (empty nesters) show less evidence of strain than active parents.

Childless marriages were more likely to be happy ones, even among the older couples for whom childlessness was associated with poor health; and the childless marriages tended to improve with time, while parents' marriages tended to deteriorate.[7]

Women with Infertility Problems

When couples have infertility problems, however, even happy marriages are badly shaken as the partners try to come to grips with this crisis. Studies have found, however, that their happiness edges back up over time. They communicate better with their spouses, share more opinions equally, and have fewer extramarital affairs than parents do.[8] In one study that compared mothers with voluntarily and involuntarily childless wives, the women with long-term infertility problems reported feeling less control over their lives. They also felt angry, frustrated and unfulfilled because they couldn't produce a baby and reported lower levels of psychological well-being. As might be expected, these wives felt that life was emptier and less rewarding than mothers and voluntarily child-free wives reported. At the same time, however, the involuntarily (as well as the voluntarily) childless wives—who on average had been coping with their infertility for five years—not only reported much more satisfaction with their freedom and flexibility, including privacy, relaxation, and feelings of independence, than the mothers did, but also *still* rated their marriages as happier, more satisfying and loving than the mothers did. Infertile women not only reported greater happiness in how they spent their free time, but also in how much friendship, love, affection, and respect they received in life.[9]

Overall, married men have been found to be in better mental health than married women—evidently because women are overloaded by their roles as mothers, wives, and daughters, while men "are taken care of" by their wives. When researchers tried to sort out more specifically why married women didn't fare as well, an interesting finding emerged: married women who worked were better off than married women who stayed home, and "having children in the household generally contribute[d] to poor mental health." Since work tends to boost a married woman's mental health, the researchers concluded that it was not necessarily the number of tasks that mothers must perform that affected their mental health, but rather the "incessant demands" of children, the craving for privacy and time alone, and feelings of loneliness contributing to frustration, alienation, and social isolation that tended to compromise a married mother's mental health.[10]

Hard Times

For women who are childless by default or for a combination of reasons—including infertility, bad timing, and husbands who don't want children—the issue of children may be more frequently laced with ambivalence and doubt, tension and anxiety. Although women approach resolution in middle age, some of the women who were content and satisfied with their lives, expressed certain times when they felt more vulnerable.

The Specter of Holidays

Although holidays represented no particular problems for many of the women interviewed, especially younger women whose parents were still alive and older women who had large extended family networks, holidays were more difficult for others, particularly for women with a history of infertility. Deanna, for example, said that holidays, including Mother's and Father's Days, are the hardest times. She doesn't live near any relatives, "So I make more Christmas or holiday goodies for my husband, but I feel lonely and sad. Christmas is the loneliest time!"

Margaret spoke of how she and her husband (victims of unexplained infertility) used to share the holidays with her mother who would fly in or with friends who invited them over. She has only one brother, married with no children, who lives far away and is emotionally distant. Recently, though, with her mother no longer alive, and most of her friends going to *their* children's homes for the holidays, Margaret and her husband have been alone.

> When I first realized we were going to spend Christmas alone, it was a shocker, and it loomed in my mind for weeks. What was it going to be like? I dreaded it. My husband said, "Well, we're a family, maybe the smallest you can have, but we're still a family." So I made the traditional dinner, and made many, many phone calls during the day to feel connected, and you know, although I was miserable beforehand, it was every bit as nice.

For Julie, a never-married woman, Christmas is the most difficult time. She's always invited to one of her brothers' homes, but she feels like the odd one out:

> I sometimes feel like I want to leave town at these times. I feel they feel they have to invite me so I'm not left alone. I feel like "Poor Old Aunt Julie" at these times.

Terri, who gave up the hope for children a decade ago when the doctors gave her a final verdict of permanent infertility, said:

> As time goes on, the need to have children is less and less, but there are times when it comes up, and it shocks you every time because you forgot about it. Like Mother's Day. You don't think about having children for a while, and then suddenly, the restaurants are jammed with everybody out for brunch or dinner. That's when I really feel left out of the norm.

As for the other holidays, Terri feels very comfortable having "been adopted" by friends with children: "We're always included as part of the family and we love the kids."

For Dorothy, with a history of infertility, the hardest time is Passover.

> Passover to me is a very important time. Usually we spend it with my brother-in-law, but this past year he and his wife went to their daughter's because she was expecting a baby. I got on the phone and started calling people. Everyone had plans with their children, and although some tried to make me feel good, inviting me to their children's, it's just not the same. That's when I feel a lack.

Many of the women interviewed went to relatives for Thanksgiving and Christmas; younger women usually went to their parents' if alive and still living in the home they grew up in. If their parents were elderly or deceased, the women tended to go to a sibling's home or to a niece's or nephew's if the women themselves were quite elderly.

Several women in their forties and fifties created their own holiday traditions, a strategy that some child-free-living proponents such as Merle Bombardieri, author of the Resolve fact sheet, "Child-Free Decision-Making" and the Carters in *Sweet Grapes* recommend. Some women, for example, invited over family members who didn't have children (because when children are involved, holidays are usually either held at their own homes or at a grandparent's) or with "alternative families," what one women called, a "widows' and orphans' Thanksgiving." She'd invite over single friends, friends without children, etc. "Now that my sister's kids are grown, though, we're talking about spending next year as volunteers in a soup kitchen for the homeless or elderly and making that a holiday tradition." One woman made it a point to travel during the Christmas holidays; another had an annual holiday party for adults.

Tammy talked of "cocooning" with her husband, but wonders what it will be like when she's older.

> I'll cook like crazy, and we'll spend Thanksgiving or Christmas or Easter with the VCR and a coffee table full of food. Cocooning is nice, but it's not "family" to me. My father, who is in his eighties, is my only real link to this whole family life. In years to come, when he's no longer around, it will be strange and difficult for me. I think that may be a time when I have some regrets about not having a family group/kids of my own.

Several of the women interviewed minimized the holidays. Lynn, for example, considers the holidays an opportunity to put her feet up and a time when no one will bother her. "Of course it feels okay," she said. "If it didn't, I'd go someplace. Holidays just don't mean anything to me, and teaching is such a demanding job that holidays mean days off for a break."

The Timeless Twilight Zone of "Peter Pan"

Some women observed that their not having children was sheltering them in a sort of ageless twilight zone. While mothers passed through stages of life through their children growing older, women without children said they felt much more "stageless." Also, not having to take on the duties of parenthood allowed them to stay childlike, even immature, creating a sort of female Peter Pan effect (not to be confused with the Peter Pan Syndrome, a psychological term used to describe men who won't grow up).

At a twentieth college reunion, Laura recalled that some of her classmates had kids going off to college, while a few came to the reunion pregnant. The discussions among the women weren't keyed into issues for women who are forty, but rather to the stages of their children. From infancy to preschool to Little League to a child getting her driver's license, a mother's life is strongly linked to these stages. She'll have much more in common with other parents who have children in the same stages regardless of her age. Without children, Laura felt not ageless, but agelessly free floating.

Most life-cycle and midlife research is organized around children and their stages; whereas parents go through transitions from one stage to the next, those without children seem much less likely to. A small study at Smith College of intentionally child-free couples in midlife, for example, found that the couples, unlike parents, observed no particular transitions in their lives together. [11]

Some women liked not being pushed into middle age by having children. Said forty-one-year-old Tammy, now married for the second time: "I *am* a kid. I'm in a kind of prolonged adolescence." When she remarried at thirty-five, she left her career as an advertising copywriter to work on her own at home. "Without a 'real' job, I try to keep my responsibilities to a minimum. I like to play. I still feel I have a lot of possibilities in my future, and I like the freedom I have."

Women who choose to be child-free are particularly apt to integrate their fantasy of staying as a child into their adult selves, says Carole A. Wilk, author of *Career Women and Childbearing*.[12] Ambivalent women, on the other hand, may be resisting having to grow up, suggests Wilk. These women may not only fight giving up the child side of themselves, but also their youth, their freedom for responsibility, and even the "pressure of having to deal with one's own finite life cycle."[13] Interestingly, some of the most ageless children's classics—*Peter Pan, Alice in Wonderland, Mary Poppins*, and the Dr. Seuss books—were written by authors who did not have children. Having a child, after all, requires that one forsake childhood and become a real grown-up.

Thirty-eight-year-old Natalie agrees with Wilk that remaining child-free allows her to never have to grow up:

> Somehow, if you have kids, it forces you to become an adult. You become the mom and you're the adult. One by one I see my friends get really tied down. I think there's probably a part of me that doesn't want to grow up. I don't want that kind of life. I'm still a kid and that's nice, although that's not part of my real decision not to have children.

Other women, though, were bothered by this Peter Pan effect of never having children. But Barbara couldn't quite put her finger on why it bothered her so much:

> I've never gone through the growing phases that my friends have. And it's not realistic this way. Everybody wants to be young forever, but one of the things that forces you along the way are children and their stages. But not having children, not going through the phases, you mentally stay put for a long time without even thinking about aging and phases. I don't think that's good. I don't know why for sure, but I don't think it's good.

Fear of Regrets

Some women had no regrets, but the one thing that continued to haunt them was whether they would in the future. "Am I making a big mistake? Will I grow to regret this?"

Every decision risks being regretted at some point. When a life decision is made and you proceed through that door, all the other paths through all the other doors are forever unknowns. You can never know what your life might have been like if you'd gone to a different college, married a different lover, taken a different job. But life's decisions aren't "wrong" or "right"; they are differing paths through which we have certain experiences, both good and bad, and learn lessons along the way. Though regrets about never having a child may haunt a woman from time to time, there's no way to know if that child would have been a blessing at a time needed most or a heartbreak. Just as a mother never knows what curves her life might have taken had she not made the irrevocable decision to have children, the child-free woman never knows the flip side of her irrevocable decision.

Janice, who always thought she'd be a less than perfect mother, fearing she'd be "distracted, impatient, resentful and overbearing," said that she's always been somewhat ambivalent about parenting: "But I think I'd feel far worse if I became a parent and *then* regretted it than sometimes regretting not doing it."

And indeed, some mothers do regret their parenthood. One 1960s study found that only three in one hundred mothers would definitely *not* do it again.[14] But in the early 1970s, when Shirley Radl interviewed 200 mothers for *Mother's Day is Over*, only six felt truly fulfilled by their mothering role and well-suited for the task of nurturing children. As for the vast majority of mothers, Radl reported:

> Many women come to feel, as I do, that the scales of motherhood do not really balance out for them, that the rewards of motherhood—and they are indeed there, and nothing here is meant to suggest otherwise—are not great enough to offset the difficulties and plain unpleasantness of so much of the job.[15]

Radl also wrote that while most mothers find joy in their children, they do not like motherhood.

In 1975, *McCall's* found that one in ten women would not have children if they could go back again.[16] When Ann Landers asked her readership in 1976 how they felt about doing it, a staggering seventy percent of the thousands of letters she received flatly said no, the rewards were too few and the sacrifices too great. Of course, the people who answered Landers were far from a representative sample. Eighty percent were women, and they were probably the ones who felt so strongly that they were compelled to respond.

What about other, less biased surveys? A 1978 *Better Homes and Gardens* survey found one in ten would choose to be child free.[17] According to *The Motherhood Report: How Women Feel about Being Mothers* and its study of 1,100 mothers of all ages, one in four of the mothers felt motherhood was basically great vs. one in five who said that being a mother gave them very little pleasure or rewards. The majority—fifty-five percent—said they were overwhelmingly ambivalent about the experience. The rewards of motherhood won out by a small margin, yet that "did not negate the tremendous difficulty, pain, and heartache of the role."[18]

The Motherhood Report also found that although almost half of the mothers felt loving and positive toward their children, fifteen percent had basically only negative feelings toward their kids with little, if anything, good to say; and another thirty-seven percent were fraught with ambivalence, caused by equally negative and positive feelings about their children.[19]

In the final tally, what was their bottom line? Would they do it again? "Motherhood is a living tapestry, with dark threads of frustration and stress interwoven with and inseparable from golden strands of joy."[20] Four percent said they would definitely not do it again; fifteen percent were uncertain.

Ellen, the forty-seven-year-old psychotherapist who knows she won't have children, said that she refuses to look over her shoulder and think about regrets:

> You can't go back, so why even think that way? I was the way I was and made certain choices. I don't want to live with regrets. Sometimes, I feel like Lot's wife: if I looked back I'd turn into a pillar of salt. Instead, I look ahead and seek ways to grow, be productive, and do things that are meaningful to me.

In her book, *My Mother, My Self*, Nancy Friday, herself married and child free, speaks of a female psychiatrist who tells her she will always regret never having had a child. Friday is instantly filled with anxiety until she collects her wits again: "Today, should a person talk about these regrets, my reply would be that I will never try skydiving, or be the president of the United States. These must be very fulfilling, too. I have learned to live without them."[21]

The Carters in *Sweet Grapes* stress that those who make active choices will be least apt to have regrets. The drifters, on the other hand, are most vulnerable to regret. They may spend years suppressing their feelings, avoiding the issue, never processing what not having children means for them, and therefore never getting to a stage of affirming, planning, and taking forthright advantage of a different life. Say the Carters: "Choice is the anchor that keeps you from drifting into regret. It is through choice that you come to embrace your life without children. . . ."[22]

An antidote to regret, or fear of regret ("anticipatory regret"), then seems to be making active choices to pursue goals that are challenging and meaningful. Wallowing in a pool of regret, or fear of regret, only paralyzes the swimmer; it is the sprinter who makes decisions and swims with them who will look back at a satisfying life well planned and well spent.

Death's Darkening Shadow

The most vulnerable time for any woman is when loved ones begin to die, especially a parent or husband. When a parent grows mortally ill, it is a daughter, the childless daughter if there is one, who typically provides the care required. Women who don't have children may feel particularly vulnerable at these times, thinking about who will be there for them when they're at this stage. When a parent dies, the childless daughter may be jolted into feeling her own mortality, her own adulthood now that the parent is no longer there to rely on, and her role in breaking the chain of perpetuating her family line.

The most difficult time, though, must be when a husband or mate dies. Four out of five of today's women can expect to outlive their mates by some sixteen years. Wives without children may be particularly hard hit because of the close interdependence and intimacy such relationships foster. Women with children have a bolster to get through the pain and isolation of the death and funeral itself although soon after, widows are largely on their own. Grown children must return to their families and jobs. Widows tend to turn to other widows for company and support. Women who have practiced the lifelong skill of reaching out to others—which never-married women have been found to be the most skilled at—whether they have children or not, will find themselves most at ease and with the most supports by continuing to reach out in widowhood.

Times of death are bound to bring on bouts of sadness, melancholy, and vulnerability. Of all the women interviewed, three got choked up, and these three all mentioned what seemed like a rash of deaths around them. They felt for the first time in their lives the gloomy shadow that the cloak of death can cast. Interestingly, none were widows; in fact, all were married. But for the first time in their lives, they said, they felt impacted by their childlessness in the face of deaths around them.

Barbara had had years of endometriosis during her thirties and couldn't adopt because she and her husband had different religions.

> By age thirty-six, my bleeding episodes finally stopped, and I realized then I wasn't going to be able to have children. But it wasn't an earth-shattering thing to me, especially not compared to finally being done with all that bleeding. I didn't cry, didn't go through any of that emotional stuff.
>
> For years I just didn't think about it. I was too preoccupied.

She was running the family business—her dad had died and her two older brothers lived across the continent—and going on three or four vacations a year ("We do that a lot! You know, Hawaii, different places in the Caribbean, cruises, whatever. Sometimes for a week, maybe two at a time"), having friends and family over to the family's lake summer house, running around town as an active member on the boards of several community organizations she believed in (NOW, president of the chamber of commerce, Martin Luther King scholarships, Planned Parenthood, church finance committee, and more), and eating dinner out almost every night (she never cooked because she hated it!).

And then, Barbara's brother-in-law was suddenly killed, and his widow and three children moved back to town. Barbara's sister-in-law went back to school and Barbara helped out with the kids. Then her father-in-law died. "Suddenly, we were saddled with two mothers and three kids and I never thought about having children after that," she said.

Barbara's mother's health continued to decline, first with a near-fatal heart attack. She needed around-the-clock care, which the family could fortunately afford, so Barbara found help but visited every day for five years. When her mother suddenly had a stroke and was put on a respirator against her plans and wishes, "I cannot tell you what I went through at that point. She was ninety-five percent brain dead and for a month I had to deal with the agony of obtaining a court order to 'pull the plug.' "

Within months of her mother's death, her brother died unexpectedly while traveling in Hong Kong. Although Barbara was still married to her husband of twenty years, it felt as if all her blood relatives were now dead—her other brother, who is ten years older, lives very far away and Barbara has very little contact with him.

My brother's death was another torture. It took three weeks to get the body back, and now I can't stop thinking about blood family. I know it's selfish on my part, but who can I count on? Who's going to care about the heirlooms here that have been in our family for nine generations, like my great-great-great-grandmother's quilt. My brother's kids don't care about it. I know I shouldn't worry about those things, but I do.

I worry about who's going to be around if I get sick; who'll arrange for things. Who's going to be there to say, "Put her in a nursing home"?. It's the blood family issue that concerns me most now.

When you think about what you do with your life, have I missed children? No. I'm really close with my close friends' kids; they call me aunt, and we always have their birthday parties at our summer house. I have nieces and nephews in town on my husband's side, and we always make sure my husband stays close to them. During the holidays, my best friend who's Jewish has always come, since we've been babies, to dig the tree and fight about the angel on top. I'm her children's godmother.

And we've always done really neat things. We've always had two houses, boats, we belong to the country club and yacht club, we eat out every night, always take vacations; we've never been on a budget or had to sacrifice.

But right now it's a crisis for me. You caught me at a bad time.

What are my regrets about not having children? Normally, they'd be a glimmer, but that glimmer's been real magnified lately. I think it'll pass, but now I worry.

I interviewed sixty-eight-year-old Dorothy at a similar time. She married when she was twenty-three, and never knew why she didn't get pregnant. By her mid-thirties, her doctor laughed when she asked for a diaphragm. By that time, she didn't want children.

I had really wanted children, but I learned to cope with it. Eventually, I decided this is what God had in mind for me. Okay. That's it. I remember other couples would tell us we didn't know how lucky we were. In my thirties, forties, and fifties, I didn't think about it much. I was able to live a very wonderful life; we could do a lot of things that our friends couldn't afford because they needed the money for children.

But in the past few years, several of Dorothy's closest friends as well as her parents have passed away. She finds herself getting melancholy from time to time about not having children and grandchildren.

Now, the most painful part of not having a child is looking into the future. At my age, the present is the future. It's a time in your life when the important things are your children and grandchildren, and everybody has the children and grandchildren, and we don't have the extended family.

But Dorothy's heart had opened to all the little children her friends did have. She had all their photos in a frame on her television and spent hours making needlepoint rainbows for their rooms, needlepoint tic-tac-toe sets, even needlepoint alphabet building blocks.

I happen to love children, I really do. I look at all the babies and see somebody else in them. But there will not be us—this is it, and that bothers me. What's going to happen to all of our photos, for example?

Forty-three-year-old Gail was also feeling vulnerable in the aftermath of her sister-in-law's sudden death. Suddenly she felt mortal as she realized her life was half over. For the first time in twenty years, she was wrestling with "the residuals" of her decisions and reassessing how she wants to spend the rest of her life. She's considering a geographical move, a career change perhaps. It's time, she says, to process the loss she never mourned, and to get on with her life. She knew she was entering a major transition in her life, but it was just beginning.

I'm suddenly seeing a lot of death now. You start hearing a lot more. A sense of loss is heightened and escalated by all the changes around you surrounding death, and it tends to dredge up whatever you didn't do in your life. All this stuff comes up now in the second half of life, and you either address it in a positive way or it'll get the better of you. You have to take care of yourself—emotionally and physically. It could end at any minute.

But what if it doesn't? What if you make it to a ripe old age? Just how scary and lonely are the older years without children?

CHAPTER FIFTEEN

Looking Ahead and Growing Older

I worry about a future without kids. What if I outlive my husband? I don't have any brothers or sisters, so I'll be pretty isolated as far as family.

—TAMMY, 41

My only regret about being childless concerns itself with aging and being alone. I have a very small family and once in a while I think about how it would be if I had children when I was older. Then I wonder if I'd miss it.

—LOUISE, 42

We've looked at many reasons why women don't have children. We've looked at differences between mothers vs. women without children. We've examined psychological issues that women confront as they move through their childbearing years into the time when they come to terms with the finality of not having children. We've looked at the situation and the ups and downs from both sides in the here and now. But how do feelings and thoughts about not having children change, if at all, as women grow older? Do some problems become more acute? Do others recede into non-issues? This chapter will look into what tends to happen in middle and older age.

Middle Age

As we have seen, once women move out of the childbearing years, the issue of having children gradually fades. Not having them doesn't feel as different anymore. Friends and co-workers aren't preoccupied with babies anymore. Fewer and fewer people ask about their friends' plans to start a family. Louise felt relieved to be done with all those prying questions:

> In my late twenties and through my thirties, I'd very often be asked about my parental state. Now that I am forty-two, the curiosity has stopped in other people.

Forty-five-year-old Karen, married and child free said:

> One of the things I liked best about turning forty was that people finally believed me when I said I wasn't interested in having children. They finally stopped asking me about it.

The bouts of agonizing doubts eventually recede into an acceptance of a child-free lifestyle and that you can't have it all, but you can give your all to whatever you choose. Career-minded women are well established and typically very successful at what they wanted to do. Ambition may shift away from a career to taking advantage of financial freedom and deciding to scale down professionally. This midlife period for many women was a time to reassess their lives. Forty-three-year-old Gail, for example, was just entering her transition, trying to determine her goals for the second half of her life. Cathy, forty-one, was well on her way to a new career as an emergency medical technician. Ilene at fifty and Ann at forty-five had both just "dropped out" from high-powered careers, opting for less demanding, more balanced lifestyles. Janet, forty-five, who had gotten her Ph.D. and worked full time for twenty years, had just quit her job to take the next year to leisurely explore her options. Randy, fifty and widowed, on the other hand, was through her transition, brought on by her husband's sudden death eight years ago. For the first time in her life, she gave her career one hundred percent, and glowed in the satisfaction it gave her. As a top magazine editor and expert in her field, she was being quoted in national publications frequently and asked to lecture around the country. Fran at fifty-four had just left Manhattan, after working there as a stockbroker for thirty years and was starting a new life on the West Coast. Betsy, fifty-seven, married and psychologically child free from a young age, was enjoying an early retirement launched more than a decade ago.

But at the same time, parents have grown much older and more frail. Middle-aged daughters start helping them out more. The gradual shift of intergenerational caretaking is bound to trigger women to think about their own old age and consider who will be doing this for them when they're older. But these thoughts weren't scaring the women, but rather were triggers for starting to think about their old age and planning for it. Janice, though she was only forty-four, knew she didn't want to retire in the city in which she was now working:

> I don't want to spend the rest of my life here, but I do want to spend most of my life wherever that place is. I don't want to wait until I retire to move, either—I'd have to abandon my network of people who mean a lot to me.

> So my husband and I are now in the active pursuit of where we want to live out our lives. I want to make sure I have at least fifteen years in the same place while I'm still very active. I'm sure we'll move in the next year or so.

But these concerns were the foundation for plans, and the majority of middle-aged women had upbeat attitudes and a sense of enjoying what they had. Although there's only scant research on how the middle-aged without children fare during this period of the life cycle, what little there is shows that the child free are just as happy as parents. One study of seventy-two middle-aged (ages forty-five to fifty-nine) married persons, for example, found couples with no children just as highly satisfied with life as "empty nesters." The researchers concluded: "The equivalence of life satisfaction for empty-nest and childless individuals suggests that parenthood is not a necessary prerequisite for happiness during middle age."[1] The childless group, however—which included both voluntarily and involuntarily childless couples—was a little less content with their not having children than the parents' were in having children. They weren't *displeased*, the authors stressed, just not as content with their state, probably because part of the sample included couples who had wanted but couldn't have children.

Another small study looked at six child-free couples between the ages of thirty-eight and sixty-five who had all decided against children before they married. Although the couples wondered what old age would be like, they liked their lives, and were thoroughly enjoying their flexibility, mobility, and careers. The researchers also found them feeling fulfilled by having achieved "generativity" through their pets, careers, and/or volunteer work.[2]

But middle age is still a time of good health and active, busy social and professional lives. What happens after retirement when health begins to fail? Are the fears that some women harbor about regret growing as they get older justified?

Older Age

Sure I'm worried about what it'll be like when I'm widowed, but not because I don't have children. That doesn't make any difference from what I can see.

So said Dolores, sixty-five, married her entire adult life and child free. As women grew old, they seemed to grow less and less concerned about regrets in old age, probably because they felt they were already old and having children didn't seem to matter. Carol, ninety-two, has been married for fifty-three years. She's seen some of her friends' children come through in old age and some not being of any support or benefit to their parents. She's never had any expectations regarding children and so has always acted accordingly. As she put it, "You have to make an effort and plan."

Clara, eighty-four, widowed and childless because of infertility, says she would have liked to have had children, but wasn't about to dwell on it all her life.

I don't have concerns about growing older. You have to just push forward and not brood over things. I'm sure it's been harder for me, and I'd have given anything to have children of my own but God's provided me with wonderful friends and relatives. It's amazing how they stick by you.

If you let it get under your skin, you could let it really bother you, but you've got to accept these things and rise above it. You've got to read, be active, stay interested in other people, help out when you can, and forget yourself. You just can't be self-centered, that's all.

Ruth, eighty-five, also widowed and a former victim of infertility, was living in a nursing home. She, too, judged her life by what she *had*, rather than by what she lacked:

> I'm not concerned about not having children at this stage—I'm grateful for what I have. One man here's going blind, another just had a stroke, and one lady has no legs. You just have to be happy. You always see someone worse off than you. Children wouldn't have made a difference.

Only *one* woman over fifty (out of thirty-two over age fifty) was feeling deeply concerned about old age, and that was Dorothy, mentioned in the last chapter, because she was feeling shaky in the wake of several recent deaths. Most of the older women lived around other older women, either in retirement communities or in communities where they'd lived all their lives. From their standpoint, they didn't see their neighbors' children being a great source of gratification for their parents. Whether they're right or not (and we'll see below that they are to some extent), isn't as important as the observation that they don't feel different or deprived because they don't have children. It's not so much a sense of sour grapes, but their sincere observation that their friends didn't seem better off because of their children.

Edith, eighty-two, divorced since her early twenties, lives in a Century Village senior housing apartment complex in Florida.

> I don't think when you get older it makes a gosh darn bit of difference whether you have children or not. I see women here who are alone. They have children, oh, what the heck, the children live their own lives. You can't expect a child to give up his or her life to take care of a parent. There's one sick woman here, her daughter lives up in New York. I have to call her every day to see if she's all right. This woman is lonelier than I am knowing she has children and they're not there for her. Her daughter calls and says "Hi, Mom, how are ya, I'm so busy it's crazy." I don't think women with children will tell you the truth if they're very lonely.

Phyllis, seventy-six, always single, who lives in a senior housing apartment complex in upstate New York, expressed a similar sentiment:

> I see more bitterness in old people here, especially among older women who think they've done things for their kids all their lives and now they're not there for them now. That's my experience.

Seniors with children do, in fact, have frequent social contact with their adult children—about seventy-five percent of older persons see one child at least weekly. Yet several studies suggest that there's little, if any, link between an elderly parent's contact with his/her grown children and their morale. Seniors report that they get much more satisfaction from contact with their peers.[3] Although the childless may idealize what it would be like to have grown children and young grandchildren, they need to remember that a lot of intergenerational contact is "not pleasant and gratifying" for the older generation, stress family sociologists.

> Older people who have expected close relationships with their offspring often feel neglected . . . and disappointed . . . In many . . . cases, intergenerational relations are strained by such influences as value conflicts and dependency of the parents which results in resentment on the part of the offspring. . . .
>
> Whereas older people may experience pride and vicarious pleasure from the successes and experiences of their offspring and grandchildren, it is perhaps just as likely that shame, embarrassment, and vicarious pain will result from identification with younger members.[4]

After analyzing the happiness ratings in six national surveys, with a total sampling of 2,365 men and women over the age of fifty, the researchers concluded that, "Overall, there is little evidence that important psychological rewards are derived from the later stages of parenthood. . . . it seems that having had children had very little impact on the average psychological well-being of older Americans."[5]

Nevertheless, regardless of how gratifying or fulfilling contact with grown children is, gerontologists agree that "there is extensive documentation to suggest that children provide seventy to eighty percent of their elderly parents' emotional, health, and social needs."[6] Yet, two out of every ten seniors don't have children, and another one in ten is totally estranged from their children.[7] That means that almost one-third of seniors today live without any contact or help from children.

The bad news is that these individuals are at greater risk for being lonely and needing support services, gerontologists say. Without the role of mother and grandmother, childless women not only lack important sources of support but have one less role to contribute to their social identity and self-esteem.

Childlessness is also a predictor for greater social isolation (not having frequent face-to-face contact with relatives and/or acquaintances/friends) especially as health wanes. Studies conflict about whether *healthy* childless women have more or less contact with friends and neighbors (unmarried women tend to have the most, married women without children the least), though there seems a bit more evidence suggesting that parents have more contact. Women without children in poor health and/or from working-class backgrounds, however, clearly tended to be more isolated.[8] However, those without children tended to be better off financially and in better health.[9]

The good news is that the childless elderly, especially women, have not been found to be deprived or disadvantaged. Sociologist Pat Keith, author of *The Unmarried in Later Life*, concluded in 1989 that "childlessness, for the most part, tends to be benign."[10] The reason is because these women had spent a lifetime of nurturing nonrelative relationships, thereby forming "a network of friends who contribute to their life quality in a way that is parallel to (though obviously different from) the contribution of children to parents."[11]

Also, although seniors without children are at greater risk for social isolation, being socially isolated does not necessarily mean feeling dissatisfied, deprived, or disadvantaged, says Pat Keith. Her study of 1,674 single older women (ages fifty-three to seventy-three) found that although more childless women lived alone and were more socially isolated than mothers, they were just as happy and satisfied with their social contacts as widowed and divorced mothers.[12] Timothy Brubaker, author of *Later Life Families* agrees:

> As a group, [the childless elderly] are more socially isolated than the older persons who had children but are not anymore lonely and are as likely to have someone in whom to confide. Apparently, the childless elderly develop a social network of friends and relatives whom they trust, even though they have contact with them less frequently.[13]

Also, the *number* of friends a senior has is not the critical factor for emotional well-being, gerontologists point out. What's most important is having *at least one* confidante. "Just one significant interpersonal relationship is so overwhelmingly powerful [and] has important implications for . . . childless older women," reported two experts at Ohio University.[14]

Although parents had *more* friends, researchers found the following:

> Today's childless elderly have levels of well-being that match and sometimes exceed those of parent elderly. That the childless are able to construct a parallel quality of life suggests either that children are not crucial in that quest or that the childless are able to establish effective alternatives to the benefits derived from children.[15]

Another study, which looked at the attitudes and well-being of 719 women, ages sixty to seventy-five, also found that women without children tended to benefit from alternative networks and were content about their childless state. They continued to focus on the advantages of being child free, just as mothers focused on the advantages of having children. Concluded the three researchers:

> It is clear . . . that childless older women surveyed . . . did not conform to the classic unsatisfied, unhappy stereotype. Rather they appeared to perceive certain advantages to their life status, as did the parents surveyed. Each group valued its own rewards for their lifestyle and perceived costs in the other.[16]

What's important in old age is having support networks, and although some elderly don't have children from which to form such networks, unmarried (including widowed) seniors without children tend to turn to siblings first, then nieces and nephews, and then friends.[17] Charlotte at seventy-one feels that her two older sisters are her greatest source of emotional sustenance. Sylvia at seventy-two speaks to her nieces every day, especially since their mother, Sylvia's sister, died ten years ago. Iris at seventy-seven is widowed and derives her emotional closeness from her husband's sister and three friends who live nearby. Ruth at eighty-five considers her brother's son her greatest source of joy. He visits once a week and manages all her business affairs. It is these close relationships, regardless of whether they're with family or friends, that buffer stress and illness in old age.[18]

Married women's primary confidantes tend to be their husbands, sometimes to the exclusion of other important social supports. Two sociologists who studied 2,194 married older persons, with and without children (1989), found that while the married childless had fewer social supports and confidantes, their marriages tended to be more supportive than parent couples. They concluded that "for the [married] childless, weak support from neighbors and confidantes may be complemented by stronger marital support."[19]

And, in fact, many women interviewed for this book (as well as for Diana Burgwyn's book, *Marriage Without Children*) stressed how strong and fulfilling their marriages were. Many expressed that their husbands were their best friends and met all their emotional needs. Said Sylvia:

> I've never needed any support for not having children. You have to understand what my husband's like—I didn't need any support from anybody. We spend as much time together as we can. We have very similar interests. I don't think it makes any difference in your old age whether you have children, the way things go these days. I'm just happy with the life I've had with my husband. I think we've an unusual relationship and maybe it's because we haven't had children. I don't know.

One danger, in fact, is the tendency married women without children have to invest the vast majority of their time and energy into their husbands, forming an exceptionally close bond. The danger is, if they become widowed, they're less well positioned than other women to buffer that pain of bereavement with other relationships and tend to be more bereft for years, compared with women who never married.

"The never-married appear to have become comfortable in a world that includes time alone, and do not experience it as a loss, as much as do the widowed," says social worker/gerontologist Susan Rice in the *Journal of Gerontological Social Work*. When comparing thirty never-married women with widowed childless women, Rice found that the never-married consistently reported higher levels of life satisfaction even though the widows had more social support. One reason may be that twice as many never-married women had been professionals, compared with widows, which may have contributed to self-esteem and life satisfaction. A previous study, for example, which found mothers and never-married women as fulfilled had concluded that meaningful careers appeared to contribute to fulfillment for never-married women much the way that marriage and children did for mothers.[20] But Rice suspects that the never-married were happier because their lives and social roles had remained consistent; the widows had to cope with a dramatic role change when they lost their husbands.

"[T]he never married have, in a way, had an easier task, since they have been practicing the skill of adapting to the roles of single women all their lives," says Rice. They are also happier because they are more "enmeshed" in their roles with others, and "the never-married seem better able to have accepted the choices available to them."[21]

Pamela, the sixty-one-year-old ever-single retired dancer, described her singleness like this:

> There is something that one learns in living alone, in learning to be responsible to and for yourself. You gain a kind of strength you couldn't gain in a marriage and with children. There's a certain kind of joy you achieve without being melancholy or bitter, that leaves you free to do whatever you want when you want. It's not self-indulgence, but it's important, sometimes even an ecstasy with moments of revelation of some sort. There's a great benefit to it. I like it.

What's critical, Rice points out, is feeling connected to others, having meaningful attachments to friends or family, and, therefore, having a social support system. As Karen Lindsey points out in *Friends As Family*, such networks can be spun out of relationships from work, a neighborhood, and social and religious organizations.

Being alone isn't necessarily the same as loneliness; isolation isn't the same as desolation. Nonfamilial kinship networks, though fluid and shifting throughout our lives, are being recognized more and more as contributing to one's social identity and well-being. "Such surrogate families of circumstance or of one's own choosing can stand in for or enrich the biological family, or, more often, operate as a legitimate kinship unit quite apart from the family itself," writes Cheryl Merser, author of *Grown-Ups: A Generation in Search of Adulthood*.[22] With nuclear families scattered across the continent and/or broken and transformed by divorce and remarriage, many women, mothers or not, are turning more and more to friends and neighbors as important sources of social support in old age.

As Marjory Stoneman Douglas, an only child, divorced since her twenties, and never a mother in her 100 years said: "I don't need a family. I have friends."

The women interviewed for this book were fostering relationships with relatives and friends. Many had lived in the same community for fifty years and never planned to move. They felt well woven into a web of neighbors and friends who would always be there. Marjory Stoneman Douglas has been living in the same house for seventy-five years; Clara has been in her area all her life, and now widowed at eighty-four, she's within a few miles of fifteen to twenty families of relatives. Lillian, eighty-seven, has lived in her small city for almost sixty years and is still very connected to the spiritual group she helped found thirty years ago. Florence, fifty-three, lives in the same city she was born in, and she's been active in her church for fifteen years. Most of her relatives live nearby, and she feels confident they'll be there for her when she needs help.

Women of the baby boom generation, however, have been

much more mobile, often living far from relatives. But their generation grew up in the spirit of community. In *Lifetrends: the Future of Baby Boomers and Other Aging Americans,* the authors predict that that community spirit will persist into old age, forming connections and supports among each other like no other previous generation:

> Of course, the baby boomers are likely to be the elder community-builders par excellence. Their formative years were spent reaching out to their peers to cope with life changes through group strength. . . . As boomers age . . . they will reach out instinctively to one another for mutual aid. "Networking" will become a deeper, more encompassing concept. . . . The networks boomers form . . . will be psychological and sometimes actual lifelines.[23]

Many women were confident that their planning, financial resources, and independent spirits would continue to serve them well in old age. When and if they became enfeebled, they planned to have their decisions prearranged. Others didn't have concrete plans, but were confident they would cope with the situation when it occurred. Judy Long, however, had the most startling response of all. She planned to maintain control to the very end:

> As long as I'm able to change and be flexible in my life, I'll be happy. When I can no longer work, I think it'll be a major change. I suspect at some point I won't be able to live alone anymore, and at a point I probably won't be able to do anything very useful.
>
> As long as I can get around, I'll still do volunteer work and help out, but at the point when I can't, I don't want to live the way my grandmother did at the end, hanging on helplessly for years. This life is very precious, but that's not living. I've got a living will in place, but that only protects you in certain situations.
>
> When my physical problems overwhelm me and I can't live the way I want to, I'll probably kill myself.

Judy was serious; she had already spoken to her physician sister about the right combination of sleeping pills and sedatives one needs to die peacefully. She planned to have it all in place when the time came.

Just as the baby boomers have been trend-setters from the day they were born, they will probably continue to set the trends to the day they die. Already, new kinds of services and institutions are springing up across America to support the elderly. Many seniors are moving to retirement communities, often miles from their families, but with services geared to the elderly already in place. As older people become frailer and impaired, more and more are moving into adult congregate living units—sort of communes for the elderly. Each senior has her own small apartment but may eat meals in a common dining room and use the recreational rooms for planned social activities, shared television watching, and socializing. Most of the services they need as seniors—medical, beauty, banking—come to the units. If a senior needs nursing-home-level care, she may move into another wing of the unit—part of the institution and close to her friends still living in the other wings.

Another option becoming more popular is seniors moving in with each other. Seniors without children often move in with siblings and friends twice as often as elderly parents do.[24] Another increasingly common alternative is family senior care facilities, where a small group of seniors live in the home of a family that cares for them.

Although many baby boomers will have children, many will have just one or two. That means that fewer children will be available to aging parents as the boomer generation grows old. At the same time, as millions of Americans move into older age, new services will increasingly become available.

Many of the older women interviewed for this book commented that having children and grandchildren now would probably indeed be a pleasure. Yet they also indicated, and research backs them up, that today's seniors without children are doing fine. And there's every reason to believe that the baby boom generation, with its smaller families and state-of-the-art services tailored to their generation's needs, will do even better.

CONCLUSIONS

I think that people, whether they have a feminist consciousness or not, realize that there are plenty of life choices, of which having children is one, but only one. Granted, it's a very important one, and one that should not be made lightly. But there's no doubt that those who don't have one can still lead a rich and rewarding life.

I'm aware that family life leads to some of the most ecstatic and most painful experiences human beings have, and it's not like you get to choose ahead of time what the balance is going to be in any given family. Not having children is a trade-off, and I think the down sides are really the flip of the good sides.

—LAURA, 45

We all make choices, though some are more active decisions than others. Some women have made the active, positive choice not to have children, while others didn't mean not to have children at all.

Regardless of the choice and circumstance, millions of women in America today will not have or adopt children. As we've seen, there is no evidence that they will grow old to be lonely or alone, bereft of good friends and loving kindred spirits. As the baby boom generation grows older, several trends are clear. Many boomers will be part of blended and alternative families—including "typical" two-parent families, divorced singles living half in and out of single-parent households, blended stepfamilies, gay couples, and singles with and without children, as well as record numbers of people living alone. They will age in an era with more services and options in place than have ever been available before. Most will have had small families and have a history of seeking out others in a spirit of community. Women who reach out and form attachments and who in some way have a purpose beyond themselves will be enriched by those connections and fulfilled with a sense of purpose, whether with or without children.

In spite of all the problems caused by neglectful or abusive parents and the anti-motherhood sentiments of the 1970s, we again glorify motherhood for all. Women without children are again neglected in these so-called "pro-choice" liberated times. Before feminism can truly achieve its goal, *all* women need to be free to control their reproductive destiny without any loss of respect or identity.

As members of this invisible and silent minority journey down the road less traveled, the one without children, a thousand possibilities lay ahead. Although such women may at times wonder about the child never born, it's important to remember that, just as motherhood may be streaked with ambivalence, so, too, may be nonmotherhood. Women without children may not have as clear an idea about what may lay ahead, yet one truth emerges: their road is open to endless choices and possibilities.

SOURCES

Chapter One   Three Women Without Children

1. Marjory Stoneman Douglas, *Marjory Stoneman Douglas: Voice of the River, An Autobiography* (Sarasota, Florida: Pineapple Press, 1987), p. 55.
2. Ibid., p. 56.
3. Ibid., p. 72.
4. Ibid., p. 72.
5. Ibid., p. 84.
6. Ibid., p. 89.
7. Ibid., p. 127.
8. Ibid., p. 187.
9. Ibid., p. 256.
10. See Jean E. Veevers, *Childless by Choice* (Toronto: Butterworth & Co., 1980), p. 60. Her landmark study of 127 voluntarily childless couples published in 1980 is considered the most comprehensive work ever completed on such couples. She found that one in five of the wives she interviewed who chose to not have children were only children, compared with only one in twenty in the general population.

Chapter Two   Tracking the Trends Before the Baby Boomers

1. Bernice Lott, *Becoming A Woman: The Socialization of Gender* (Springfield, Illinois: Charles C. Thomas, 1981), p. 163.

251

2. William Manchester, *The Glory and The Dream: A Narrative History of America 1932–72.* (New York: Bantam Books, 1973), p. 41.

3. Donald W. Hastings, and Robinson J. Gregory, "Incidence of Childlessness for United States Women, Cohorts Born 1891–1945," *Social Biology*, 21:178–184, Summer, 1974, as cited in Margaret Kathryn Ambry, "Social Decision-Making and the Decision to Be Voluntarily Childless" (Thesis: Cornell University, 1981).

4. J. A. Sweet and L. L. Bumpass, *American Families and Households* (New York: Russell Sage Foundation, 1987), p. 130.

5. Diana Burgwyn, *Marriage Without Children* (New York: Harper & Row, 1981), p. 4.

6. Manchester, *The Glory and the Dream*, p. 780.

7. Ibid., p. 781.

8. Ann Dally, *Inventing Motherhood: The Consequences of An Ideal* (New York: Schocken Books, 1982), p. 150.

9. Ambry, *Social Decision-Making*, p. 34.

10. Adrienne Rich, *Of Woman Born: Motherhood As Experience and Institution* (New York: W.W. Norton & Co., Inc., 1976), p. 25.

Chapter Three   Tracking the Trends of the Baby Boomers

1. Kathleen Gerson, *Hard Choices: How Women Decide About Work, Career, and Motherhood* (Berkeley: University of California Press, 1985), p. 216.

2. Anna Quindlen, "Mother's Choice," *Ms.* Magazine, February 1988, p. 55.

3. For a well-articulated description of how women of this age group grappled with tough issues about work and motherhood, see Gerson, *Hard Choices*, p. 10.

4. Lance Morrow, "Wondering if Children are Necessary," *Time*, March 5, 1979, p. 47.

5. Morrow, op.cit.

6. Werner Fornos, Population Institute, speech to the National Editors Club, National Public Radio, August 1, 1990.

7. Claudia Willis, "Onward, Women!" *Time*, December 4, 1989, p. 82.

8. Cynthia Harrison, "A Richer Life: A Reflection on the Women's Movement," in Sara E. Rix, ed., *The American Woman: 1988–89: A Status Report* (New York: W.W. Norton & Co., 1988), pp. 63–64.

9. Gerson, *Hard Choices*, p. 239.

10. Sara E. Rix, ed., *The American Woman: 1988–89*, p. 363.

11. Willis, op.cit., p. 82.

12. Ibid.

13. Cardell K. Jacobson, Tim B. Heaton, and Karen M. Taylor, "Childlessness Among American Women," *Social Biology*, Fall/Winter 1988, p. 187.

14. *Time*, Special Issue, "Women: The Road Ahead," Fall 1990, p. 50.

15. Ibid., p. 52.

16. Census Bureau, "Status of the Family," *Monthly Labor Review*, March 1990, pp. 10–11.

17. Martha Smilgis, "The Dilemmas of Childlessness," *Time*, May 2, 1988, p. 88.

18. See Chapter Five, The Never Married, for more discussion on this phenomenon.

19. Michael Humphrey and Heather Humphrey, *Families with a Difference: Varieties of Surrogate Parenthood*, (London: Routledge, 1988), p. 4.

20. Robert Boyd, "Minority Status and Childlessness," *Sociological Inquiry*, vol. 59 (3), Summer 1989, pp. 331–342.

21. Arland Thornton and Deborah Freedman, "The Changing American Family," *Population Bulletin*, 38, pp. 1–43, 1983.

22. Gannett News Service, "U.S. Birth Rate Highest Since 1972," *Ithaca Journal*, May 8, 1990.

23. Unless otherwise noted, these fertility statistics come from the Bureau of the Census, *Fertility of American Women: June 1988*, Current Population Reports, Series F-20, No. 436.

24. Alan Riding, "Western Europe, Its Births Falling, Wonders Who'll Do All the Work," the *New York Times*, July 22, 1990.

25. Karl Zinsmeister, "The American Dream: The Family's Tie," *Current*, February 1987, p. 12.

26. Rosemarie Nave-Herz, "Childless Marriages," *Marriage and Family Review*, vol. 14(1–2) 1989, pp. 239–250.

27. Gina Johnson, et al., "Infertile or Childless by Choice? A Multipractice Survey of Women Aged 35 and 50," *British Medical Journal*, vol. 294, March 28, 1987, p. 804.

28. "Status of Family," *Monthly Labor Review*, March 1990, pp. 10–11.

29. Ibid.

30. Humphrey and Humphrey, *Families with a Difference*, p. 5.

31. *Time*, Special Issue, op.cit., p. 14.

Chapter Four   Who Doesn't Have Children?

1. Sharon Houseknecht, "Voluntary Childlessness," in Marvin B. Sussman and Suzanne K. Steinmetz, eds. *Handbook of Marriage and the Family* (New York: Plenum Press, 1987), p. 369, referring to the National Center for Health Statistics estimate in 1980.
2. Kathleen E. Kiernan, "Who Remains Childless?" *Journal of Biosocial Science*, 1989, vol. 21, pp. 387–398.
3. Ibid.
4. Cardell K. Jacobson, Tim B. Heaton, and Karen M. Taylor, "Childlessness Among American Women," *Social Biology*, Fall/Winter 1988, pp. 198–190.
5. Jacobson, et al, p. 193.
6. Steven L. Nock, "The Symbolic Meaning of Childbearing," *Journal of Family Issues*, vol. 8, No. 4, December 1987, pp. 373–393.
7. Susan Bram, "Childlessness Revisited: A Longitudinal Study of Voluntarily Childless Couples, Delayed Parents, and Parents," *Lifestyles: A Journal of Changing Patterns*, vol. 8(1), Fall 1985, pp. 46–66.
8. Kathleen Gerson, *Hard Choices: How Women Decide About Work, Career, and Motherhood* (Berkeley: University of California Press, 1985), p. 75.
9. Ibid., p. 78.
10. Ibid., p. 196.
11. Ibid., p. 109.
12. Ibid., p. 152.
13. Ibid., p. 192.

Chapter Five   The Never Married

1. Barbara Levy Simon, *Never Married Women* (Philadelphia: Temple University Press, 1987), p. 1.
2. Ibid., pp. 29 and 186.
3. Katherine Allen, *Single Women/Family Ties* (Newbury Park, California: Sage Publications, 1989), p. 23.
4. Ibid., p. 23.
5. Pat M. Keith, *The Unmarried in Later Life* (New York: Praeger, 1989), p. 4.
6. *New York Times*, February 22, 1986, quoted in Simon, p. 4.
7. Felicity Barringer, "Study on Marriage Patterns Revised, Omitting Impact of Women's Careers," *New York Times*, November 11, 1989, p. 10.

8. Mary Barberis, "Women and Marriage: Choice or Chance?" in *The American Woman: 1988–89*, Sara E. Rix, ed. (New York: W.W. Norton & Co., 1988), pp. 271–272.

9. Laura Mansnerus, "In Happiness Quotient, The Unmarried Gain," *New York Times*, June 15, 1988.

10. Simon, *Never Married Women*, p. 31.

11. *New York Times*, August 2, 1990.

12. Nancy L. Peterson, *Our Lives for Ourselves: Women Who Have Never Married* (New York: G.P. Putnam's, 1981), p. 114.

13. *Time*, Special Issue "Women: the Road Ahead," Fall 1990, p. 73.

14. *Fertility of American Women: June 1988*, p. 15.

15. Allen, *Single Women/Family Ties*, p. 119.

16. Peterson, *Our Lives for Ourselves*, p. 247.

Chapter Six   Choosing to Be Child Free

1. M. Ory, "The Decision to Parent or Not: Normative and Structural Components," *Journal of Marriage and the Family*, vol. 40 (3), 1978, pp. 531–539, as cited in Rogers and Larson, p. 50.

2. Jean E. Veevers, *Childless by Choice* (Toronto: Butterworth & Co., 1980), p. 64.

3. Elaine Campbell, *The Childless Marriage* (London and New York: Tavistock Publications, 1985), p. 138.

4. Sharon K. Houseknecht, "Voluntary Childlessness," in Marvin B. Sussman and Suzanne K. Steinmetz, eds., *Handbook of Marriage and the Family* (New York: Plenum Press, 1987), p. 377.

5. M. Ory, "The Decision to parent or Not", as cited in Lisa Kay Rogers and Jeffrey H. Larson, "Voluntary Childlessness: A Review of the Literature and a Model of the Childlessness Decision," *Family Perspective*, 22, (1), 1988, pp. 43–58.

6. Veevers, *Childless by Choice*, p. 59.

7. Ibid., p. 60.

8. Rogers and Larson, "Voluntary Childlessness," p. 45.

9. Molly McKaughan, *The Biological Clock* (New York: Doubleday, 1987), p. 43.

10. Bonnie Burman and Diane de Anda, "Parenthood or Nonparent-hood: A Comparison of Intentional Families," *Lifestyles: Journal of Changing Patterns*, vol. 8(2), Winter 1987, pp. 69–74.

11. This distinction was made originally by Elaine Campbell in *The Childless Marriage*. See also Veevers, *Childless by Choice*.

12. Karen A. Polonko, John Scanzoni, and Jay D. Teachman, "Childlessness and Marital Satisfaction," *Journal of Family Issues*, vol. 3, No. 4, December 1982, pp. 545–573.

13. Louis Genevie, Ph.D., and Eva Margolies, M.A., *The Motherhood Report: How Women Feel About Being Mothers* (New York: Macmillan Publishing Company, 1987), p. 15.

14. Ibid., pp. 5–10.

15. Ibid., p. 30.

16. Carin Rubenstein, "The Baby Bomb," *New York Times Good Health Magazine*, October 8, 1989, p. 34.

17. L. Silka and S. Kiesler, "Couples Who Choose to Remain Childless," *Family Planning Perspectives*, 1977, Vol. 9, pp. 16–25, as referenced in Sharon Houseknecht, "Voluntary Childlessness," op.cit., p. 384.

18. Marian Faux, *Childless by Choice: Choosing Childlessness in the Eighties* (Garden City, New York: Anchor/Doubleday, 1984), p. 162.

19. Genevie and Margolies, *The Motherhood Report*, pp. 56–57.

20. Veevers, *Childless by Choice*, pp. 20–27.

21. McKaughan, *The Biological Clock*, p. 37.

22. Houseknecht, "Voluntary Childlessness," p. 381.

23. Ibid., p. 381.

24. Veevers, op.cit., p. 80.

25. Kathleen Gerson, *Hard Choices: How Women Decide About Work, Career, and Motherhood* (Berkeley: University of California Press, 1985), p. 150.

26. Veevers, op.cit., p. 83.

27. Rogers and Larson, "Voluntary Childlessness," p. 46.

28. Burman and de Anda, "Parenthood or Nonparenthood," p. 69.

29. Cardell K. Jacobsen, Tim B. Heaton, and Karen M. Taylor, "Childlessness Among American Women," *Social Biology*, Fall/Winter 1988, p. 193.

30. F. Baum and D. R. Cope, "Some Characteristics of Intentionally Childless Wives in Britain," *Journal of Biosocial Science*, 1980, vol. 12, pp. 287–299, as referenced in Houseknecht, op.cit, p. 384; other studies with similar findings are referenced in Rogers and Larson, op.cit, p. 44.

Chapter Seven No Time Was the Right Time

1. Cynthia Harrison, "A Richer Life: A Reflection on the Women's Movement," in Sara E. Rix, ed., *The American Woman: 1988–89: A Status Report* (New York: W.W. Norton & Co., 1988), p. 73.

Chapter Eight   When Men Don't Want to Father

1. Anaïs Nin, *The Diary of Anaïs Nin, Vol. One, 1931–1934* (New York: Swallow Press and Harcourt, Brace & World, Inc, 1966), p. 339.

2. Letty Cottin Pogrebin, "Fathers Must Earn Their 'Rights'" *New York Times*, June 17, 1990.

3. Louis Genevie, Ph.D., and Eva Margolies, M.A., *The Motherhood Report: How Women Feel About Being Mothers* (New York: Macmillan Publishing Company, 1987), pp. 319 and 336.

4. Tamar Lewin, "Father's Vanishing Act Called Common Drama," *New York Times*, June 4, 1990, p. A18. This article refers to Frank Furstenberg's research at the University of Pennsylvania. He studied 1,000 children from fractured families.

5. Nicholas Davidson, "Life Without Father," *Policy Review*, Winter 1990, as excerpted in the *Herald Examiner*, Vol. 4., No. 4, September 1990.

6. Lewin, "Father's Vanishing Act Called Common Drama." op.cit.

7. Kathleen Gerson, *Hard Choices: How Women Decide About Work, Careers, and Motherhood*, (Berkeley: University of California Press, 1985), pp. 144–46.

8. Ibid., p. 142.

9. Personal interview.

10. Nan Bauer Maglin and Nancy Schneidewind, *Women and Stepfamilies: Voices of Anger and Love* (Philadelphia: Temple University Press, 1989), p. 13.

11. Jerry Gerber, Janet Wolff, Walter Klores, and Gene Brown, *Lifetrends: The Future of Baby Boomers and Other Aging Americans* (New York: Stonesong Press, Macmillan Publishing Company, 1989), p. 36.

12. Richard A. Gardner, *The Parents' Book About Divorce* (New York: Doubleday, 1977), as quoted in Claire Berman, *Making It As a Stepparent: New Roles/New Rules* (New York: Harper & Row, 1986), p. 12.

13. Berman, *Making It As A Stepparent: New Roles/New Rules*, p. 14.

14. Maglin and Schneidewind, *Women and Stepfamilies: Voices of Anger and Love*, p. 8.

15. This story is adapted from Christine's story in Maglin and Schneidewind's book, pp. 19–28.

16. Lawrence Kutner, "Adopting a Stepchild," *New York Times*, June 7, 1990.

17. Karen Savage and Patricia Adams, *The Good Stepmother: A Practical Guide* (New York: Crown Publishers, Inc., 1988), p. 152.

Chapter Nine   Infertility and Medical Interference

1. Constance Shapiro, *Infertility and Pregnancy Loss: A Guide for Helping Professionals* (San Francisco: Jossey-Bass Publishers, 1988), p. 42 and 187.

2. Gilda Radner, *It's Always Something* (New York: Avon Books, 1989), p. 32.

3. Ibid.

4. This survey was conducted by Reverend Mr. John Van Regenmorter for Resolve and cited by Jean and Michael Carter in *Sweet Grapes: How To Stop Being Infertile and Start Living Again* (Indianapolis: Perspectives Press, 1989), p. 82.

5. For discussions on the stages involved in infertility, see Anne Martin Matthews and Ralph Matthews, "Beyond the Mechanics of Infertility: Perspectives on the Social Psychology of Infertility and Involuntary Childlessness," *Family Relations*, 35, October 1986, pp. 476–487, and B. E. Menning, *Infertility: A Guide for the Childless Couple* (Englewood Cliffs, New Jersey: Prentice-Hall, 1977).

6. See Constance Shapiro, *Infertility and Pregnancy Loss: A Guide for Helping Professionals* (San Francisco, Jossey-Bass, Inc., 1988) for a more complete discussion on the emotional aspects of infertility.

7. See Ronald M. Sabatelli, Richard L. Meth, and Stephen M. Gavazzi, "Factors Mediating the Adjustment to Involuntary Childlessness," *Family Relations*, 37, July 1988, pp. 338–343.

8. Ralph Matthews and Anne Martin Matthews, "Infertility and Involuntary Childlessness: the Transition to Nonparenthood," *Journal of Marriage and the Family*, 48, August 1986, pp. 641–649.

9. Judith Viorst, *Necessary Losses*, (New York: Ballantine, 1986), p. 3.

10. Philip J. Hilts, "New Study Challenges Estimates on Odds of Adopting a Child," *New York Times*, Dec. 10, 1990.

11. Charlene E. Miall, "The Stigma of Adoptive Parent Status: Perceptions of Community Attitudes Toward Adoption and the Experience of Informal Social Sanctioning," *Family Relations Journal of Applied and Child Studies*, vol. 36(1), January 1987, pp. 34–39.

12. Susan and Elton Klibanoff, *Let's Talk About Adoption* (Boston: Little Brown, 1973), as cited in Carter and Carter, *Sweet Grapes*.

13. For further discussion on this transformation, see Chapter Eight in Jean Carter and Michael Carter, *Sweet Grapes: How to Stop Being Infertile and Start Living Again* (Indianapolis: Perspectives Press, 1989).

14. Robin Marantz Henig, "Chosen and Given," *New York Times Magazine*, November 11, 1988, pp. 70–71.

15. Carter and Carter, *Sweet Grapes*, p. 68.

16. Ibid.

17. Ibid., p. 80.

18. Ibid., p. 27.

19. Viorst, *Necessary Losses*, pp. 366–367.

20. Merle Bombardieri, *The Baby Decision* (New York: Rawson Associates 1981), is available from the author ($9.95 trade paperback; $15.95, cloth) when check is made out to Wellspring Counseling Center and sent to Bombardieri at 26 Trapelo Road, Belmont, MA 02178. "Child-Free Decision-Making," a twelve-page fact sheet is available for $2 from Resolve, 5 Water St., Arlington, MA 02174 or by calling 617–643–2424.

21. Bombardieri, op.cit., p. 2.

22. Carter, op.cit., p. 88.

23. Ibid., p. 88.

24. T. A. Leitko and A. L. Greil, "Involuntary Childlessness, Gender, Female Employment, and Emotional Distress," a paper presented at a meeting of the American Sociological Association, Washington, D.C., August, 1985, and cited in Shapiro's *Infertility and Pregnancy Loss*, op.cit., p. 20.

25. M. D. Mazor, "Emotional Reactions to Infertility," in M. D. Mazor and H. F. Simons, eds., *Infertility: Medical, Emotional, and Social Consequences* (New York: Human Sciences Press, 1984), as cited in Shapiro, op.cit., p. 20.

Chapter Ten   Women Who Love Women

1. Sandra Pollack and Jeanne Vaughn, eds., *Politics of the Heart: A Lesbian Parenting Anthology* (Ithaca, New York: Firebrand Books, 1987), p. 49.

2. Elizabeth Gibbons, "Psychosocial Development of Children Raised by Lesbian Mothers: A Review of the Research," in Ester D. Rothblum and Ellen Cole, *Lesbianism: Affirming Nontraditional Roles* (New York: Haworth Press, 1989), p. 65.

3. Irena Klepfisz, "Women Without Children/Women Without Families/Women Alone," *Dreams of an Insomniac: Feminist Essays, Speeches, and Diatribes* (Eighth Mountain Press: 1990).

4. Harriet Alpert, personal interview.

5. Nancy D. Polikoff, "Lesbians Choosing Children," in Pollack and Vaughn, p. 51.

6. Klepfisz, op.cit.

7. Sandra Pollack, personal interview.

8. Pollack and Vaughn, *Politics of the Heart*, p. 50.

Chapter Eleven   When Not Having Children Is a Loss

1. As quoted in Molly McKaughan, *The Biological Clock* (New York: Doubleday, 1987), p. 43.

2. Including those by Faux, Veevers, Burgwyn, and Campbell.

3. Judith Viorst, *Necessary Losses* (New York: Ballantine, 1986). See p. 278 for a discussion on internalization.

4. Irena Klepfisz, "Women Without Children/Women Without Families/Women Alone," *Dreams of an Insomniac: Feminist Essays, Speeches, and Diatribes* (Eighth Mountain Press: 1990).

5. Norval D. Glenn and Sara McLanahan, "The Effects of Offspring on the Psychological Well-Being of Older Adults," *Journal of Marriage and the Family*, May 1981, pp. 409–421.

6. Klepfisz, p. 62.

7. Jean E. Veevers, *Childless by Choice* (Toronto: Butterworth & Co., 1980), p. 143.

8. Nancy Peterson, *Our Lives for Ourselves* (New York: G.P. Putnam's, 1981), p. 182.

9. Ibid.

10. Klepfisz, "Women Without Children/Women Without Families/Women Alone," p. 63.

11. Viorst, *Necessary Losses*, p. 365.

12. Carole A. Wilk, *Career Women and Childbearing: A Psychological Analysis of the Decision Process* (New York: Van Nostrand Reinhold Company, 1986), p. xv.

13. Ibid.

14. Bureau of the Census, Current Population Reports, "Fertility of American Women: June 1988, Series P-20, No. 436.

15. "Women Work It," *New Woman*, September 1990, p. 32.

16. Wilk, op.cit., p. 278.

17. For more complete discussions on why people have children, see Robert E. Gould, M.S., "The Wrong Reasons To Have Children," reprinted from the *New York Times Magazine*, May 3, 1970, and published in Ellen Peck and Judith Sanderowitz, *Pronatalism—The Myth of Mom and Apple Pie* (New York: T. Y. Crowell, 1974) and Lois Wladis Hoffman and Martin L. Hoffman, "The Value of Children To Parent," in J. T.

Fawcett, ed., *Psychological Perspectives on Population* (New York: Basic Books, 1973), pp. 19–76.

18. Elaine Campbell, *The Childless Marriage* (London and New York: Tavistock Publications, 1985), pp. 103–104.

19. Deborah Oakley, "Low-Fertility Childbearing Decision-Making," *Social Biology*, Fall/Winter 1986, p. 249.

20. See Arthur G. Neal, H. Theodore Groat, and Jerry W. Wicks, "Attitudes about Having Children: A Study of 600 Couples in the Early Years of Marriage," *Journal of Marriage and the Family*, 51, May 1989, pp. 313–328. This is a Bowling State University study of 600 married couples without children.

21. Karl Zinsmeister, "The American Dream: The Family's Tie," *Current*, 1987, reprinted from *Public Opinion*, September/October 1986, pp. 3–6, 60.

22. Jessie Bernard, *Future of Motherhood* (New York: Dial Press, 1975), p. 48.

23. Paula Weideger, *Womb Worship, MS.* magazine, February 1988.

24. Roberta Joseph, "Deciding Against Motherhood: One Woman's Story," *Utne Reader*, Jan./Feb. 1990 and excerpted originally from the New York lifestyle weekly *7 Days*, August 23, 1989.

25. Victor J. Callan, "Perceptions of Parents, the Voluntarily and Involuntarily Childless: A Multidimensional Scaling Analysis, *Journal of Marriage and the Family*, 47(4), November 1985, pp. 1045–1050.

Chapter Twelve   Nurturing and Networking

1. Karen Lindsey, *Friends As Family* (Boston: Beacon Press, 1981), p. 115.

2. Nancy Friday, *My Mother, My Self: The Daughter's Search for Identity* (New York: Delacorte Press, 1977), p. 21.

3. Ibid., p. 37.

4. Dan Hurley, "Getting Help From Helping," *Psychology Today*, January 1988, p. 64.

5. Cheryl Merser, "*Grown-Ups: A Generation In Search of Adulthood* (New York: G.P. Putnam's, 1987), p. 208.

6. Jean E. Veevers, *Childless by Choice* (Toronto: Butterworth & Co., 1980), pp. 34–37.

7. Ibid., pp. 34–37.

8. Jon Nordheimer, "High-Tech Medicine at High-Rise Costs is Keeping Pets Fit," *New York Times*, September 17, 1990.

9. Lena Williams, "Influence of Pets Reaches New High," *New York Times*, August 18, 1988.

10. "Pet Owners Go to the Doctor Less," *New York Times*, August 2, 1990.

11. Ibid.

12. For more on friendships for never-married women, see Barbara Levy Simon, *Never Married Women* (Philadelphia: Temple University Press, 1987), pp. 89–111, as well as Lindsey's *Friends as Family*.

Chapter Thirteen   Wealth, Health, and Time to Enjoy Them

1. "Cost of Raising a Child Rises Sharply," Gannett News Service, *Ithaca Journal*, Jan. 18, 1990.

2. Andrea Rock, "Can You Afford Your Kids?" *Money*, July 1990, pp. 88–99.

3. Jean E. Veevers, *Childless by Choice* (Toronto: Butterworth & Co., 1980), p. 88.

4. R. H. Reed and Susan McIntosh, "Costs of Children," in E. R. Morss and R. H. Reeds, eds., *Economic Aspects of Population Change*, vol. 2 (Washington, D.C.: U.S. Commission on Population Growth and the American Future, 1972)), pp. 356–46, as cited in Marian Faux, *Childless by Choice*.

5. Jacob Mincer and Haim Ofek, "Interrupted Work Careers," National Bureau of Economic Research, Working Paper No. 479, 1980, as cited in Sandra L. Hofferth, *Effects of Number and Timing of Births on Family Well-being over the Life Cycle* (Washington, D.C.: Urban Institute, 1981), p. 15.

6. Barbara Ehrenreich and Deirdre English, "Blowing the Whistle on the 'Mommy Track,'" *MS.*, July/August 1989, p. 56.

7. Claudia Willis, "Onward, Women!" *Time*, December 4, 1989, p. 82.

8. "Three's A Crowd," *Newsweek*, September 1, 1986, p. 74.

9. U.S. Department of Commerce News, "Wives' Earnings Growing Twice as Fast as Husbands' Earnings," Census Bureau Reports, July 26, 1989.

10. David Bloom and Neil Bennett, "Childless Couples," *American Demographics*, August 1986.

11. Newsweek, op.cit. Similar findings were obtained in Susan Bram's study of childless couples vs. parents. She found that childless women (as well as couples who were delaying their childbearing) earned about

$5,500 more than parents. See Bram, "Childlessness Revisited," *Lifestyles*, vol. 8(1), Fall, pp. 46–66.

12. John P. Robinson, "Who's Doing the Housework," *American Demographics*, December 1988, pp. 24–28.

13. Boone A. Turchi, *The Demand for Children: The Economics of Fertility in the United States* (Cambridge, MA: Ballinger, 1975), as cited in Sandra L. Hofferth, *Effects of Number and Timing of Births on Family Well-being over the Life Cycle*, p. 138.

14. Robinson, op.cit., pp. 24–28.

15. "Americans' Use of Time Project: Bringing Up Baby," Survey Research Center, University of Maryland, as published in *MS.*, September 1989, p. 86. For one of the most detailed analyses on time-use studies, though dated, see John P. Robinson, *How Americans Use Time: A Social-Psychological Analysis of Everyday Behavior* (New York: Praeger Publishers, 1977). For a detailed analysis on sixty unmarried women and time use, see Ivory Holmes, *The Allocation of Time by Women Without Family Responsibilities* (Washington, D.C.: University Press of America, 1983).

16. Robinson, *American Demographics*, op.cit.

17. *Time*, Special Issue, "Women, the Road Ahead," Fall 1990, p. 26.

18. Arlie Hochschild, *The Second Shift* (New York: Viking, 1989), pp. 3–4.

19. Bram, op.cit.

20. G. N. Ramu, "Voluntarily Childless and Parental Couples: A Comparison of Their Lifestyle Characteristics," *Lifestyle: A Journal of Changing Patterns*, 7(3), Spring 1985, p. 141.

21. Personal interview with Louise Brinton, Ph.D., chief of Environmental Studies Section, National Cancer Institute, National Institutes of Health, and epidemiologist on female cancers.

22. M. G. Lee, A. Bachelot, and C. Hill, "Characteristics of Reproductive Life and Risk of Breast Cancer in a Case-Control Study of Young Nulliparous Women, *Journal of Clinical Epidemiology*, vol. 42 (12), 1989, pp. 1227–1233.

23. Personal interview with Linda Carson, J. Fanning, et al, "Endometrial Adenocarcinoma Histologic Subtypes," *Gynecological Oncology*, 32(3), March 1989, pp. 288–291. Other studies which have documented this same connection are in Chinese, Japanese, and Swedish, but their abstracts are translated on the database, "Medline," and may be found under the subject heading, "Nulliparity."

24. "Fighting the Silent Attacker," *Time*, December 1, 1986. See also

E. O. Talbott, et al, "Reproductive History of Women Dying of Sudden Cardiac Death: A Case-Control Study," *International Journal of Epidemiology*, vol. 18 (3), September 1989, pp. 589–94.

25. Suzanne Haynes, Elaine Eaker, and Manning Feinleib, "The Effect of Employment, Family, and Job Stress on Coronary Heart Disease in Patterns in Women," in Ellen B. Gold, *The Changing Risk of Disease in Women: An Epidemiological Approach* (Lexington, MA: Collamore Press, D.C. Heath & Co., 1984), pp. 40–41.

26. Personal interview.

27. R. Lindsay, "Prevention of Osteoporosis, *Clinical Orthopedics*, September 1987 (222), pp. 44–59, and J. C. Stevenson, et al., "Determinants of Bone Density," in "Normal Women: Risk Factors for Future Osteoporosis?" *British Medical Journal*, April 8, 1989, pp. 924–928.

28. Personal interview.

29. Jeffrey Sobal, "The Social Epidemiology of Obesity," *Human Ecology Forum*, Spring 1990, p. 18.

30. Ibid.

31. Karen S. Renne, "Childlessness, Health, and Marital Satisfaction," *Social Biology*, vol. 23 (3), 1976, pp. 183–197.

32. Judith Rempel, "Childless Elderly: What Are They Missing," *Journal of Marriage and the Family*, May 1985, pp. 343–348.

33. Sandra L. Hofferth, *Effects of Number and Timing of Births on Family Well-Being Over the Life Cycle*, (Washington, D.C.: Urban Institute, 1981), p. 324.

34. Lois M. Verbrugge, "Marital Status and Health," *Journal of Marriage and the Family*, May 1979, p. 267, and "Yes, Married People Do Live Much Longer," *New York Times*, May 15, 1990.

35. "New Twist to Marriage and Mortality," *Science News*, vol. 138, October 27, 1990, p. 267.

Chapter Fourteen   The Ups and Downs of Child-Free Living

1. Ann Landers, "Skip the Kids, They'd Rather Have Fun," October 28, 1989.

2. Lisa Kay Rogers and Jeffry H. Larson, "Voluntary Childlessness: A Review of the Literature and a Model of the Childlessness Decision," *Family Perspective*, vol. 22 (1), 1988, p. 44.

3. Elaine Campbell, *The Childless Marriage*, (London and New York: Tavistock Publications, 1985), p. 39.

4. Kate Harper, *The Childfree Alternative* (Brattleboro, Vermont: Harper-Moretown, 1980), p. 169.

5. Karen Peterson, Gannett News Service, "Study: When Kids Leave Home, Parents' Marriage Gets Better," *Ithaca Journal*, August 22, 1990.

6. Karen Polonko, et al, "Childlessness and Marital Satisfaction," *Journal of Family Issues 3* (4), December 1982, pp. 545–573.

7. Karen S. Renne, "Childlessness, Health, and Marital Satisfaction," *Social Biology*, vol. 23(3), 1976, p. 196.

8. Victor Callan, "The Personal and Marital Adjustment of Mothers and of Voluntarily and Involuntarily Childless Wives," *Journal of Marriage and the Family 49*, November 1987, pp. 847–856.

9. Ibid.

10. Walter R. Gove and Michael R. Geerken, "The Effect of Children and Employment on the Mental Health of Married Men and Women," *Social Forces*, vol. 56(1), September 1977, p. 75.

11. Greg Seltzer, "Midlife and the Intentionally Childless Couple: An Exploratory Study," thesis for Master of Social Work, Smith College School for Social Work, 1986, p. 38.

12. Carole A. Wilk, *Career Women and Childbearing: A Psychological Analysis of the Decision Process* (New York: Van Nostrand Reinhold Company, 1986), p. 193.

13. Ibid., p. 220.

14. R. Blood and D. Wolfe, *Husbands and Wives: the Dynamics of Married Living* (New York: Free Press, 1960), as reported in Martha Garrett Russell, Richard N. Hey, Gail A. Thoen, and Tom Walz, "The Choice of Childlessness, A Workshop Model," *Family Coordinator*, April 1973.

15. Shirley Radl, *Mother's Day Is Over* (New York: Charterhouse, 1973), pp. 18–19.

16. *McCall's* Monthly Newsletter for Women, "Parents Who Wouldn't Do It Again," *McCall's*, November 1975, as reported in Russell, et al, op.cit.

17. "What's Happening to the American Family?" Survey by *Better Homes and Gardens* published in NON Newsletter, July 1978, and cited in Diana Burgwyn, *Marriage Without Children* (New York: Harper & Row, 1981), p. 10.

18. Louis Genevie, Ph.D., and Eva Margolies, M.A., *The Motherhood Report: How Women Feel About Being Mothers* (New York: Macmillan Publishing Company, 1987), p. xxvi.

19. Ibid., p. 192.

20. Ibid., p. 412.

21. Nancy Friday, *My Mother, My Self* (New York: Delacorte Press, 1977), p. 429.

22. Jean Carter and Michael Carter, *Sweet Grapes: How to Stop Being Infertile and Start Living Again* (Indianapolis: Perspectives Press, 1989), p. 93.

Chapter Fifteen   Looking Ahead and Growing Older

1. James E. Bell and Nancy Eisenberg, "Life Satisfaction in Midlife Childless and Empty-Nest Men and Women," *Lifestyles: A Journal of Changing Patterns* 7 (3), Spring 1985, pp. 146–155.

2. Greg Seltzer, "Midlife and the Intentionally Childless Couples: An Exploratory Study," thesis for Master of Social Work, Smith College School for Social Work, 1986.

3. Norval Glenn and Sara McLanahan, "The Effects of Offspring on the Psychological Well-Being of Older Adults," *Journal of Marriage and the Family*, May 1981, pp. 409–421.

4. Ibid.

5. Ibid.

6. John A. Krout, *The Aged in Rural America*, (New York: Greenwood Press, 1986), p. 124.

7. Pat Keith, *The Unmarried in Later Life* (New York: Praeger Publishers, 1989), p. 119.

8. Christine A. Bachrach, "Childlessness and Social Isolation Among the Elderly," *Journal of Marriage and the Family*, August 1980, pp. 627–636.

9. Judith Rempel, "Childless Elderly: What Are They Missing?" *Journal of Marriage and the Family*, May 1985, p. 343.

10. Keith, *The Unmarried in Later Life*, p. 188.

11. Rempel, op.cit., pp. 343–348.

12. Keith, op.cit., p. 186.

13. Timothy Brubaker, *Later-Life Families* (Beverly Hills: Sage Publications, 1985), p. 64.

14. Jane E. Myers and Sally Navin, "To Have Not: The Childless Older Woman," *Humanistic Education and Development*, March 1984, pp. 91–99.

15. Rempel, op.cit.

16. Betsy Houser, Sherry Beckman, and Linda Beckman, "The Rela-

tive Rewards and Costs of Childlessness for Older Women," *Psychology of Women Quarterly*, vol. 8(4), Summer 1984.

17. Charlotte Ikels, "Delayed Reciprocity and the Support Networks of the Childless Elderly," *Journal of Comparative Family Studies*, vol. XIX(1), Spring 1988, pp. 99–112, and Brubaker, *Later-Life Families*, p. 63.

18. Krout, *The Aged in Rural America*, p. 129.

19. Nasako Ishi-Kuntz and Karen Seccombe, "The Impact of Children Upon Social Support Networks Throughout the Life Course," *Journal of Marriage and the Family*, vol. 51, August 1989, pp. 777–790.

20. L. Baker, "The Personal and Social Adjustment of the Never-Married Woman," *Journal of Marriage and the Family*, vol. 30, August 1968, pp. 473–479.

21. Susan Rice, "Single Older Childless Women: Differences Between Never-Married and Widowed Women in Life Satisfaction and Social Support," *Journal of Gerontological Social Work*, vol. 13 (3/4), 1989, pp. 35–47.

22. Cheryl Mercer, *"Grown-Ups": A Generation in Search of Adulthood* (New York: G.P. Putnam's, 1987), p. 162.

23. Jerry Gerber, Janet Wolff, Walter Klores, and Gene Brown, *Lifetrends: the Future of Baby Boomers and Other Aging Americans*, (New York: Stonesong Press, Macmillan Publishing Company, 1989), p. 238.

24. Judith Stryckman, "Childlessness: Its Impact Among the Widowed Elderly," *Gerontologist*, vol. 21, 1981.

For Further Reading

(More references can be found in the end notes of each chapter.)

On Decision-Making:

Bombardieri, Merle. *The Baby Decision*. New York: Rawson Associates, 1981. (Available from the author, $9.95 trade paperback; $15.95 cloth. Make check out to Wellspring Counseling Center and send to the author at 26 Trapelo Road, Belmont, MA 02178.)

Bombardieri, Merle. *Childfree Decision-Making*. A twelve-page packet for infertile couples who would like to consider a child-free future. Available for $2 from Resolve National, 5 Water St., Arlington, MA 02174, (617) 643-2424.

Carter, Jean and Mike Carter. *Sweet Grapes: How to Stop Being Infertile and Start Living Again.* Perspectives Press, 1989. (Perspectives Press: PO Box 90318, Indianapolis, IN 46290.)

Dowrick, Stephanie and Sibyl Grundberg, ed. *Why Children?* New York and London: Harcourt Brace Jovanovich, 1980. The stories of eighteen women, and why they chose to have or not have children.

Elvenstar, Diane C. *Children: To Have or Have Not?* San Francisco: Harbor Publishing, 1982. This book discusses many issues regarding parenthood and includes questionnaires and exercises to help the reader clarify her/his own attitudes and beliefs. Couples in the process of deciding are interviewed. Infertility and how that affects the decision, however, is hardly discussed.

Fabe, Marilyn and Norma Wikler. *Up Against The Clock: Career Women Speak on the Choice to Have Children.* New York: Random House, 1979. Interviews with ten women, some of whom chose to combine children and career, some who decided to be single mothers, and some who decided to remain child free.

McKaughan, Molly. *The Biological Clock: Reconciling Careers and Motherhood in the 1980s.* New York: Doubleday, 1987.

Pies, Cheri. *Considering Parenthood: A Workbook for Lesbians.* San Francisco: Spinsters/Aunt Lute, 1985. This book explores parenting issues and dilemmas unique to lesbians and is chock full of exercises that are useful for both lesbians and straights.

Shealy, C. Norman, M.D., and Mary Charlotte Shealy. *To Parent or Not?* Virginia Beach: The Donning Company, 1981.

Whelan, Elizabeth M. *A Baby? . . . Maybe!* New York: The Bobbs-Merrill Company, Inc., 1975. An overview of the advantages and disadvantages of being a parent without pushing the reader.

On Being a Single Woman

Allen, Katherine R. *Single Women/Family Ties: Life Histories of Older Women.* Newbury Park: Sage Publications, 1989. A study of thirty working-class women born in 1910; fifteen never-married compared with fifteen widowed.

Austrom, Douglas R. *The Consequences of Being Single.* New York: Peter Lang, 1984. A study of 1038 single persons in Canada.

Bakos, Susan Crain. *This Wasn't Supposed to Happen: Single Women Over 30 Talk Frankly about Their Lives.* New York: Continuum, 1985. Discussions about sex, kids, work, and being single. Many of the interviewees are single mothers. There is very little discussion about not having children.

Lindsey, Karen. *Friends as Family*. Boston: Beacon Press, 1981. How single women can create extended family networks through friends, neighborhoods, workplaces.

Peterson, Nancy L. *Our Lives for Ourselves*. New York: G.P. Putnam's Sons, 1981. Interviews with eighty women, ages twenty to seventy-eight who never married but some of whom have children.

Renvoize, Jean. *Going Solo: Single Mothers by Choice*. Boston: Routledge & Kegan, Paul, 1985. Theoretical and practical coverage of women deciding to become mothers without a mate. Includes discussions of the women's movement, of men, family, and effects on children as well as interviews with thirty-one women.

Simon, Barbara Levy. *Never-Married Women*. Philadelphia: Temple University Press, 1987. A study of fifty women, ages sixty-six to one hundred one, and their work, intimate relationships, and aging patterns. There is very little discussion about not having children.

On Living without Children

Burgwyn, Diana. *Marriage Without Children*. New York: Harper & Row, 1981.

Faux, Marian. *Childless By Choice: Choosing Childlessness in the Eighties*. Garden City, N.Y.: Anchor/Doubleday, 1984.

Harper, Kate. *The Child-Free Alternative*. Brattleboro, Vermont: The Stephen Greene Press, 1980. Interviews with five married couples, and five single women, all of whom chose not to have children. Most of those interviewed were in their thirties at the time of the interview.

On Being a Stepmother

Burns, Cherie. *Stepmotherhood: How to Survive Without Feeling Frustrated, Left Out, or Wicked*. New York: Times Books, 1985.

Lofas, Jeanette with Dawn Sova. *Step-Parenting: A Complete Guide to the Joys, Frustrations, and Fears of Stepparenting!* New York: Zebra, 1985.

Lowe, Patricia. *The Cruel Stepmother*. Englewood Cliffs, New Jersey: Prentice-Hall, Inc., 1970.

Savage, Karen and Patricia Adams. *The Good Stepmother: A Practical Guide*. New York: Crown Publishers, 1988.

On Lesbians

Pollack, Sandra, and Jeanne Vaughn, eds. *Politics of the Heart: A Lesbian Parenting Anthology.* Ithaca, New York: Firebrand Books, 1987. Although the focus of this book is on mothering, several essays address the issues of lesbians and nonmothering.

Pies, Cheri. *Considering Parenthood: A Workbook for Lesbians.* San Francisco: Spinsters/Aunt Lute, 1985.

On Infertility

Glazer, Ellen Sarasohn and Susan Lewis Cooper. *Without Child: Experiencing and Resolving Infertility.* Lexington, MA: Lexington Books, 1988.

Liebmann-Smith, Joan. *In Pursuit of Pregnancy: How Couples Discover, Cope with, and Resolve Their Fertility Problems.* New York: Newmarket Press, 1987.

Shapiro, Constance. *Infertility and Pregnancy Loss: A Guide for the Helping Professionals.* San Francisco: Jossey-Bass Publishers, 1988.

Salzer, Linda P. *Infertility: How Couples Can Cope.* Boston: G.K. Hall & Company, 1986.

INDEX

271

ABOUT THE AUTHOR

Susan S. Lang's articles have appeared in dozens of publications, including *Vogue, Family Circle, Woman's Day, American Health, McCall's, Parade, Cosmopolitan, Omni, Reader's Digest, New Woman,* and *Science Digest*. A graduate of Cornell University, she was a senior staff writer for Cornell and a researcher and assistant to Dr. Carl Sagan. This is Lang's third book. She lives in Ithaca, New York.